The Penguin Poets

BRITISH POETRY SINCE 1945

Edward Lucie-Smith was born in Jamaica in 1933. His works include *A Tropical Childhood* (1961), *Confessions and Histories* (1964), *Towards Silence* (1968) and *Well-wishers* (1972). A selection of his poems appeared in *Penguin Modern Poets 6*. He has edited two other anthologies for Penguins and several for other publishers, has also written a number of books on art, and is well known as an art critic and journalist.

BRITISH POETRY SINCE 1945

Edited with an Introduction by
Edward Lucie-Smith

Penguin Books

Penguin Books Ltd, Harmondsworth, Middlesex, England
Viking Penguin Inc., 40 West 23rd Street, New York, New York 10010, U.S.A.
Penguin Books Australia Ltd, Ringwood, Victoria, Australia
Penguin Books Canada Ltd, 2801 John Street, Markham, Ontario, Canada L3R 1B4
Penguin Books (N.Z.) Ltd, 182–190 Wairau Road, Auckland 10, New Zealand

First published 1970
Reprinted 1971, 1973, 1974, 1976, 1978, 1980, 1982
Revised edition 1985

Printed and bound in Great Britain by
Cox & Wyman Ltd, Reading
Set in 9/11 Linotron Bembo

FOR ERIC WALTER WHITE

CONTENTS

Contents

Contents

FOUR: EXPRESSIONISTS

FIVE: THE GROUP

SIX: INFLUENCES FROM ABROAD

Contents

SEVEN: POST-MOVEMENT

Contents

Contents

Twelve: University Wits

From the Introduction to the First Edition

This book has a simple purpose. It tries to offer the reader a reasonably comprehensive survey of the poetry which has been written in Britain since the war: 'Britain', here, being taken to mean England, Scotland, Wales and Northern Ireland. My reason for dividing the latter from the rest of Ireland is that the most recent poetry to emerge from Belfast seems more greatly influenced by English models, such as Hughes or Larkin, than by indigenous ones, such as Yeats or Patrick Kavanagh.

Inevitably a book of this kind is open to all kinds of objections. There are some poets whom I have quite unrepentantly omitted, for example. There are others whom I would have liked to include, but was unable to do so for reasons of space. My concern, throughout, has been to present a clear, concise and coherent picture of what has been happening in English poetry. Occasionally, my self-imposed limits have led to lacunae. I am, for instance, well aware of the influence which William Empson's work had on many poets in the 1950s, but he has published nothing of much consequence since *The Gathering Storm* appeared in 1940.* Nor am I inclined to underrate the impact which Auden's pre-war work has had on poets such as Peter Porter and Adrian Mitchell – but Auden's long residence in America seemed to make him an American rather than a British writer for the purposes of this book.

The most controversial feature of the anthology is perhaps its system of categorization – not merely the decision to have a 'composed order', instead of some more mechanical principle (such as an order by dates of birth), but the kind of critical judgements which the categories imply. I recognize that, in many cases, a poet might have been put in one section just as easily as in another: Hugh MacDiarmid and W. S. Graham have been separated from the rest of the Scotsmen, for example, and the large section labelled 'Influences From Abroad' is a mixed bag indeed. I should not like it to be thought that I think of these

* William Empson died in 1984

categories as absolutely rigid divisions. Some, it is true, have a factual or historical basis: the Movement poets were all of them represented in Robert Conquest's anthology *New Lines*; the Group poets are all of them present in *A Group Anthology*. The only purpose of my categorizations is to provoke the reader to judge for himself. This is *one* way of looking at the poetry which is being written in Britain today; but the reader may well be able to provide himself with another and more convincingly logical method of approach.

INTRODUCTION TO THE
REVISED EDITION

There is always a risk in trying to revise an old anthology. The danger is that it will promptly unravel like an old sweater. Snip one thread, and you undo all the rest. *British Poetry since 1945* was first published in 1970. It was an attempt at a complete survey of the way poetry had developed in the years since the war. Nearly fifteen more years have passed, and the book has been seven times reprinted without substantial change. Clearly, therefore, it has fulfilled at least some part of its original purpose, which was to introduce the poetry of their own time to a wide spectrum of readers. Equally clearly, the time has now come to revise the book if it is to continue to be useful.

What was going through my mind, when I began to compile it? It seemed to me that what was then lacking was an extremely broadly based, non-partisan anthology – that the enthusiast or potential enthusiast for contemporary verse deserved the compliment of being encouraged to make up his or her own mind. In this, *British Poetry since 1945* differed from A. Alvarez's *The New Poetry*, published eight years previously in 1962, which passionately and unashamedly advocated a cause. One kind of poetry was to be preferred, and the others consigned to outer darkness. A similar, though more moderate, line was taken by Penguin's more recent *Contemporary British Poetry*, edited by Blake Morrison and Andrew Motion and published in 1982. As the joint editors' introduction makes plain, Alvarez's book was very much in their minds when they selected their own approach. They wanted to isolate a new tendency in British poetry, and to make out a case for it, perhaps at the expense of other kinds of poetry being written at the same time.

Contemporary British Poetry provoked a reply in the form of Michael Schmidt's rival collection, *Some Contemporary Poets of Britain and Ireland*, published by Carcanet Press in 1983. Significantly, despite the fact that this second anthology was made in opposition to the first, there is a substantial overlap in the contents of the two collections. A number of poets – Tony Harrison, Derek Mahon, Tom Paulin, Peter Scupham, Andrew

Motion – are represented in both. As it happens, they are all also included in the revised edition of this book. This is due, not to craven conformity on any of our parts, but to the fact that people concerned with poetry, despite their superficial differences, do seem to have at the moment certain broad areas of agreement about what is happening to the art.

Yet, though I detect an area of agreement between myself and the makers of the anthologies I have just mentioned, my aim here does remain different from theirs. No more than in the first version of the book do I ask the reader to support one kind of poetry against another; though I do assume that he or she, confronted with the wide variety of styles which are now practised by contemporary poets, will inevitably prefer one or some of these approaches to the others.

All the same, isn't there something rather disingenuous about a pretence to total objectivity, so far as the business of making anthologies is concerned? Those of us who anthologize, whatever our faults of judgement, have a real appetite for poetry, and appetites of this sort are apt to follow their own laws, accepting some flavours and spitting out others. I would answer the objection by saying that yes, of course, there are poets whose work means so little to me, even in a purely negative sense, that I have almost automatically left them out. There are also others whom I omitted reluctantly, for lack of space. Often direct comparisons have decided the issue – I have come to feel that a particular poet doesn't quite measure up, when placed beside another writer of the same sort who illustrates the same tendency. And this is something which brings me to a more genuinely controversial aspect of this book, both in its unrevised and its revised form, than the omissions which critics and fellow anthologists will inevitably seize on (to publish an anthology is to turn oneself into a pheasant on the first day of August). The system of categorization, which has been preserved from the first edition, though adjusted here and there to fit new sets of poetic circumstances, is surely the point where the claim to absolute objectivity tumbles to the ground. By putting poets and poems into compartments, I inevitably imply, and often quite openly commit myself to, judgements about the importance and quality of the writing. These judgements could have been avoided quite easily by putting the poets in alphabetical order, or arranging them by date of birth. They could have been fudged over by choosing a kind of symphonic arrangement – one which implies various affinities and contrasts, but makes them apparent only in a vague, subliminal way.

There is no avoiding the fact that making an anthology is a form of criticism, just as to paraphrase a single poem involves making a judgement on the text. The aim with this book always was, and of course still is, to offer the reader a framework, a means of understanding the way in which poetry has developed during the period under review.

Having said this, let me point to at least some of the ways in which the judgements put forward in the first version of this anthology have been belied by later events. I claimed, for example, in my introduction to the book, that:

> Poets in Britain are still coming to terms, not only with Britain's changed position in the world and the sudden upsurge of American literature, but with the fact of modernism itself. The past quarter of a century, with its pattern of action and reaction, has seen a painful adjustment to the fact that the modern sensibility is here to stay.

I now wonder if that adjustment really took place, at least in the sense which I described, and if it did, whether it wasn't ephemeral. The additions I have made to this book, whatever their other characteristics, have the general effect of making the collection seem more conservative, and indeed more insular, than it was previously. That seems to me to reflect the mood of the time. The high tide of American influence has receded. Poets like William Carlos Williams, Charles Olson and Robert Creeley no longer seem to excite the English poetry world as they did fifteen years ago. The native American poet whose influence is most visible in recent British verse is Robert Lowell, whom I once described as 'the most praised American poet in recent years and surely the least followed'. The praise given to Lowell's work is no longer universal. His attitudes have been the subject of sharply amusing attacks by writers such as John Fuller and James Fenton, but his technical influence is now conspicuous. It is nowhere more apparent than in the work of Tony Harrison, who has made a big impact on the British poetry-reading public during the last decade. Some technical innovations which are often attributed to Harrison by critics here, such as the running-over of ''s' on to the next line when it is attached to a rhyme-word, are in fact typical of Lowell's most characteristic style.

Another conspicuous influence on British poetry in recent years – and here too I am forced to contradict my earlier self – is the late, American Auden. In the first edition of *British Poetry since 1945*ￒ I claimed that Auden's post-1945 work had had little impact in England. That was true in 1970, though perhaps I then underrated the late Auden's importance to Peter Porter, one of the established poets who has grown most noticeably in stature since then. But now no one could underestimate the 'American' Auden's appeal, both to the poets whom I have classified as 'University Wits' and to some of the Northern Irish poets, particularly Derek Mahon.

The influence of post-war German poetry on what has been written in England since 1945, an influence disseminated through the fine translations by Michael Hamburger and Christopher Middleton, remains a fact, but neither contemporary German poetry, nor the East European and Spanish poetry which was translated in some quantity in the late 1960s and early 1970s, have affected the course of British poetry as much as it seemed they were doing and were going to do at the time when my first sampling was made. Yet the translations exist, and they continue to be read. Poets remain subliminally aware of these alien voices, and if this kind of poetry is less talked of, and if, too, the pace at which translations are made and published has slackened, some important new resources have been added to the poetic stock. In addition to this, one or two poets have been looking again at the heritage of French modernism, even though French verse written during this century has always seemed very alien to what most English poets are trying to do. A conspicuous new attempt to domesticate French ideas was made by Geoffrey Hill in *The Mystery of the Charity of Charles Péguy*, published in 1983.

In general, however, it must be said that the full reconciliation between the modernist spirit and British poetry which I looked forward to in 1970 has yet to take place. The most discussed new poets, often brilliantly accomplished within the fairly strict technical and emotional limits they have chosen for themselves, are often not only conservatives, but ones bold enough to flaunt their own conservatism. Indeed, they seem to look upon a declared hostility to modernism as being in itself a form of innovation – which perhaps, taken in a broader cultural context, it actually is. Certainly it helps to define their aims and function within the general literary framework.

The paradox of the 'new poetry' of the 1980s not being new at all can be seen most clearly by turning to the work of members of the so-called 'Martian School', and particularly to that of its leader, Craig Raine. In his poems one soon becomes aware of an inner, extremely traditionalist core, only a little disguised by the coruscating outer surface. His poems seem to me to be a highly successful reconciliation of tendencies which ought to cancel one another out. In one sense, he belongs to the lineage of Ted Hughes. It was Hughes who put an emphasis on the function of metaphor which is still felt by nearly all British poets. He led readers to think of the power of metaphor as being the primary poetic power, and the rest – rhythm, form, what is loosely called 'tone' – as something subsidiary. When he fails (and his failures are always at a high level) it is because the parts are more powerful than the whole: the poem becomes a series of thunderous special effects. Or, to change my own metaphor like a series of box-cars, noisily jarring one against the other as the engine shunts them. Raine takes over Hughes's belief in the primacy of metaphor, but translates everything into a minor key. In his hands the poem becomes, not a train of massive box-cars, but an assemblage of glittering verbal trinkets. Metaphors are used, not to stun the reader as Hughes does, but to distract him from the ordinariness of the ordinary. As his best-known poem, 'A Martian Sends a Postcard Home', suggests, Raine uses poetry to alienate us from the quotidian, and through this alienation to make us experience it afresh. This, of course, is precisely what the Metaphysical poets, and especially the later members of the school, did in the seventeenth century. By returning to these poets as a source of inspiration, Raine reveals how deeply rooted he is in the tradition of university English studies.

The question of the link between the academic study of English and the poetry currently being produced in Britain is a fundamental one. Very many of the poets represented in this book teach or have taught at universities, most of them in departments of English. An even larger number have university degrees in English. The poet here has not perhaps become as much the prisoner and pensioner of the academic system as he is in America, but it must also be recalled that there are big differences between English and American ideas about how a university English course should function. I am not speaking here of the comparative lack of 'creative writing' courses in Britain, but of things which seem to me more important. The American sense of the past, of what is established and historic, remains different from ours. On their side of the Atlantic, for example, the year 1800 seems considerably more distant. Most of American literary history has taken place since that date; the bulk of ours happened before it. In addition to this, the word 'English' is interpreted differently. Americans are naturally inclined to pay attention to their own literature as part of a general academic course, rather than treating it as a specialist subject, a little apart from the mainstream. In the twentieth century the modernist element has been an integral part of this American literature, and has perhaps been especially conspicuous in poetry. The result is that the study of modernist approaches and attitudes is a necessary background to the study of classic American texts – texts which in British terms may seem too recent even to merit inclusion as part of a standard degree course. These differences in approach mean that the academic study of English in England maintains a distinction between the classic and the modern which no longer exists in the United States. Critics – and following them poets – still feel compelled to espouse one cause or the other. On the whole it is the academic approach – using this word in a non-pejorative sense – which is once again carrying the day.

Touching on this topic, I am of course aware of the anomalous nature of my own position. In France it has long been customary for poets and those concerned with poetry to adopt art-criticism rather than teaching as their second profession. The tradition was founded by Baudelaire and much reinforced by the enormous influence which Guillaume Apollinaire exerted over the fortunes of modern art. In America, too, the leading poets and other members of the avant-garde have often been closely linked. Black Mountain College is associated not only with Olson, but also with Albers, Rauschenberg and Cage; poets as different from one another as John Ashbery and Frank O'Hara have been an accepted part of the New York art-scene. In England there have indeed been attempts in the years since 1945 to bring all kinds of modernist creativity together. But these have always taken place away from London (Liverpool in the late 1950s and in the 1960s is still the best example), while London itself remains the centre of English creative life. In the metropolis the division between the contemporary visual arts (generally regarded as the standard-bearers of modernism) and the world of contemporary poetry remains almost exaggeratedly distinct – so much so that one has to have the privilege of an entrée into both camps to be fully aware of how sharp it has become. Quite simply, the poets and the artists have more or less turned their backs on one another. It is almost impossible to use the standards and values universally accepted by those concerned with one art to measure achievement in the other. In the long run, it seems to me that the divorce will be bad for both poets and artists.

The suspicion between advocates of what I have called the academic approach – favoured by most, though not all, British poets (some of them brilliantly successful in using it) – and the modernist strategy favoured by most, but not all, visual artists has existed in British culture almost since the century began, and is certainly not a novel feature of the poetry being written in Britain today. In 1970, however, the frontier did not seem so clearly visible – the barbed wire was only a few strands in places, the minefields were not yet laid, the wooden watchtowers not yet built. One reason why it was less noticeable was the so-called 'Little Press Movement' – a proliferation of small publishers who devoted themselves to poetry, putting out material of extremely variable standard, some of which at least was a genuine challenge to established taste. The Little Presses still exist today, but the decline in their influence is very visible. Its highwater mark was reached more than a decade ago, when a major publishing house – Jonathan Cape – briefly allied itself to the Goliard Press. The disappearance of imprints like Fulcrum, which published so many important and beautifully produced collections of verse, is to be regretted not only for its own sake, but because it seems to have left homeless a number of writers whose work does not fit more conventional lists. To their honour, some mainstream publishers have taken on writers who used to be thought of as difficult and experimental. A case in point is Roy Fisher's *Poems 1955–1980*, published by Oxford University Press. But the usual process, whereby the avant-garde is absorbed and digested by the establishment, seems to have been slow in taking place.

What has happened instead is unexpected – a challenge issued by one kind of poetic conservatism to another, under the banners of different imprints. It is rather like the confrontation between the 'wets' and the monetarists of Mrs Thatcher's Toryism. It is too glib, however, to call the remarkable list of poets published by the Carcanet Press an ultra-conservative opposition, an attack made from the right (in terms of aesthetics) on received notions of how poetry should be made. Carcanet have published work by decidedly experimental poets such as Christopher Middleton. *Pataxanadu*, the title of one of Middleton's volumes, neatly proclaims his spectrum of literary allegiances. But the press has also consistently come to the rescue of poets such as John Heath-Stubbs, whose academic classicism is of a different sort from the commonly accepted variety. Particularly significant is its championship of the work of C. H. Sisson – pessimistic, stoical and grittily impressive. This is perhaps the best single indication of the direction Carcanet has chosen to pursue and of its difference from the mainstream.

My instinct, in trying to accommodate the book to the changes which have taken place in British poetry in the years since 1970, has been to add rather than delete, though for reasons of space a few deletions have inevitably imposed themselves. First and foremost I have added names. One or two are poets who had written a good deal but whose importance was not fully understood when the book was published – C. H. Sisson is the prime example. Most of the additions are poets who have established themselves as interesting writers only in the years since the original choice was made. One section has been greatly expanded – that devoted to poets originating from or working in Ulster. The continuing poetic upsurge in Northern Ireland was perhaps the most exciting phenomenon of the 1970s. I have also added a new section of poets whom I have chosen to label 'University Wits', conspicuous for the civilized elegance of their work. And in addition to adding new poets I have, though with great restraint, added some more recent poems to the existing representation of a few writers who seem to have developed in a particularly interesting way. Among them are Seamus Heaney and Peter Porter. To have altered the representation of every poet who has continued to write since the anthology was put together would inevitably have set in train the unravelling process I mentioned in my first paragraph. In its new guise this is therefore a bi-focal view of British poetry in the years since the Second World War. Some of its contents are seen with the eyes of 1970, which, given the cyclic nature of taste, may also turn out to be the eyes of 1990 or of 1995. The rest is seen with the eyes of the present moment: George Orwell's fateful 1984.

EDWARD LUCIE-SMITH

PART ONE: SOURCES

One of the peculiarities of English poetry in the post-war period has been an absence of dominating father-figures. Auden's departure for America on the eve of the war seemed to snap some thread of continuity which has never been retied. His pre-war work continued to be influential – though perhaps rather less so than that of William Empson – but it was not until the 1970s that the verse he published during his American years began to have a major impact in England. The poets whom I have grouped together here offer a view of the various, and often conflicting influences which were available to younger poets. Not all of these writers have been in the ascendant at the same moment. The Movement poets admired Edwin Muir and Robert Graves; and sometimes, but not always, John Betjeman. MacDiarmid was a dominant force in Scotland, and more recently he had an impact on aspiring modernists south of the border. A renewed interest in the difficult work of David Jones also seemed to reflect a revival of hermetic modernism. Particularly significant in this respect was the rediscovery of the work of Basil Bunting, a disciple of Pound's whose early work appeared in the thirties, just as Auden was beginning to sweep the board. It will be noticed, however, that though the poets I have grouped together here differ widely from one another, the majority have one thing in common: before the war they would have been regarded as peripheral to the main tradition. Muir and MacDiarmid are Scotsmen; Jones and Bunting are belated scions of the twenties; and Graves is a Georgian who has refined his art and turned it in the direction of the romantic classicism of Landor.

EDWIN MUIR

1887–1959

A Scot, like MacDiarmid, Edwin Muir seems to have had more import-
ance for the development of poetry in England than in Scotland. Many
of the Movement poets admired him greatly: the quiet, deliberately
unshowy quality of his work seemed to represent something which they
themselves strove for. And, in a sense, Muir stands at the parting of the
ways between modernism and traditionalism, insularity and its opposite.
He spent much of his life abroad; with his wife, Willa Muir, he was the
translator of Kafka. But he is far enough from the kind of modernism
championed by Pound. The single poem printed here is perhaps his most
famous, and is the finest representative of the fusion of qualities which
I have described.

The Combat

It was not meant for human eyes
That combat on the shabby patch
Of clods and trampled turf that lies
Somewhere beneath the sodden skies
For eye of toad or adder to catch.

And having seen it I accuse
The crested animal in his pride,
Arrayed in all the royal hues
Which hide the claws he well can use
To tear the heart out of the side.

Body of leopard, eagle's head
And whetted beak, and lion's mane,
And frosty-grey hedge of feathers spread
Behind – he seemed of all things bred.
I shall not see his like again.

As for his enemy, there came in
A soft round beast as brown as clay;
All rent and patched his wretched skin;

A battered bag he might have been,
Some old used thing to throw away.

Yet he awaited face to face
The furious beast and the swift attack.
Soon over and done. That was no place
Or time for chivalry or for grace.
The fury had him on his back.

And two small paws like hands flew out
To right and left as the trees stood by.
One would have said beyond a doubt
This was the very end of the bout,
But that the creature would not die.

For ere the death-stroke he was gone,
Writhed, whirled, huddled into his den,
Safe somehow there. The fight was done,
And he had lost who had all but won.
But oh his deadly fury then.

A while the place lay blank, forlorn,
Drowsing as in relief from pain.
The cricket chirped, the grating thorn
Stirred, and a little sound was born.
The champions took their posts again.

And all began. The stealthy paw
Slashed out and in. Could nothing save
These rags and tatters from the claw?
Nothing. And yet I never saw
A beast so helpless and so brave.

And now, while the trees stand watching, still
The unequal battle rages there.
The killing beast that cannot kill
Swells and swells in his fury till
You'd almost think it was despair.

Hugh MacDiarmid
(C. M. Grieve)

1892–1978

Hugh MacDiarmid's importance as a pioneer has long been established, but attention tended to be concentrated on his work in Scots. His finest poetry in this manner appears in *A Drunk Man Looks at a Thistle* (1926), which has long been accepted as a classic. In the middle thirties MacDiarmid abandoned the new language which he had so ingeniously created from the ruins of an old one, and started to write poetry in standard English. It took a long time for this to win acceptance, either in Scotland or outside it. Among the reasons for this are the tough scientific diction of the later poetry and dislike of MacDiarmid's very personal brand of Communism (characteristically, he rejoined the Communist Party, from which he had been expelled in 1938 because of his Scottish Nationalism, in the aftermath of the Hungarian uprising). To me, these objections seem trivial when put beside the intellectual sweep of his work. The first extract printed here is taken from the long poem in *In Memoriam James Joyce*: MacDiarmid selected the passage for inclusion in his *Collected Poems*. The other two poems are extracts from the long poem *Impavidi Progrediamur*.

In the Fall

From *In Memoriam James Joyce*

Let the only consistency
In the course of my poetry
Be like that of the hawthorn tree
Which in early Spring breaks
Fresh emerald, then by nature's law
Darkens and deepens and takes
Tints of purple-maroon, rose-madder and straw.

Sometimes these hues are found
Together, in pleasing harmony bound.
Sometimes they succeed each other. But through
All the changes in which the hawthorn is dight,
No matter in what order, one thing is sure
– The haws shine ever the more ruddily bright!

And when the leaves have passed
Or only in a few tatters remain
The tree to the winter condemned
       Stands forth at last
   Not bare and drab and pitiful,
But a candelabrum of oxidized silver gemmed
By innumerable points of ruby
Which dominate the whole and are visible
Even at considerable distance
As flame-points of living fire.
That so it may be
With my poems too at last glance
Is my only desire.

All else must be sacrificed to this great cause.
I fear no hardships. I have counted the cost.
I with my heart's blood as the hawthorn with its haws
Which are sweetened and polished by the frost!

See how these haws burn, there down the drive,
In this autumn air that feels like cotton wool,
When the earth has the gelatinous limpness of a body dead as
  a whole
While its tissues are still alive!

Poetry is human existence come to life,
.The glorious energy that once employed
Turns all else in creation null and void,
The flower and fruit, the meaning and goal,
Which won all else is needs removed by the knife
Even as a man who rises high
Kicks away the ladder he has come up by.

This single-minded zeal, this fanatic devotion to art
Is alien to the English poetic temperament no doubt,
'This narrowing intensity' as the English say,
But I have it even as you had it, Yeats, my friend,
And would have it with me as with you at the end,
I who am infinitely more un-English than you
And turn Scotland to poetry like those women who
In their passion secrete and turn to
Musk through and through!

So I think of you, Joyce, and of Yeats and others who are dead
As I walk this Autumn and observe
The birch tremulously pendulous in jewels of cairngorm
The sauch, the osier, and the crack-willow
Of the beaten gold of Australia;
The sycamore in rich straw-gold;
The elm bowered in saffron;
The oak in flecks of salmon gold;
The beeches huge torches of living orange.

Billow upon billow of autumnal foliage
From the sheer high bank glass themselves
Upon the ebon and silver current that floods freely
Past the shingle shelves.
I linger where a crack-willow slants across the stream,
Its olive leaves slashed with fine gold.
Beyond the willow a young beech
Blazes almost blood-red,
Vying in intensity with the glowing cloud of crimson
That hangs about the purple bole of a gean
Higher up the brae face.

And yonder, the lithe green-grey bole of an ash, with its boughs
Draped in the cinnamon-brown lace of samara.
(And I remember how in April upon its bare twigs
The flowers came in ruffs like the unshorn ridges
Upon a French poodle – like a dull mulberry at first,
Before the first feathery fronds
Of the long-stalked, finely-poised, seven-fingered leaves) –
Even the robin hushes his song
In these gold pavilions.

Other masters may conceivably write
Even yet in C major
But we – we take the perhaps 'primrose path'
To the dodecaphonic bonfire.

They are not endless these variations of form
Though it is perhaps impossible to see them all.
It is certainly impossible to conceive one that doesn't exist.

gean: wild cherry.

But I keep trying in our forest to do both of these,
And though it is a long time now since I saw a new one
I am by no means weary yet of my concentration
On phyllotaxis here in preference to all else,
All else – but my sense of sny!

The gold edging of a bough at sunset, its pantile way
Forming a double curve, tegula and imbrex in one,
Seems at times a movement on which I might be borne
Happily to infinity; but again I am glad
When it suddenly ceases and I find myself
Pursuing no longer a rhythm of duramen
But bouncing on the diploe in a clearing between earth and air
Or headlong in dewy dallops or a moon-spairged fernshaw
Or caught in a dark dumosity, or even
In open country again watching an aching spargosis of stars.

Bagpipe Music

From *Impavidi Progrediamur*

Let me play to you tunes without measure or end,
Tunes that are born to die without a herald,
As a flight of storks rises from a marsh, circles,
And alights on the spot from which it rose.

Flowers. A flower-bed like hearing the bagpipes.
The fine black earth has clotted into sharp masses
As if the frost and not the sun had come.
It holds many lines of flowers.
First faint rose peonies, then peonies blushing,

phyllotaxis: the arrangement or order of leaves upon an axis or stem. *sny*: a shipbuilding term for the 'run' of the hull of a ship. Here presumably used by extension, to mean 'the tendency of the natural order'. *tegula*: strictly speaking, a scale-like structure covering the base of the fore-wing in insects. *imbrex*: the unit of a system of overlapping, or imbrication. *duramen*: the heartwood of a tree. *diploe*: that part of the leaf which comes between the two layers of the epidermis. *dumosity*: that which is full of brambles and briers. *spargosis*: the distention of the breasts caused by too much milk, hence (presumably) by metaphoric transference, a way of describing the Milky Way.

Then again red peonies, and, behind them,
Massive, apoplectic peonies, some of which are so red
And so violent as to seem almost black; behind these
Stands a low hedge of larkspur, whose tender apologetic
    blossoms
Appear by contrast pale, though some, vivid as the sky above
    them,
Stand out from their fellows, iridescent and slaty as a pigeon's
    breast.
The bagpipes – they are screaming and they are sorrowful.
There is a wail in their merriment, and cruelty in their triumph.
They rise and they fall like a weight swung in the air at the end
    of a string.
They are like the red blood of those peonies.
And like the melancholy of those blue flowers.
They are like a human voice – no! for the human voice lies!
They are like human life that flows under the words.
That flower-bed is like the true life that wants to express itself
And does . . . while we human beings lie cramped and fearful.

Glasgow 1960

From *Impavidi Progrediamur*

Returning to Glasgow after long exile
Nothing seemed to me to have changed its style.
Buses and trams all labelled 'To Ibrox'
Swung past packed tight as they'd hold with folks.
Football match, I concluded, but just to make sure
I asked; and the man looked at me fell dour,
Then said, 'Where in God's name are *you* frae, sir?
It'll be a record gate, but the cause o' the stir
Is a debate on "la loi de l'effort converti"
Between Professor MacFadyen and a Spainish pairty.'
I gasped. The newsboys came running along,
'Special! Turkish Poet's Abstruse New Song.
Scottish Authors' Opinions' – and, holy snakes,
I saw the edition sell like hot cakes.

ROBERT GRAVES

born 1895

The marked influence which Robert Graves had over younger English poets in the middle fifties (rivalled only by that of William Empson) was based in part on the fact that his work formed a middle ground between modernism and old-fashioned Georgianism. Graves *had* been a Georgian poet, and without betraying these roots had slowly and painfully wrought for himself a style purged of earlier mannerisms. In the fifties he wrote some of his most beautiful poems. On the whole, the Movement poets found the way in which he wrote more acceptable than what he was saying – Elizabeth Jennings praised his 'reticence' and 'diffidence'; Donald Davie spoke of his work as 'an object lesson in how much style can do'; Robert Conquest admired his freedom from 'unnatural tricks'. Graves's worship of the Muse – the central doctrine of his work – was tactfully ignored. It seems to me that Graves's real merit was to be a love poet, and a very good one, at a time when love poets were few.

Counting the Beats

You, love, and I,
(He whispers) you and I,
And if no more than only you and I
What care you or I?

Counting the beats,
Counting the slow heart beats,
The bleeding to death of time in slow heart beats,
Wakeful they lie.

Cloudless day,
Night, and cloudless day,
Yet the huge storm will burst upon their heads one day
From a bitter sky.

Where shall we be,
(She whispers) where shall we be,
When death stikes home, O where then shall we be
Who were you and I?

Not there but here,
(He whispers) only here,
As we are, here, together, now and here,
Always you and I.

Counting the beats,
Counting the slow heart beats,
The bleeding to death of time in slow heart beats,
Wakeful they lie.

The Straw

Peace, the wild valley streaked with torrents,
A hoopoe perched on his warm rock. Then why
This tremor of the straw between my fingers?

What should I fear? Have I not testimony
In her own hand, signed with her own name
That my love fell as lightning on her heart?

These questions, bird, are not rhetorical.
Watch how the straw twitches and leaps
As though the earth quaked at a distance.

Requited love; but better unrequited
If this chance instrument gives warning
Of cataclysmic anguish far away.

Were she at ease, warmed by the thought of me,
Would not my hand stay steady as this rock?
Have I undone her by my vehemence?

The Face in the Mirror

Grey haunted eyes, absent-mindedly glaring
From wide, uneven orbits; one brow drooping
Somewhat over the eye
Because of a missile fragment still inhering,
Skin deep, as a foolish record of old-world fighting.

Crookedly broken nose – low tackling caused it;
Cheeks, furrowed; coarse grey hair, flying frenetic;
Forehead, wrinkled and high;
Jowls, prominent; ears, large; jaw, pugilistic;
Teeth, few; lips, full and ruddy; mouth, ascetic.

I pause with razor poised, scowling derision
At the mirrored man whose beard needs my attention,
And once more ask him why
He still stands ready, with a boy's presumption,
To court the queen in her high silk pavilion.

DAVID JONES

1895–1974

The extreme complexity of David Jones's work makes it difficult to discuss in a small space. A poet-artist, Jones was the Celtic and twentieth-century equivalent of William Blake. At the same time, he stands in the modernist tradition. The way in which his principal works, *In Parenthesis* and *The Anathemata*, are constructed puts them in the same category as Joyce's *Ulysses* or *The Cantos* of Ezra Pound. The principle upon which he worked may be deduced from a statement made by the poet himself: 'I believe that there is, in the principle that informs the poetic art, a something which cannot be disengaged from the mythus, deposits, *matière*, ethos, whole *res* of which the poet himself is a product.' Among the more important 'deposits', besides those of personal experience (*In Parenthesis* is essentially a narrative of the First World War), are the Christian faith and Welsh legend. The two fragments printed here were part of a work in progress.

A, a, a, Domine Deus

I said, Ah! what shall I write?
I inquired up and down.
          (He's tricked me before
with his manifold lurking-places.)
I looked for His symbol at the door.
I have looked for a long while
          at the textures and contours.
I have run a hand over the trivial intersections.
I have journeyed among the dead forms
          causation projects from pillar to pylon.
I have tired the eyes of the mind
          regarding the colours and lights.
I have felt for His Wounds
          in nozzles and containers.
I have wondered for the automatic devices.
I have tested the inane patterns
          without prejudice.

David Jones

I have been on my guard
          not to condemn the unfamiliar.
For it is easy to miss Him
          at the turn of a civilization.

I have watched the wheels go round in case I might see the
living creatures like the appearance of lamps, in case I might see
the Living God projected from the Machine. I have said to the
perfected steel, by my sister and for the glassy towers I thought I
felt some beginnings of His creature, but *A, a, a, Domine Deus*,
my hands found the glazed work unrefined and the terrible
crystal a stage-paste . . . *Eia Domine Deus*.

The Hunt[1] ★

          . . . and the hundreds and twenties
of horsed *palatini*
          (to each *comitatus*
one Penteulu)
          that closely hedge
          with a wattle of weapons
the first among equals
          from the wattled *palasau*
the torqued *arglwyddi*
          of calamitous jealousy[2]
     (if there were riders from the Faithful Fetter-locked War-Band
there were riders also from the Three Faithless War-Bands: the
riders who receive the shaft-shock
          in place of their radiant lords
the riders who slip the column
          whose lords alone
          receive the shafts)[3]
     when the men of proud spirit and the men of mean spirit, the
named and the unnamed of the Island and the name-bearing
steeds of the Island and the dogs of the Island and the silent lords
and the lords of loud mouth, the leaders of familiar visage from
the dear known-sites and the adjuvant stranger lords with aid
for the hog-hunt from over the Sleeve[4]

★ Footnotes – see end of poem.

and the wand-bearing lords that are kin to Fferyllt[5] (who learned from the Sibyl the Change Date and the Turn of Time) the lords who ride after deep consideration and the lords whose inveterate habit is to ride the riders who ride from interior compulsion and the riders who fear the narrow glances of the kindred.

Those who would stay for the dung-bailiff's daughter and those who would ride through the shining *matres* three by three sought to stay them.[6]

The riders who would mount though the green wound unstitched and those who would leave their mounts in stall if the bite of a gadfly could excuse them.

The innate Combroges[7] by father by mother without mixed without brok'n without mean descent, all the lords from among the co-equals and the quasi-free of limited privilege, whose insult price is unequal but whose limb-price is equal for all the disproportion as to comeliness and power because the dignity belonging to the white limbs and innate in the shining members, annuls inequality of status and disallows distinctions of appearance.[8]

When the free and the bond and the mountain mares and the fettled horses and the four-penny curs and the hounds of status in the wide, jewelled collars
     when all the shining Arya[9] rode
with the diademed leader
    who directs the toil
    whose face is furrowed
with the weight of the enterprise
  the lord of the conspicuous scars whose visage is fouled with the hog-spittle whose cheeks are fretted with the grime of the hunt-toil:
    if his forehead is radiant
like the smooth hill in the lateral light
    it is corrugated
like the defences of the hill
    because of his care for the land
and for the men of the land.

If his eyes are narrowed for the stress of the hunt and because of the hog they are moist for the ruin and for love of the recumbent bodies that strew the ruin.

If his embroidered habit is clearly from a palace wardrobe it

is mired and rent and his bruised limbs gleam from between the
rents, by reason of the excessive fury of his riding when he rode
the close thicket as though it were an open launde

       (indeed, was it he riding the forest-ride
or was the tangled forest riding?)

  for the thorns and flowers of the forest and the bright elm-
shoots and the twisted tanglewood of stamen and stem clung
and meshed him and starred him with variety

  and the green tendrils gartered him and briary-loops galloon
him with splinter-spike and broken blossom twining his royal
needlework

       and ruby petal-points counter
the countless points of his wounds

  and from his lifted cranium where the priced tresses dragged
with sweat stray his straight brow-furrows under the twisted
diadem

       to the numbered bones
of his scarred feet

       and from the saturated forelock
of his maned mare

       to her streaming flanks
and in broken festoons for her quivering fetlocks
he was caparison'd in the flora

       of the woodlands of Britain
and like a stricken numen of the woods

       he rode
with the trophies of the woods

       upon him
who rode

       for the healing of the woods
and because of the hog.

  Like the breast of the cock-thrush that is torn in the hedge-war
when bright on the native mottle the deeper mottling is and
brighting the diversity of textures and crystal-bright on the deli-
cate fret the clear dew-drops gleam: so was his dappling and his
dreadful variety

       the speckled lord of Prydain
in his twice-embroidered coat

       the bleeding man in the green
and if through the trellis of green

       and between the rents of the needlework

the whiteness of his body shone
        so did his dark wounds glisten.

And if his eyes, from their scrutiny of the hog-track and from considering the hog, turned to consider the men of the host (so that the eyes of the men of the host met his eyes) it would be difficult to speak of so extreme a metamorphosis.

        When they paused at the check
when they drew breath.

And the sweat of the men of the host and of the horses salted the dew of the forest-floor and the hard-breathing of the many men and of the many dogs and of the horses woke the fauna-cry of the Great Forest[10] and shook the silent flora.

        And the extremity of anger
alternating with sorrow
        on the furrowed faces
of the Arya
        transmogrified the calm face
of the morning
        as when the change-wind stirs
and the colours change in the boding thunder-calm
        because this was the Day
of the Passion of the Men of Britain
        when they hunted the Hog
life for life.

Author's Notes:

1. This fragment is part of an incomplete attempt based on the native Welsh early medieval prose-tale, Culhwch ac Olwen, in which the predominant theme becomes the great hunt across the whole of southern Wales of the boar Trwyth by all the war-bands of the Island, led by Arthur.

2. The words *palatini*, Penteulu, *arglwyddi*, and jealousy all rhyme. The word *palasau* (palaces) is pronounced approximately pal-ass-eye, accent on the middle syllable. The Penteulu was the term used for the Captain of the Guard of the horse-troop which constituted the *comitatus* of a Welsh ruler. Pronounce pen-tye-lee, accent on the middle syllable. *Arglwyddi* (lords) pronounce approximately arr-gloo-with-ee – stress accent on penultimate syllable. Perhaps arg-glwith-ee conveys it better.

3. This passage in brackets refers to certain incidents and persons (such as Gronw the Radiant) mentioned in the Triads of the Three Faith-

ful War-Bands and the Three Unfaithful War-Bands of the Island of Britain.

4. In the Culhwch narrative mention is made of aid coming from across the Channel, and at Cardigan the hog kills *gwilenhin brenin freinc*, Gwilenhin, King of France.

5. Fferyllt or Fferyll is the Welsh form of the name Vergil. Pronounce approximately fair-rillt. Owing to the medieval association of Vergil with prophetic and magical powers, any alchemist was called *fferyllt* and later the word became used of any chemist.

6. The term *maer biswail*, 'dung bailiff', was used of the overseer of the villeins who worked on the court farmlands, thus making the jocular distinction between him and the Maer (from Lat. *major*) of the province, an important executive official.

The 'shining *matres*, three by three' refers to a possible connexion between the female cult-figures sculptured in groups of three of Romano-Celtic Antiquity, called *Deae Matres* and the term *Y Mamau*, The Mothers, used of the fairies in some parts of Wales.

7. Combroges (pronounce com-bro-gees, accent on middle syllable), 'men of the same *patria*' from which word, Cymry, the Welsh people, derives. Compare Allobroges, a people of Savoy mentioned by Classical writers and glossed as meaning 'men of a different *patria*'.

8. This passage refers to various complex distinctions listed in the code known as 'The Laws of Hywel Dda'.

9. The word Arya means the nobles or high-men, and has nothing whatever to do with race. Among the Sumerians, Chinese, Mongols and the Hamitic tribes of Africa, wherever there was a warrior-culture and the cult of the sky-god, the tribal king or chieftain tended to personify that god, and be addressed by the same title. As noted by Mr Christopher Dawson in *The Age of the Gods*, in the case of the Etruscans a whole mixed people are known to history as 'the Lords', merely because their female cult-figure was Turan, The Lady, and their male cult-figure Maristuran, Mars the Lord.

10. The initial letters are in capitals because the reference is not only to a large tract of forest-land but to a district name, Fforest Fawr, an upland area of Breconshire which formed part of the itinerary taken by the boar, Trwyth, and Arthur's hunt.

BASIL BUNTING

born 1900

The most surprising apotheosis of the post-war years has been that of the long-neglected Basil Bunting. A conscientious objector during the First World War, Bunting was imprisoned and mistreated. During the twenties, he was for a time a professional music critic. Later, he became a disciple of Pound's, and went to live near him at Rapallo. Pound included his work in the *Activist Anthology*. During the Second World War (having abandoned his conscientious objection), Bunting was sent to Persia, where he stayed on after the war ended, first of all in the British diplomatic service, and later as a journalist. Expelled from Persia by Mossadeq, he eventually found work on a local newspaper in Newcastle, in his native Northumberland. Though he had published a small private edition in Milan in the thirties and a larger collection in Texas in 1950, his work remained unknown in England until its rediscovery by an enthusiastic band of young disciples. The publication of the long autobiographical poem *Briggflatts* abruptly established Bunting's reputation. Cyril Connolly described it as 'perhaps the most distinguished long poem to have been published since *Four Quartets*'. *Briggflatts* does, in fact, bring something distinctively English to the Pound tradition, a highly-wrought, deliberately musical quality which has both Marvell and Milton behind it. A slightly earlier and shorter poem, *The Spoils*, is printed here.

الانفال لله

The Spoils

These are the sons of Shem, after
their families, after their tongues,
in their lands, after their nations.

Man's life so little worth,
do we fear to take or lose it?
No ill companion on a journey, Death
lays his purse on the table and opens the wine.

ASSHUR:
As I sat at my counting frame to assess the people,
from a farmer a tithe, a merchant a fifth of his gain,
marking the register, listening to their lies,
a bushel of dried apricots, marking the register,
three rolls of Egyptian cloth, astute in their avarice;
with Abdoel squatting before piled pence,
counting and calling the sum,
ringing and weighing coin,
casting one out, four or five of a score,
calling the deficit;
one stood in the door
scorning our occupation,
silent: so in his greaves I saw
in polished bronze
a man like me reckoning pence,
never having tasted bread
where there is ice in his flask,
storks' stilts cleaving sun-disk,
sun like driven sand.
Camels raise their necks from the ground,
cooks scour kettles, soldiers oil their arms,
snow lights up high over the north,
yellow spreads in the desert, driving blue westward
among banks, surrounding patches of blue,
advancing in enemy land.
Kettles flash, bread is eaten,
scarabs are scurrying rolling dung.
Thirty gorged vultures on an ass's carcass
jostle, stumble, flop aside, drunk with flesh,
too heavy to fly, wings deep with inner gloss.
Lean watches, then debauch:
after long alert, stupidity:
waking, soar. If here you find me
intrusive and dangerous, seven years was I bonded
for Leah, seven toiled for Rachel:
now in a brothel outside under the wall
have paused to bait on my journey.
Another shall pay the bill if I can evade it.

LUD:
When Tigris floods snakes swarm in the city,

coral, jade, jet, between jet and jade, yellow,
enamelled toys. Toads
crouch on doorsteps. Jerboas
weary, unwary, may be taught to feed
from a fingertip. Dead camels, dead Kurds,
unmanageable rafts of logs
hinder the ferryman, a pull and a grunt,
a stiff tow upshore against the current.
Naked boys among water-buffaloes,
daughters without smile
treading clothes by the verge,
harsh smouldering dung:
a woman taking bread from her oven
spreads dates, an onion, cheese.
Silence under the high sun. When the ewes go out
along the towpath striped with palm-trunk shadows
a herdsman pipes, a girl shrills
under her load of greens. There is no clamour
in our market, no eagerness for gain;
even whores surly, God frugal,
keeping tale of prayers.

ARPACHSHAD:
Bound to beasts' udders, rags no dishonour,
not by much intercourse ennobled,
multitude of books, bought deference:
meagre flesh tingling to a mouthful of water,
apt to no servitude, commerce or special dexterity,
at night after prayers recite the sacred
enscrolled poems, beating with a leaping measure
like blood in a new wound:
These were the embers . . . Halt, both, lament . . .:
moon-silver on sand-pale gold,
plash against parched Arabia.
What's to dismay us?

ARAM:
By the dategroves of Babylon
there we sat down and sulked
while they were seeking to hire us
to a repugnant trade.
Are there no plows in Judah, seed or a sickle,

no ewe to the pail, press to the vineyard?
Sickly our Hebrew voices far from the Hebrew hills!

ASSHUR:
We bear witness against the merchants of Babylon
that they have planted ink and reaped figures.

LUD:
Against the princes of Babylon, that they have tithed of the best
leaving sterile ram, weakly hog to the flock.

ARPACHSHAD:
Fullers, tailors, hairdressers, jewellers, perfumers.

ARAM:
David dancing before the Ark, they toss him pennies.
A farthing a note for songs as of the thrush.

ASSHUR:
Golden skin scoured in sandblast
a vulture's wing. 'Soldier,
O soldier! Hard muscles, nipples like spikes.
Undo the neck-string, let my blue gown fall.'
Very much like going to bed with a bronze.
The child cradled beside her sister silent and brown
Thighs in a sunshaft, uncontrollable smile,
she tossed the pence aside in a brothel under the wall.

LUD:
My bride is borne behind the pipers,
kettles and featherbed,
on her forehead jet, jade, coral under the veil;
to bring ewes to the pail, bread from the oven.
Breasts scarcely hump her smock,
thighs meagre, eyes
alert without smile
mock the beribboned dancing boys.

ARPACHSHAD:
Drunk with her flesh when, polished leather,
still as moon she fades into the sand,
spurts a flame in the abandoned embers,
gold or silver. Warmth of absent thighs
dies on the loins: she who has yet no breasts
and no patience to await tomorrow.

ARAM:
Chattering in the vineyard,
breasts swelled, halt and beweep
captives, sickly, closing repugnant thighs.
Who lent her warmth to dying David, let her seed
sleep on the Hebrew hills, wake under Zion.

What's begotten on a journey but souvenirs?
Life we give and take, pence in a market,
without noting beggar, dealer, changer;
pence we drop in the sawdust with spilt wine.

II

They filled the eyes of the vaulting
with alabaster panes,
each pencil of arches spouting
from a short pier,
and whitewashed the whole, using
a thread of blue to restore
lines nowhere broken,
for they considered capital
and base irrelevant.
The light is sufficient
to perceive the motions of prayer
and the place cool.
Tiles for domes and aivans
they baked in a corner,
older, where Avicenna may have worshipped.
The south dome, Nezam-ol-Molk's,
grows without violence from the walls
of a square chamber, Taj-ol-Molk
set a less perfect dome
over a forest of pillars.
At Veramin
Malekshah cut his pride in plaster
which hardens by age, the same
who found Khayyam a better reckoner
than the Author of the Qor'an.
Their passion's body was bricks and its soul algebra.
Poetry
they remembered

too much, too well.
'Lately a professor in this university'
said Khayyam of a recalcitrant ass,
'therefore would not enter, dare not face me.'
But their determination to banish fools foundered
ultimately in the installation of absolute idiots.
Fear of being imputed
naive impeded thought.
Eddies both ways in time:
the builders of La Giralda
repeated
heavily, languidly,
some of their patterns in brick.
I wonder what Khayyam thought
of all the construction and organization afoot,
foreigners, resolute Seljuks, not so bloodthirsty
as some benefactors of mankind; recalling
perhaps Abu Ali's horror of munificent patrons;
books unheard of or lost elsewhere
in the library at Bokhara,
and four hours writing a day
before the duties of prime minister.

For all that, the Seljuks avoided
Roman exaggeration and the leaden mind of Egypt
and withered precariously on the bough
with patience and public spirit.
O public spirit!

Prayers to band cities and brigade men
lest there be more wills than one:
but God is the dividing sword.

A hard pyramid or lasting law
against fear of death and
murder more durable than mortar.

Domination and engineers
to fudge a motive you can lay your hands on
lest a girl choose or refuse waywardly.

From Hajji Mosavvor's trembling wrist
grace of tree and beast
shines on ivory

in eloquent line.
Flute,
shade dimples under chenars
breath of Naystani chase and traces
as a pair of gods might dodge and tag between stars.
Taj is to sing, Taj,
when tar and drum
come to their silence, slow,
clear, rich, as though
he had cadence and phrases from Hafez.
Nothing that was is,
but Moluk-e Zarrabi
draws her voice from a well
deeper than history.
Shir-e Khoda's note
on a dawn-cold radio
forestalls, outlasts the beat.
Friday. Sobhi's tales
keeping boys from their meat.

A fowler spreading his net
over the barley, call,
calls on a rubber reed.
Grain nods in reply.
Poppies blue upon white
wake to the sun's frown.
Scut of gazelle dances and bounces
out of the afternoon.
Owl and wolf to the night.
On a terrace over a pool
vafur, vodka, tea,
resonant verse spilled
from Onsori, Sa'di,
till the girls' mutter is lost
in whisper of stream and leaf,
a final nightingale
under a fading sky
azan on their quiet.

They despise police work,
are not masters of filing:
always a task for foreigners

to make them unhappy,
unproductive and rich.

Have you seen a falcon stoop
accurate, unforeseen
and absolute, between
wind-ripples over the harvest? Dread
of what's to be, is and has been –
were we not better dead?
His wings churn air
to flight.
Feathers alight
with sun, he rises where
dazzle rebuts our stare
wonder our fright.

III

All things only of earth and water
to sit in the sun's warmth
breathing clear air.
A fancy took me to dig,
plant, prune, graft;
milk, skim, churn;
flay and tan.
A side of salt beef
for a knife chased and inscribed.
A cask of pressed grapes
for a seine-net.
For a peace until harvest
a jig and a hymn.

How shall wheat sprout
through a shingle of Lydian pebbles
that turn the harrow's points?
Quarry and build, Solomon,
a bank for Lydian pebbles:
tribute of Lydian pebbles
levy and lay aside,
that twist underfoot
and blunt the plowshare,

countless, useless, hampering
pebbles that spawn.

Shot silk and damask white
spray spread from
artesian gush of our past.
Let no one drink unchlorinated
living water but taxed tap, sterile,
or seek his contraband mouthful
in bog, under thicket, by crag, a trickle,
or from embroidered pools
with newts and dytiscus beetles.

One cribbed in a madhouse
set about with diagnoses;
one unvisited; one uninvited;
one visited and invited too much;
one impotent, suffocated by adulation;
one unfed: flares on a foundering barque,
stars spattering still sea under iceblink.
Tinker tapping perched on a slagheap
and the man who can mend a magneto.
Flight-lieutenant Idema, half course run
that started from Grand Rapids, Michigan,
wouldnt fight for Roosevelt,
'that bastard Roosevelt', pale
at Malta's ruins, enduring
a jeep guarded like a tyrant.
In British uniform and pay
for fun of fighting and pride,
for Churchill on foot alone,
clowning with a cigar, was lost
in best blues and his third plane that day.

Broken booty but usable
along the littoral, frittering into the south.
We marvelled, careful of craters and minefields,
noting a new-painted recognizance
on a fragment of fuselage, sand drifting into dumps,
a tank's turret twisted skyward,
here and there a lorry unharmed
out of fuel or the crew scattered;

leaguered in lines numbered for enemy units,
gulped beer of their brewing,
mocked them marching unguarded to our rear;
discerned nothing indigenous, never a dwelling,
but on the shore sponges stranded and beyond the reef
unstayed masts staggering in the swell,
till we reached readymade villages clamped on cornland,
empty, Arabs feeding vines to goats;
at last orchards aligned, girls hawked by their mothers
from tent to tent, Tripoli dark
under a cone of tracers.
Old in that war after raising many crosses
rapped on a tomb at Leptis; no one opened.

Blind Bashshar bin Burd saw,
doubted, glanced back,
guessed whence, speculated whither.
Panegyrists, blinder and deaf,
prophets, exegesists, counsellors of patience
lie in wait for blood,
every man with a net,
Condole with me with abundance of secret pleasure.
What we think in private
will be said in public
before the last gallon's teemed
into an unintelligible sea –
old men who toil in the bilge to open a link,
bruised by the fling of the ship and sodden
sleep at the handpump, Staithes, filthy harbour water,
a drowned Finn, a drowned Chinee;
hard-lying money wrung from protesting paymasters.

Rosyth guns sang, Sang tide through cable
for Glasgow burning:
          'Bright west,
          pale east,
          catfish on the sprool.'
Sun leaped up and passed,
bolted towards green creek
of quiet Chesapeake,
bight of a warp no strong tide strains. Yet
as tea's drawing, breeze backing and freshening,

who'd rather
make fast Fortune with a slippery hitch?
Tide sang. Guns sang:
>   'Vigilant,
>   pull off fluffed woollens, strip
>   to buff and beyond.'
In watch below
meditative heard elsewhere
surf shout, pound shores seldom silent
from which heart naked swam
out to the dear unintelligible ocean.
From Largo Law look down,
moon and dry weather, look down
on convoy marshalled, filing between mines.
Cold northern clear sea-gardens
between Lofoten and Spitzbergen,
as good a grave as any, earth or water.
What else do we live for and take part,
we who would share the spoils?

Author's Notes:

'*The Spoils*' was written in 1951 and printed in *Poetry*, Chicago.

Let readers who lack Arabic forgive me for explaining that the epigraph, *al anfal li'llah* is from the Qor'an, sura viii, and means 'The spoils are for God.' I named the sons of Shem at random from the Bible's list.

Some Persian words have no English equivalent. An *aivan* is a high arch backed by a shallow honeycomb half-dome or leading into a mosque. *Chenar, Platanus orientalis*, is grander than its London cousins; *tar*, a stringed instrument used in Persian classical music. *Vafur* signifies the apparatus of opium smoking, pipe, pricker, tongs, brazier, charcoal and the drug, shining like a stick of black sealing wax. The *azan* is the mo'ezzin's call to prayer. You hardly hear its delicate, wavering airs at other times, but an hour before sunrise it has such magic as no other music, unless perhaps the nightingale in lands where nightingales are rare.

Proper names explain themselves and can be found in books of reference. A few are not yet filed. *Hajji Mosavvor*, greatest of modern miniature painters, suffered from *paralysis agitans*. *Naystani*, a celebrated virtuoso of the nose-flute. *Taj* sings classical odes with authenticity; *Moluk-e Zarrabi* moulds them to her liking. *Shir-e Khoda* begins

Teheran's radio day with a canto of the epic. *Sobhi* is the most perfect teller of tales, his own.

Gaiety and daring need no naming to those who remember others like *Flight-lieutenant Idema*.

Abu Ali is, of course, Ibn Sina – Avicenna.

JOHN BETJEMAN

1906–84

The publication of John Betjeman's *Selected Poems* in October 1948 was one of the significant events of the early years after the war. Before it, Betjeman had been accounted a very lightweight and minor figure; now he suddenly found himself catapulted into the position of the most popular poet in England. He retained it with some ease for the rest of his life. Part of the attraction of Betjeman's work is its humour, and another part is its cunning neo-Victorianism. But there is more to it than that. The tensions between an apparently 'traditional' form and a distinctly modern content link Betjeman to Larkin, whom he foreshadows. Betjeman and Larkin publicly admired one another's work. It is also an injustice to label Betjeman merely a 'funny' poet. His best work is deeply melancholic, as can be seen from two of the poems printed here.

Indoor Games Near Newbury

In among the silver birches winding ways of tarmac wander
   And the signs to Bussock Bottom, Tussock Wood and Windy
                                     Brake,
Gabled lodges, tile-hung churches, catch the lights of our
                                    Lagonda
As we drive to Wendy's party, lemon curd and Christmas
                                    cake.
    Rich the makes of motor whirring,
    Past the pine-plantation purring
        Come up, Hupmobile, Delage!
  Short the way your chauffeurs travel,
    Crunching over private gravel
        Each from out his warm garáge.

Oh but Wendy, when the carpet yielded to my indoor pumps
    There you stood, your gold hair streaming,
    Handsome in the hall-light gleaming
There you looked and there you led me off into the game of
                                    clumps

Then the new Victrola playing
And your funny uncle saying
'Choose your partners for a fox-trot! Dance until its *tea* o'clock!'
'Come on, young 'uns, foot it featly!'
Was it chance that paired us neatly,
I, who loved you so completely,
You, who pressed me closely to you, hard against your party
frock?
'Meet me when you've finished eating!' So we met and no one
found us.
Oh that dark and furry cupboard while the rest played hide
and seek!
Holding hands our two hearts beating in the bedroom silence
round us,
Holding hands and hardly hearing sudden footstep, thud and
shriek.
Love that lay too deep for kissing –
'Where *is* Wendy? Wendy's missing!'
Love so pure it *had* to end,
Love so strong that I was frighten'd
When you gripped my fingers tight and
Hugging, whispered 'I'm your friend.'

Good-bye Wendy! Send the fairies, pinewood elf and larch tree
gnome,
Spingle-spangled stars are peeping
At the lush Lagonda creeping
Down the winding ways of tarmac to the leaded lights of home.
There, among the silver birches,
All the bells of all the churches
Sounded in the bath-waste running out into the frosty air.
Wendy speeded my undressing,
Wendy is the sheet's caressing
Wendy bending gives a blessing,
Holds me as I drift to dreamland, safe inside my slumber-wear.

Devonshire Street W.1

The heavy mahogany door with its wrought-iron screen
   Shuts. And the sound is rich, sympathetic, discreet.
The sun still shines on this eighteenth-century scene
   With Edwardian faience adornments – Devonshire Street.

No hope. And the X-ray photographs under his arm
   Confirm the message. His wife stands timidly by.
The opposite brick-built house looks lofty and calm
   Its chimneys steady against a mackerel sky.

No hope. And the iron knob of this palisade
   So cold to the touch, is luckier now than he
'Oh merciless, hurrying Londoners! Why was I made
   For the long and the painful deathbed coming to me?'

She puts her fingers in his, as, loving and silly,
   At long-past Kensington dances she used to do
'It's cheaper to take the tube to Piccadilly
   And then we can catch a nineteen or a twenty-two.'

N.W.5 & N.6

Red cliffs arise. And up them service lifts
Soar with the groceries to silver heights.
Lissenden Mansions. And my memory sifts
Lilies from lily-like electric lights
And Irish stew smells from the smell of prams
And roar of seas from roar of London trams.

Out of it all my memory carves the quiet
Of that dark privet hedge where pleasures breed,
There first, intent upon its leafy diet,
I watched the looping caterpillar feed
And saw it hanging in a gummy froth
Till, weeks on, from the chrysalis burst the moth.

I see black oak twigs outlined on the sky,
Red squirrels on the Burdett-Coutts estate.
I ask my nurse the question 'Will I die?'

As bells from sad St Anne's ring out so late,
'And if I do die, will I go to Heaven?'
Highgate at eventide. Nineteen-eleven.

'You will. I won't.' From that cheap nursery-maid,
Sadist and puritan as now I see,
I first learned what it was to be afraid,
Forcibly fed when sprawled across her knee
Lock'd into cupboards, left alone all day,
'World without end.' What fearsome words to pray.

'World without end.' It was not what she'ld do
That frightened me so much as did her fear
And guilt at endlessness. I caught them too,
Hating to think of sphere succeeding sphere
Into eternity and God's dread will
I caught her terror then. I have it still.

LOUIS MACNEICE

1907–63

Many of the chief poets of the thirties seemed to falter after the war, and none more visibly than Louis MacNeice. His poetry written in the immediate post-war period has a dismaying flatulence, nowhere more detectable than in *Autumn Sequel*, which was published in 1953. But after this began a process of recovery. His work simplified itself; he no longer embarked on the elaborate poem-sequences which characterized his work just after the war. His new work combined an underlying gravity with the flippant, glittering surface which had delighted the readers of his early poetry. To achieve these successes, MacNeice seems to have renounced a great deal. Sometimes the new poems are stoical; at other times they are frankly despairing, the wry jokes of a man prey to irreversible melancholia. The great debate about 'confessional verse' was just beginning when MacNeice published these later volumes: it seems surprising that his name was not mentioned more often when the subject came up.

The Wiper

Through purblind night the wiper
Reaps a swathe of water
On the screen; we shudder on
   And hardly hold the road,
All we can see a segment
Of blackly shining asphalt
With the wiper moving across it
   Clearing, blurring, clearing.

But what to say of the road?
The monotony of its hardly
Visible camber, the mystery
   Of its invisible margins,
Will these be always with us,
The night being broken only
By lights that pass or meet us
   From others in moving boxes?

Boxes of glass and water
Upholstered, equipped with dials
Professing to tell the distance
　We have gone, the speed we are going,
But never a gauge nor needle
To tell us where we are going
Or when day will come, supposing
　This road exists in daytime.

For now we cannot remember
Where we were when it was not
Night, when it was not raining,
　Before this car moved forward
And the wiper backward and forward
Lighting so little before us
Of a road that, crouching forward,
　We watch move always towards us,

Which through the tiny segment
Cleared and blurred by the wiper
Is sucked in under the axle
　To be spewed behind us and lost
While we, dazzled by darkness,
Haul the black future towards us
Peeling the skin from our hands;
　And yet we hold the road.

The Truisms

His father gave him a box of truisms
Shaped like a coffin, then his father died;
The truisms remained on the mantelpiece
As wooden as the playbox they had been packed in
Or that other his father skulked inside.

Then he left home, left the truisms behind him
Still on the mantelpiece, met love, met war,
Sordor, disappointment, defeat, betrayal,
Till through disbeliefs he arrived at a house
He could not remember seeing before,

And he walked straight in; it was where he had come from
And something told him the way to behave.
He raised his hand and blessed his home;
The truisms flew and perched on his shoulders
And a tall tree sprouted from his father's grave.

The Taxis

In the first taxi he was alone tra-la,
No extras on the clock. He tipped ninepence
But the cabby, while he thanked him, looked askance
As though to suggest someone had bummed a ride.

In the second taxi he was alone tra-la
But the clock showed sixpence extra; he tipped according
And the cabby from his muffler said: 'Make sure
You have left nothing behind tra-la between you.'

In the third taxi he was alone tra-la
But the tip-up seats were down and there was an extra
Charge of one-and-sixpence and an odd
Scent that reminded him of a trip to Cannes.

As for the fourth taxi, he was alone
Tra-la when he hailed it but the cabby looked
Through him and said: 'I can't tra-la well take
So many people, not to speak of the dog.'

After the Crash

When he came to he knew
Time must have passed because
The asphalt was high with hemlock
Through which he crawled to his crash
Helmet and found it no more
Than his wrinkled hand what it was.

Yet life seemed still going on:
He could hear the signals bounce
Back from the moon and the hens

Fire themselves black in the batteries
And the silence of small blind cats
Debating whether to pounce.

Then he looked up and marked
The gigantic scales in the sky,
The pan on the left dead empty
And the pan on the right dead empty,
And knew in the dead, dead calm
It was too late to die.

The Habits

When they put him in rompers the habits
Fanned out to close in, they were dressed
In primary colours and each of them
Carried a rattle and a hypodermic;
His parents said it was all for the best.

Next, the barracks of boys: the habits
Slapped him on the back, they were dressed
In pinstripe trousers and carried
A cheque book, a passport, and a sjambok;
The master said it was all for the best.

And then came the women: the habits
Pretended to leave, they were dressed
In bittersweet undertones and carried
A Parthian shaft and an affidavit;
The adgirl said it was all for the best.

Age became middle: the habits
Made themselves at home, they were dressed
In quilted dressing-gowns and carried
A decanter, a siphon, and a tranquillizer;
The computer said it was all for the best.

The age became real: the habits
Outstayed their welcome, they were dressed
In nothing and carried nothing.
He said: If you won't go, I go.
The Lord God said it was all for the best.

Dylan Thomas

1914–53

Dylan Thomas's place in the literary history of the post-war years is still somewhat in question, even if his position as a folk-hero seems secure. His life – as memorialized in such books as John Malcolm Brinnin's *Dylan Thomas in America* and his widow Caitlin Thomas's *Left-over Life to Live* – seems to have had more influence than his work. The life established a stereotype: this was how poets (even Movement poets) were expected to behave, even if they seldom did. His electrifying readings prepared the way for the revival of interest in poetry as a performer's art which took place in the mid sixties. The poetry still seems more like the end of something than the beginning of something – modernism making its last, baroque gestures before the reaction against it set in. Thomas was influenced by the surrealists, but was never, even in his early work, as committed to them as David Gascoyne. His later poems represent a very typical English compromise between romanticism and surrealism: one can see the same impulse at work in the immediately post-war sculpture of Henry Moore.

Over Sir John's Hill

Over Sir John's hill,
The hawk on fire hangs still;
In a hoisted cloud, at drop of dusk, he pulls to his claws
And gallows, up the rays of his eyes the small birds of the bay
And the shrill child's play
Wars
Of the sparrows and such who swansing, dusk, in wrangling
   hedges.
And blithely they squawk
To fiery tyburn over the wrestle of elms until
The flash the noosed hawk
Crashes, and slowly the fishing holy stalking heron
In the river Towy below bows his tilted headstone.

Flash, and the plumes crack,
And a black cap of jack-

Daws Sir John's just hill dons, and again the gulled birds hare
To the hawk on fire, the halter height, over Towy's fins.
In a whack of wind.
There
Where the elegiac fisherbird stabs and paddles
In the pebbly dab-filled
Shallow and sedge, and 'dilly dilly,' calls the loft hawk,
'Come and be killed,'
I open the leaves of the water at a passage
Of psalms and shadows among the pincered sandcrabs prancing
And read, in a shell,
Death clear as a buoy's bell:
All praise of the hawk on fire in hawk-eyed dusk be sung,
When his viperish fuse hangs looped with flames under the
   brand
Wing, and blest shall
Young
Green chickens of the bay and bushes cluck, 'dilly dilly,
Come let us die.'
We grieve as the blithe birds, never again, leave shingle and elm,
The heron and I,
I young Aesop fabling to the near night by the dingle
Of eels, saint heron hymning in the shell-hung distant

Crystal harbour vale
Where the sea cobbles sail,
And wharves of water where the walls dance and the white
   cranes stilt.
It is the heron and I, under judging Sir John's elmed
Hill, tell-tale the knelled
Guilt
Of the led-astray birds whom God, for their breast of whistles,
Have mercy on,
God in his whirlwind silence save, who marks the sparrows hail,
For their souls' song.
Now the heron grieves in the weeded verge. Through windows
Of dusk and water I see the tilting whispering
Heron, mirrored, go,
As the snapt feathers snow,
Fishing in the tear of the Towy. Only a hoot owl
Hollows, a grassblade blown in cupped hands, in the looted elms

And no green cocks or hens
Shout
Now on Sir John's hill. The heron, ankling the scaly
Lowlands of the waves,
Makes all the music; and I who hear the tune of the slow,
Wear-willow river, grave,
Before the lunge of the night, the notes on this time-shaken
Stone for the sake of the souls of the slain birds sailing.

DAVID GASCOYNE

born 1916

In 1965, when his *Collected Poems* appeared, Gascoyne's reputation had reached what will probably prove to have been its lowest ebb. The new methods of criticism found his work vulnerable, clumsy in diction, and, especially in the later poems, rhythmically flaccid. They tended, on the other hand, to discount the poet's virtues – the ambition, the seriousness, the ability to project a visionary quality in spite of all flaws of detail. It now begins to look as if Gascoyne occupies a key position in the development of English poetry in the twentieth century. He was the only genuine surrealist poet writing in English, and surrealism has suddenly (and how belatedly) begun to assume major importance for the newest generation of English poets. The *Collected Poems* sold well, and one suspects that the audience they found was a young one. Gascoyne's best work is probably that written before and during the war, but the 'Elegiac Improvisation' printed here has a particular importance as a link between the new surrealism and the old.

Elegiac Improvisation on the Death of Paul Eluard[1]

A tender mouth a sceptical shy mouth
A firm fastidious slender mouth
A Gallic mouth an asymmetrical mouth

He opened his mouth he spoke without hesitation
He sat down and wrote as he spoke without changing a word
And the words that he wrote still continue to speak with his
    mouth:

Warmly and urgently
Simply, convincingly
Gently and movingly
Softly, sincerely

1. *Paul Eluard* (1895–1952): perhaps the most important surrealist poet, and certainly the most influential poet in France in the period between the two wars.

Clearly, caressingly
Bitterly, painfully
Pensively, stumblingly
Brokenly, heartbreakingly
Uninterruptedly
In clandestinity
In anguish, in arms and in anger,
In passion, in Paris, in person
In partisanship, as the poet
Of France's Resistance, the spokesman
Of unconquerable free fraternity.

And now his printed words all add up to a sum total
And it can be stated he wrote just so many poems
And the commentators like undertakers take over
The task of annotating his complete collected works.
Yet the discursivity of the void
Diverts and regales the whole void then re-enters the void
While every printed page is a swinging door

Through which one can pass in either of two directions
On one's way towards oblivion
And from the blackness looming through the doorway
The burning bush of hyperconsciousness
Can fill the vacuum abhorred by human nature
And magic images flower from the poet's speech
He said, 'There is nothing that I regret,
I still advance,' and he advances
He passes us Hyperion passes on
Prismatic presence
A light broken up into colours whose rays pass from him
To friends in solitude, leaves of as many branches
As a single and solid solitary trunk has roots
Just as so many sensitive lines cross each separate leaf
On each of the far-reaching branches of sympathy's tree
Now the light of the prism has flashed like a bird down the
dark-blue grove
At the end of which mountains of shadow pile up beyond sight
Oh radiant prism
A wing has been torn and its feathers drift scattered by flight.

Yet still from the dark through the door shines the poet's mouth
speaking

In rain as in fine weather
The climate of his speaking
In silence, calm and sunshine,
Sublime cloudburst and downpour,
The changing wind that breaks out blows away
All words – wind that is mystery
Wind of the secret spirit
That breaks up words' blind weather
With radiant breath of Logos
When silence is a falsehood
And all things no more named
Like stones flung into emptiness
Fall down through bad eternity
All things fall out and drop down, fall away
If no sincere mouth speaks
To recreate the world
Alone in the world it may be
The only candid mouth
Truth's sole remaining witness
Disinterested, distinct, undespairing mouth
'Inspiring mouth still more than a mouth inspired'
Speaking still in all weathers
Speaking to all those present
As he speaks to us here at present
Speaks to the man at the bar and the girl on the staircase
The flowerseller, the newspaper woman, the student
The foreign lady wearing a shawl in the faubourg garden
The boy with a bucket cleaning the office windows
The friendly fellow in charge of the petrol station
The sensitive cynical officer thwarting description
Like the well-informed middle-class man who prefers to remain
    undescribed
And the unhappy middle-aged woman who still hopes and can-
    not be labelled
The youth who's rejected all words that could ever be spoken
To conceal and corrupt where they ought to reveal what they
    name.

The truth that lives eternally is told in time
The laughing beasts the landscape of delight
The sensuality of noon the tranquil midnight
The vital fountains the heroic statues

The barque of youth departing for Cytheria
The ruined temples and the blood of sunset
The banks of amaranth the bower of ivy
The storms of spring and autumn's calm are Now
Absence is only of all that is not Now
And all that is true is and is here Now
The flowers the fruit the green fields and the snow's field
The serpent dance of the silver ripples of dawn
The shimmering breasts the tender hands are present
The open window looks out on the realm of Now
Whose vistas glisten with leaves and immaculate clouds
And Now all beings are seen to become more wonderful
More radiant more intense and are now more naked
And more awake and in love and in need of love
Life dreamed is now life lived, unlived life realized
The lucid moment, the lifetime's understanding
Become reconciled and at last surpassed by Now
Words spoken by one man awake in a sleeping crowd
Remain with their unique vibration's still breathing enigma
When the crowd has dispersed and the poet who spoke has gone
     home.
PAUL ELUARD has come back to his home the world.

PART TWO: POST-WAR

This is the section which corresponds most closely with Robin Skelton's anthology *Poetry of the Forties*, though most of the poems included were written after 1950. Nevertheless my aim has been to give a sampling of poets who for the most part established themselves either just before the war or during it. Patricia Beer, Thomas Blackburn and R. S. Thomas are the only exceptions. In different ways, Vernon Watkins, W. S. Graham, George Barker and John Heath-Stubbs seem to represent the kind of romanticism which the Movement was to react against. Roy Fuller's work, on the other hand, has marked affinities with that of younger poets, and Bernard Spencer's in some ways reminds one of Enright's. Causley and Stevie Smith are 'independents', almost (or so it seems) oblivious of literary fashion, though they share the taste of the 1940s for ballad-forms. R. S. Thomas and Patricia Beer illustrate the tenacious persistence of Georgianism. In a way, much the same can be said for the recently rediscovered talent of C. H. Sisson, though he strikes an extremely individual note, stoical and pessimistic.

VERNON WATKINS

1906–67

Vernon Watkins's reputation seems to have fallen in England, though it remains high abroad. He represents a curious confluence, having been both the lifelong friend of Dylan Thomas and an early encourager of Philip Larkin. His own work was that of a man who was very consciously a poet – romantic and solemn for the most part, except when (like so many poets of his particular generation) he used ballad forms. Two of the poems printed here suggest a rather unexpected affinity with Robert Bridges.

A Man With a Field

If I close my eyes I can see a man with a load of hay
Cross this garden guiding his wheelbarrow through the copse
To a long, low green-house littered with earthenware, glass and
  clay,
Then prop his scythe near the sycamore to enter it, potted with
  seeds,
And pause where chrysanthemums grow, with tomatoes'
  dragonish beads.
Stooping to fasten the door, he turns on the path which leads
To his rain-pitted bedroom of cellos, and low jugs catching the
  drops.

If I open my eyes I see this musician-turned-ploughman slow,
Plainly follow his tractor vibrating beneath blue sky,
Or cast his sickle wide, or reach full-length with the hoe.
Or blame the weather that set its blight on a crop or a plan
To mend his roof, or cut back trees where convolvulus ran,
Or attend to as many needs as the holes in a watering-can:
He would wait for the better weather; it has been a wet July.

This year his field lay fallow; he was late putting down his seed.
Cold December concealed with a sighing surplice of snow
His waste of neglected furrows, overgrown with mutinous
  weed.

Dark, bereaved like the ground, I found him feeble and sick
And cold, for neither the sticks nor his lamp with a shrunken
    wick
Would light. He was gone through the wicket. His clock con-
    tinued to tick,
But it stopped when the new flakes clustered on an empty room
    below.

Great Nights Returning

Great nights returning, midnight's constellations
Gather from groundfrost that unnatural brilliance.
Night now transfigures, walking in the starred ways,
Tears for the living.

Earth now takes back the secret of her changes.
All the wood's dropped leaves listen to your footfall.
Night has no tears, no sound among the branches;
Stopped is the swift stream.

Spirits were joined when hazel leaves were falling.
Then the stream hurrying told of separation
This is the fires' world, and the voice of Autumn
Stilled by the death-wand.

Under your heels the icy breath of Winter
Hardens all roots. The Leonids[1] are flying.
Now the crisp stars, the circle of beginning;
Death, birth, united.

Nothing declines here. Energy is fire-born.
Twigs catch like stars or serve for your divining.
Lean down and hear the subterranean water
Crossed by the quick dead.

Now the soul knows the fire that first composed it
Sinks not with time but is renewed hereafter.
Death cannot steal the light which love has kindled
Nor the years change it.

   1. *Leonids*: an annual meteor shower, which is seen around 16
November.

The Razor Shell

I am the long lean razor shell:
Do not interpret me too soon.
Streak of the wind with tawny stains,
The sky's quill-feather marked my grooves,
The sea is hidden in my veins.
I am a part of all that moves,
And more than this, of what remains.
Here on the sand in burning noon
I lie, forgotten by the swell.
I hear the breakers and the oars
Falling along the level shores
And beating down the golden grains.
Let Solomon consider well
And take me cool into his hand,
Then ask, before he count the sand:
What is that labour to the moon?

LAWRENCE DURRELL

born 1912

Durrell seems to stand for a good many of the things which the Move-
ment poets (and critics since) have been determined to disapprove. An
inveterate denizen of 'abroad', and especially of the Mediterranean lit-
toral, raffish, touched by surrealism but unable to take it very seriously,
technically rather loose and careless: it adds up to a formidable indict-
ment. Durrell proceeded to add insult to injury by becoming a best-
selling novelist, with the publication of 'The Alexandria Quartet'. Not
surprisingly, his reputation as a poet has suffered in recent years. One
doubts if he minds all that much. Durrell's virtue as a poet is that he
is an excellent entertainer; the ingredients are not always new ('A Por-
trait of Theodora', printed here, certainly owes a good deal to Cavafy)
but they are blended with a light hand.

A Portrait of Theodora

I recall her by a freckle of gold
In the pupil of one eye, an odd
Strawberry-gold: and after many years
Of forgetting that musical body –
Arms too long, wrists too slender –
Remember only the unstable wishes
Disquieting the flesh. I will not
Deny her pomp was laughable, urban:
Behind it one could hear the sad
Provincial laughter rotted by insomnia.

None of these meetings are planned,
I guess, or willed by the exemplars
Of a city's love – a city founded in
The name of love: to me is always
Brown face, white teeth, cheap summer frock
In green and white stripes and then
Forever a strawberry eye. I recalled no more
For years. The eye was lying in wait.

Then in another city from the same
Twice-used air and sheets, in the midst
Of a parting: the same dark bedroom,
Arctic chamber-pot and cruel iron bed,
I saw the street-lamp unpick Theodora
Like an old sweater, unwrinkle eyes and mouth,
Unbandaging her youth to let me see
The wounds I had not understood before.

How could I have ignored such wounds?
The bloody sweepings of a loving smile
Strewed like Osiris among the dunes?
Now only my experience recognizes her
Too late, among the other great survivors
Of the city's rage, and places her among
The champions of love – among the true elect!

Sarajevo

Bosnia. November. And the mountain roads
Earthbound but matching perfectly these long
And passionate self-communings counter-march,
Balanced on scarps of trap, ramble or blunder
Over traverses of cloud: and here they move,
Mule-teams like insects harnessed by a bell
Upon the leaf-edge of a winter sky,

And down at last into this lap of stone
Between four cataracts of rock: a town
Peopled by sleepy eagles, whispering only
Of the sunburnt herdsmen's hopeless ploy:
A sterile earth quickened by shards of rock
Where nothing grows, not even in his sleep,

Where minarets have twisted up like sugar
And a river, curdled with blond ice, drives on
Tinkling among the mule-teams and the mountaineers,
Under the bridges and the wooden trellises
Which tame the air and promise us a peace
Harmless with nightingales. None are singing now.

No history much? Perhaps. Only this ominous
Dark beauty flowering under veils,
Trapped in the spectrum of a dying style:
A village like an instinct left to rust,
Composed around the echo of a pistol-shot.[1]

Bitter Lemons

In an island of bitter lemons[2]
Where the moon's cool fevers burn
From the dark globes of the fruit,

And the dry grass underfoot
Tortures memory and revises
Habits half a lifetime dead

Better leave the rest unsaid,
Beauty, darkness, vehemence
Let the old sea-nurses keep

Their memorials of sleep
And the Greek sea's curly head
Keep its calms like tears unshed

Keep its calms like tears unshed.

1. *a pistol-shot*: Sarajevo was the scene of the assassination of Archduke Franz Ferdinand of Austria in 1914.

2. *an island of bitter lemons*: Cyprus at the period of agitation for Enosis.

GEORGE BARKER

born 1913

One of the chief figures in the poetry of the late thirties and middle forties, Barker's work has pursued an extremely erratic course since the war, to the increasing detriment of his reputation. Indeed, it has sometimes seemed that Barker's importance lay less in what he wrote than in what he *was*: the man still wholly committed to poetry in an age of part-time poets who were also full-time academics.

On a Friend's Escape from Drowning off the Norfolk Coast

Came up that cold sea at Cromer like a running grave
    Beside him as he struck
Wildly towards the shore, but the blackcapped wave
    Crossed him and swung him back,
And he saw his son digging in the castled dirt that could save.
    Then the farewell rock
Rose a last time to his eyes. As he cried out
    A pawing gag of the sea
Smothered his cry and he sank in his own shout
    Like a dying airman. Then she
Deep near her son asleep on the hourglass sand
    Was awakened by whom
Save the Fate who knew that this was the wrong time:
    And opened her eyes
On the death of her son's begetter. Up she flies
    Into the hydra-headed
Grave as he closes his life upon her who for
    Life has so richly bedded him.
But she drove through his drowning like Orpheus and tore
    Back by the hair
Her escaping bridegroom. And on the sand their son
    Stood laughing where

He was almost an orphan. Then the three lay down
    On that cold sand,
Each holding the other by a living hand.

Roman Poem III

(A Sparrow's Feather)

There was this empty birdcage in the garden.
    And in it, to amuse myself, I had hung
pseudo-Oriental birds constructed of
    glass and tin bits and paper, that squeaked sadly
as the wind sometimes disturbed them. Suspended
    in melancholy disillusion they sang
of things that had never happened, and never
    could in that cage of artificial existence.
The twittering of these instruments lamenting
    their absent lives resembled threnodies
torn from a falling harp, till the cage filled with
    engineered regret like moonshining cobwebs
as these constructions grieved over not existing.
    The children fed them with flowers. A sudden gust
and without sound lifelessly one would die
    scattered in scraps like debris. The wire doors
always hung open, against their improbable
    transfiguration into, say, chaffinches
or even more colourful birds. Myself I found
    the whole game charming, let alone the children.
And then, one morning – I do not record a
    matter of cosmic proportions, I assure you,
not an event to flutter the Volscian dovecotes –
    there, askew among those constructed images
like a lost soul electing to die in Rome,
    its feverish eye transfixed, both wings fractured,
lay – I assure you, Catullus – a young sparrow.
    Not long for this world, so heavily breathing
one might have supposed this cage his destination
    after labouring past seas and holy skies
whence, death not being known there, he had flown.
    Of course, there was nothing to do. The children

brought breadcrumbs, brought water, brought tears in their
    eyes perhaps to restore him, that shivering panic
of useless feathers, that tongue-tied little gossip,
    that lying flyer. So there, among its gods
that moaned and whistled in a little wind,
    flapping their paper anatomies like windmills,
wheeling and bowing dutifully to the
    divine intervention of a child's forefinger,
there, at rest and at peace among its monstrous
    idols, the little bird died. And, for my part,
I hope the whole unimportant affair is
    quickly forgotten. The analogies are too trite.

C. H. Sisson

born 1914

C. H. Sisson sees himself as the heir of the classic Latin poets, and at times achieves their combination of weight, density and concision. He says: 'What I aim at is to make plain statements and not more of them than I need.' His poetic career began in the 1950s, and his first book of verse was published only in 1955, when he was already past forty. Since then he has slowly gathered pace, becoming more and more prolific at an age when many poets find the Muse deserts them. Though the earlier poems are harsher in sound and bitterer in tone than those he has published more recently, there is underlying all of them a stoical pessimism, and an inclination to question the nature and purposes of a Creator whose very existence he is inclined to doubt.

Ellick Farm

The larks flew up like jack-in-the-boxes
From my moors, and the fields were edged with foxgloves.

The farm lay neatly within the hollow
The gables climbing, the barn beside the doorway.

If I had climbed into the loft I should have found a boy
Forty years back, among the bales of hay.

He would have known certainly all that I know
Seeing it in the muck-strewn cobbles below.

(Under the dark rim of the near wood
The tears gathered as under an eyelid.)

It would have surprised him to see a tall man
Who had travelled far, pretending to be him.

But that he should have been turning verses, half dumb
After half a lifetime, would least have surprised him.

The Consequence

I

There is no more to say than No
And Nothing is my farthest end.
A man has pity for his friend
But I am only glad to go.
Now therefore let the handsome crow
Pick out the eyes I would not lend.

II

We feed on death for half our lives
But vomit when we let it in.
The final pallor of the skin
Betokens that the patient thrives.
How earnestly the swimmer dives!
How eager his returning fin!

III

Old age protects itself with hope
And leans to suck the kiss of youth.
How kindly Boaz took to Ruth!
The lion with the antelope.
And what delighted fingers grope
In cradles to forget the truth!

IV

But there is twilight and the rose
And other such ephemera.
The crocus and Proserpina
Distract us to a brief repose.
And I, who have a polished heart,
Harder than any sympathy
But excellent for lechery
Or any sanctimonious part
For ever leave the truth alone;
It crunches time up like a stone

While love, the centre of the mind
Nibbles the flesh from head to feet.
The dusty streets of Sodom find
Two constables upon the beat.

v

Plato, whom reason ate like sex,
Preferred the form before the thing.
But what contentment did that bring?
Whom did that ever unperplex?
Meanwhile incessant number pecks
At form, until the scaffolding
Of all our thoughts is down, to fling
The gates of chaos on our necks.
Judas went out and hanged himself
And so should I, for I am he.
There is no Adam to set free.

vi

The forest of a long intent
Has tracks where I may lose my way
Nor was the place I am today
Intended by the way I went.
The night has only disarray;
It does not see what day mistook.
What was it that the nightmare shook?
Although I heard the drum today
The same occasions day by day
Provide me with identity.
I do what the occasions say
For nothing never is without
The thing it wants, and for its play
A futile gesture is the best.

The Desert

I

This is the only place that I inhabit:
The desert.
No drop of water: no palm trees: nothing.
No gourd, no cactus: sand
Heaped on all sides like mountainous seas
To drown in.
Luckily I cannot see myself, I am alone
No mirror, glass, plastic left by an Arab
Nothing
I cannot say it too often
Nothing.
The sand itself would diminish if I said yes.
No rascally Bedouin,
Praying mantis, or nice people
– A mirage of them, occasionally.
But they are not there, any more than I,
For all my vocables, eyes, 'I's,
Other impedimenta of the desert
– Khaki shirt, shorts, chapli,
Mess-tin, for nothing to eat;
Water-bottle, nothing in it.
It is an amusing end, because desired.

2

Alone
But to say 'alone' would be to give validity
To a set of perceptions which are nothing at all
– A set as these words are
Set down
Meaninglessly on paper, by nobody.
There were friends, they have faded into the distance;
With my disintegration the vision becomes blurred,
Rather, disintegrated, each bit
For all I know
Tied to a separate nothing, not I.
Enough of laughter, which echoes like a tin eccentric
Round the edge of the desert:

C. H. Sisson

Tears would be ridiculous
If I could shed them,
Eyes shed them, one
Then another again, weeping
For different things, not joined.

Shatter the retina so that the eyes are many
– Hailstones, now, it can be sand for all I care.
The damned unrepairable, I sit
Like a vehicle sanded up, the desert
Is frequent with images.
Could night come, that would effect a change,
But the sun blazes:
'I am all you have to fear, extreme, hot, searing
But the end is dust, and soon.'

A Visitor

Put on your coat
And go home.
Nothing is said;
Nowhere to go.

Take off your shoes,
Stretch out;
Somebody's leg;
Nothing is said.

Somebody's foot,
Somebody's toe:
Maybe at last;
Nothing is said.

Go home
Go where?
Nothing is said
In the thin air.

THOMAS BLACKBURN

1916–77

The lodestone of Blackburn's poetry was the work of W. B. Yeats. Blackburn himself said in an interview: 'I got steeped in the poetry of Yeats as a young man, I knew a great deal of his work by heart and it was only when there were certain things that I wanted to say that Yeats hadn't said that I began to seriously want to write.' Blackburn's most original poems offer a bleak geography of the domestic emotions which is in fact quite different from anything to be found in Yeats or in the Movement poets who sometimes use the same material.

En Route

It's strange, I thought, though half now stretches
Behind my back, how this road clutches
To its small grit and measuring stone,
Still more of life as I walk on;
Must all directions be subdued
By the compulsion of the road?

And strange it is, since there's no fences,
I do not take the path which glances
Aside from this, as if one strict
Intention gathered up all fact;
Is it because I'm whittled down
To the sharp stones I journey on?

Once certainly the traveller hurried
Down every path the wind unburied.
Finding, however, each new search
Swung back to the old line of march,
And that through detours I could not
Bypass myself or the road's grit,

Though still a side-lane light discloses,
I would hold back from its green mazes,
Sensing, though light it may reflect,

Once entered it would be blunt fact,
And so a double tax be owed
To the compulsion of the road.

Not that today they do not differ,
Myself and the relentless pressure
Of gravel underneath my feet,
But now I glimpse I half beget,
Step after step, what I walk on,
And know I am the origin

Of so much love and hate which gathers
Round those who with me are wayfarers.
Perhaps when to myself, the dreamer,
I wake, and understand the ardour
In which all burn, more clear I'll know
Who others are, myself also,

Than when it seemed far off, the fever
Which shakes me now. Since doom and glamour
No man can fly from or possess,
By stillness I make good their loss,
And find, upon the edge of winter,
More plain the way, as light grows fainter.

Last night I dreamt the road diminished
To a last stone, and where it perished
I met a child beside a river,
Who asked if I would bear him over.
I knelt then as if asking pardon,
But on my back his little burden

Than the whole world became much greater,
As stepping down into the water
I braced myself to find what could
Sustain my feet when I was dead,
And at long last no debt was owed
Since on my shoulders lay the road.

JOHN HEATH-STUBBS

born 1918

Heath-Stubbs's work is imbued with a nostalgia for 'classicism' – in itself a romantic characteristic. Consciously literary, elaborate, highly wrought, rather unspontaneous, it is not the kind of poetry which will ever have a large popular appeal. Yet it is work which impresses because of the poet's devotion to his craft: few writers now at work in England have a more devoted care for the language, or a deeper knowledge of it.

The Last Watch of Empire[1]

For Fred Marnau

The ultimate dream. Arms, eagles, broken banners,
And a blind battle in the naked wood.
Over the brazen birds
Those with black shining feathers that scream and tear;
The angels rending their bright hair
Amid the fog and babel of crying voices,
Where Cyril and Methodius[2] snatch at their split hearts.
Look now, this
Is the last Emperor, whose crown of iron and gold
Drops diamonds like frozen tears, like those smooth stones
The glacier bears from mythological mountains.
Now he has fled into the forest where
The elk and wild boar their yellowing bones
Abandon to the ghost-led traveller;

1. *The Last Watch of Empire*: Much of the apparatus of the poem refers to the Byzantine Empire, though the 'crown of iron and gold' is traditionally that of Lombardy.

2. *Cyril and Methodius*: the 'apostles of the Slavs', who were responsible for Christianizing the Slav regions and spreading the influence of Byzantium deep into Russia. Their adoption of a Slavic rather than a Latin liturgy was an important part of their success. Cyril lived c. 827–69, and his brother Methodius c. 825–85.

With his great hands, heavy with seals, he scratches
For acorns, beech-mast, against hibernation,
Through winters which no rising sun, no moon
Prompting the green unfolded bud, shall loosen,
In his gem-fiery chamber among the roots.
(Sleep Caesar, though the hunter's horn
Be still lamenting over your slate-grey head:
It is not time, not yet.)
Till corn and roses rise from his brain, his heart.

★

The holy Malachi,[3] in a western island, once
Prophesied this: the Roman Peter feeding
His flock amid great tribulations,
Destruction riding over the seven hills.
Now an old man, in a secret mountain cave,
Sits, with wax-white hands to bless, and hair
Light on the wind, and grey as cobwebs;
Where eleven hermits, as spry as wagtails, twitter,
Raising their spare throats to the dawn's cold beams.

A Charm Against the Toothache

Venerable Mother Toothache
Climb down from the white battlements,
Stop twisting in your yellow fingers
The fourfold rope of nerves;
And tomorrow I will give you a tot of whisky
To hold in your cupped hands,
A garland of anise-flowers,
And three cloves like nails.
And tell the attendant gnomes
It is time to knock off now,
To shoulder their little pick-axes,
Their cold-chisels and drills.
And you may mount by a silver ladder

---

3. *Malachi*: the last of the 'prophets' in the Hebrew Bible.

Into the sky, to grind
In the cracked polished mortar
Of the hollow moon.

By the lapse of warm,
And the poppies nodding like red coals,
The paths on the granite mountains,
And the plantation of my dreams.

W. S. Graham

born 1917

One cannot help feeling that W. S. Graham is a poet who has been somewhat unlucky in his timing. His best-known volume was *The Nightfishing*, which appeared in the same year as Philip Larkin's *The Less Deceived*. The contrast between the two volumes is the contrast between the 'old' poetry and the new. *The Nightfishing*, and especially the long title poem, owes an obvious debt to Dylan Thomas, and through him to the modernism of the period between the wars. Indeed, it was widely praised at the time of its publication as the logical development of Dylan Thomas's work. But in fact it marked the end of an era. The narrative printed here shows the poet's individuality more clearly.

Malcolm Mooney's Land

I

Today, Tuesday, I decided to move on
Although the wind was veering. Better to move
Than have them at my heels, poor friends
I buried earlier under the printed snow.
From wherever it is I urge these words
To find their subtle vents, the northern dazzle
Of silence cranes to watch. Footprint on foot–
Print, word on word and each on a fool's errand.
Malcolm Mooney's Land. Elizabeth
Was in my thoughts all morning and the boy.
Wherever I speak from or in what particular
Voice, this is always the record of me in you.
I can record at least out there to the west
The grinding bergs and, listen, further off
Where we are going, the glacier calves
Making its sudden momentary thunder.
This is as good a night, a place as any.

II

From the rimed bag of sleep. Wednesday,
My words crackle in the early air.
Thistles of ice about my chin,
My dreams, my breath a ruff of crystals.
The new ice falls from canvas walls.
O benign creature with the small ear-hole,
Submerger under silence, lead
Me where the unblubbered monster goes
Listening and makes his play.
Make my impediment mean no ill
But be itself a way.

A fox was here last night (Maybe Nansen's
Reading my instruments.) the prints
All round the tent and not a sound.
Not that I'd have him call my name.
Anyhow how should he know? Enough
Voices are with me here and more
The further I go. Yesterday
I heard the telephone ringing deep
Down in a blue crevasse.
I did not answer it and could
Hardly bear to pass.

Landlice, always my good bedfellows
Ride with me in my sweaty seams.
Come bonny friendly beasts, brother
To the grammarsow and the word-louse,
Bite me your presence, keep me awake
In the cold with work to do, to remember
To put down something to take back
I have reached the edge of earshot here
And by the laws of distance
My words go through the smoking air
Changing their tune on silence.

III

My friend who loves owls
Has been with me all day
Walking at my ear

And speaking of old summers
When to speak was easy.
His eyes are almost gone
Which made him hear well.
Under our feet the great
Glacier drove its keel.
What is to read there
Scored out in the dark?

Later the north-west distance
Thickened towards us.
The blizzard grew and proved
Too filled with other voices
High and desperate
For me to hear him more.
I turned to see him go
Becoming shapeless into
The shrill swerving snow.

IV

   Today, Friday, holds the white
   Paper up too close to see
Me here in a white-out in this tent of a place.
   And why is it there has to be
Some place to find, however momentarily
To speak from, some distance to listen to?
   Out at the far-off edge I hear
   Colliding voices, drifted, yes,
To find me through the slowly opening leads.
   Tomorrow I'll try the rafted ice.
Have I not been trying to use the obstacle
Of language well? It freezes round us all.

V

Why did you choose this place
For us to meet? Sit
With me between this word
And this, my furry queen.
Yet not mistake this

For the real thing. Here
In Malcolm Mooney's Land
I have heard many
Approachers in the distance
Shouting. Early hunters
Skittering across the ice
Full of enthusiasm
And making fly and,
Within the ear, the yelling
Spear steepening to
The real prey, the right
Prey of the moment.
The honking choir in fear
Leave the tilting floe
And enter the sliding water.
Above the bergs the foolish
Voices are lighting lamps
And all their sounds make
This diary of a place
Writing us both in.
Come and sit. Or is
It right to stay here
While, outside the tent
The bearded blinded go
Calming their children
Into the ovens of frost?
And what's the news?
What brought you here through
The spring leads opening?

Elizabeth you and the boy
Have been with me often
Especially on those last
Stages. Tell him a story.
Tell him I came across
An old sulphur bear
Sawing his log of sleep
Loud beneath the snow.
He puffed the powdered light
Up on to this page
And here his reek fell

In splinters among
These words. He snored well.
Elizabeth, my furry
Pelted queen of Malcolm
Mooney's Land, I made
You here beside me
For a moment out
Of the correct fatigue.
I have made myself alone now.
Outside the tent endless
Drifting hummock crests.
Words drifting on words.
The real unabstract snow.

BERNARD SPENCER

1909–63

When he died, Bernard Spencer left behind him a very small *oeuvre*. His *Collected Poems* total only ninety-six pages. In many ways, he was the type of the excellent minor poet: scrupulous, solitary, a traveller and observer. He said once in an interview: 'I think I like ordinary people, because I am *listening*, because they are my subject-matter, and I think if I got among a group of poets or writers very often I should be put off.' The poems confirm this self-portrait. What makes them live is their precision of imagery – 'A dog's pitched/barking flakes and flakes away at the sky' – and their truth to feeling.

Night-Time: Starting to Write

Over the mountains a plane bumbles in;
down in the city a watchman's iron-topped stick
bounces and rings on the pavement. Late returners
must be waiting now, by me unseen

To enter shadowed doorways. A dog's pitched
barking flakes and flakes away at the sky.
Sounds and night-sounds, no more; but then I catch
my lamp burn fiercer like a thing bewitched,

Table and chairs expectant like a play:
and – if that Unknown, Demon, what you will
stalks on the scene – must live with sounds and echoes,
be damned the call to sleep, the needs of day,

Love a dark city; then for some bare bones
of motive, strange perhaps to beast or traveller,
with all I am and all that I have been
sweat the night into words, as who cracks stones.

Bernard Spencer

Properties of Snow

Snow on pine gorges can burn blue like Persian
cats; falling on passers can tip them with the eloquent hair
of dancers or Shakespeare actors;
on roads can mute the marching of a company of infantry
(so that they seem the killed from a battle whispering by);
neglected, glues where you walk, a slippery black iron,
famous hospital-filler,
proved friend of bandages and white hip-length plaster.
Decorative and suspicious: wine broken recently on snow . . .
Spaded with tinkles and grating
from a pavement, presently huddles in a heap blotched and
    disgraced,
a pedigree pet, now repellent.

On office, on factory roofs,
or stretching, severe, to horizons on trees, fields, fences,
with no way across except the way the traveller will plough;
nothing moving, and a sky the colour of grey trousers;
blanched snow, the Chinese colour of mourning, of death,
can rob the bones of their marrow,
turn a man's face towards home.

ROY FULLER

born 1912

Roy Fuller occupies a key position in the history of British poetry in the post-war years. Essentially, it is he who forms the bridge between the poets of the thirites, and particularly W. H. Auden, and those of the fifties. He is only five years younger than Auden, and his first book of verse appeared in 1939. What he takes from the older poet he takes from the rational, civilized, well-ordered side of him: Fuller's Auden is not the poet of *The Orators*. On the other hand, Fuller is not completely a Movement writer *avant la lettre*. His wryness is more romantic than theirs; when he writes of erotic relationships he is far less domestic. He has the broader horizon which the Movement poets do not have. In his later writing he has broadened his technical range, alternating both syllabics and free verse.

Poem Out of Character

Rapidly moving from the end
To the middle of anthologies,
The poet starts to comprehend
The styles that never can be his.

The dreams of tremendous statements fade,
Inchoate still the passionate rhymes
Of men, the novel verse form made
To satirize and warn the times.

And yet at moments, as in sleep,
Beyond his book float images –
Those four great planets swathed in deep
Ammoniac and methane seas.

He walks the ruined autumn scene –
The trees a landscape painter's brown,
And through the foreground rags, serene
The faded sky, palladian town.

Or thinks of man, his single young,
The failure of the specialized,
Successful type; the curious, long
Years before earth was dramatized:

The West Wind Drift, that monstrous belt
Of sea below the planet's waist:
The twenty-one world cultures felt
Like fathers doomed to be defaced.

Yet, these vast intimations rise
And still I merely find the words
For symbols of a comic size –
Ambiguous cats and sweets and birds.

Viewed through such tiny apertures
The age presents a leaf, a hair,
An inch of skin; while what enures,
In truth, behind the barrier,

Weltering in blood, enormous joys
Lighting their faces, in a frieze
Of giantesses, gods and boys;
And lions and inhuman trees.

From 'Meredithian[1] Sonnets'

Incredulous, he stared at the amused
Official writing down his name among
Those whose request to suffer was refused.

W. H. AUDEN

II

Great suns, the streetlamps in the pinhead rain;
Surfaces gradually begin to shine;
Brunettes are silvered; taxis pass in line
On tyres that beat through moisture like a pain.

1. *Meredithian*: the sixteen-line form invented by George Meredith for
his sequence *Modern Love*.

Doubtless upon such evenings some at least
Of those events that shaped his soul occurred:
Against the streaming glass a whispered word
Whitened and faded, and the shapeless beast
Drank from the dripping gutters through the night.
But all the child expressed and feared is long
Forgotten: only what went wholly wrong
Survives as this spectator of the flight
Of lovers through the square of weeping busts
To happiness, and of the lighted towers
Where mad designs are woven by the powers;
Of normal weather, ordinary lusts.

IX

Is it the tongue enslaves him to the land?
Turning the pages of a dictionary,
He finds the snail serrates the strawberry.
On chocolate furrows birds like snowballs stand,
While horses scissor pieces of the skies;
The ploughman's lips are dreamt of in a garden
Where spheres and spheroids in the light unharden,
And shadows tremble in the shapes of eyes.
Under the birch, the peasants and the deer,
The hills run chalky fingers to the waves
Where blue bays lead into the gantried naves
And smoking spars of cities. Seasons here
Contend with brick and iron, yet in spring
Frost goes away on wagons with the coke,
And larks rise through disintegrating smoke
And see it is an island that they sing.

XIII

He reads a poem in a railway carriage
But cannot keep his glance upon the tropes,
And asks himself what is it that he hopes:
Criminal contact, fatherhood or marriage?
The child's grey eyes and tiny, dirty nails;
Its other sex; its beauty, unflawed, slim;
Its unembarrassed consciousness of him –

In which, however, he completely fails
To make out any element except
A curiosity sublime: is this
A human commerce far beyond the kiss
Such as awakened goodness where it slept
Inside the hairy capsule, or invented
Incredible ideas of innocence –
Conception lacking flesh and prurience,
And orifices marvellously scented?

STEVIE SMITH

1902–71

An unclassifiable original, Stevie Smith was a prolific poet whose earliest work appeared in 1937 – as much out of context then as it was to be later. Her apparently naïf style has a surprising flexibility, and can express a wide variety of emotions. At times she sounds like Emily Dickinson; at times like the purest Zürich Dada of 1915 (though the poet herself denied the validity of these comparisons). Certain themes recur: loneliness, a prolonged theological debate with the Christian religion, nervous animals and people in peculiar circumstances.

Not Waving but Drowning

Nobody heard him, the dead man,
But still he lay moaning:
I was much further out than you thought
And not waving but drowning.

Poor chap, he always loved larking
And now he's dead
It must have been too cold for him his heart gave way,
They said.

Oh, no no no, it was too cold always
(Still the dead one lay moaning)
I was much too far out all my life
And not waving but drowning.

Tenuous and Precarious

Tenuous and Precarious
Were my guardians,
Precarious and Tenuous,
Two Romans.

My father was Hazardous,
Hazardous,
Dear old man,
Three Romans.

There was my brother Spurious,
Spurious Posthumous,
Spurious was spurious
Was four Romans.

My husband was Perfidious,
He *was* perfidious,
Five Romans.

Surreptitious, our son,
Was surreptitious,
He was six Romans.

Our cat Tedious
Still lives,
Count not Tedious
Yet.

My name is Finis,
Finis, Finis,
I am Finis,
Six, five, four, three, two,
One Roman,
Finis.

Emily Writes Such a Good Letter

Mabel was married last week
So now only Tom left

The doctor didn't like Arthur's cough
I have been in bed since Easter

A touch of the old trouble

I am downstairs today
As I write this
I can hear Arthur roaming overhead

He loves to roam
Thank heavens he has plenty of space to roam in

We have seven bedrooms
And an annexe

Which leaves a flat for the chauffeur and his wife

We have much to be thankful for

The new vicar came yesterday
People say he brings a breath of fresh air

He leaves me cold
I do not think he is a gentleman

Yes, I remember Maurice very well
Fancy getting married at his age
She must be a fool

You knew May had moved?
Since Edward died she has been much alone

It was cancer

No, I know nothing of Maud
I never wish to hear her name again
In my opinion Maud
Is an evil woman

Our char has left
And a good riddance too
Wages are very high in Tonbridge

Write and tell me how you are, dear,
And the girls,
Phoebe and Rose
They must be a great comfort to you
Phoebe and Rose.

CHARLES CAUSLEY

born 1917

Much of Causley's work has been in ballad form; and a good deal of it looks back to his experiences as a seaman during the war. The ballads have a pace, a colour, and often a violence which sets them apart from other poets' essays in the same form. The tone swings between the humorous (Causley can sound like a less sophisticated Betjeman) and the apocalyptic.

My Friend Maloney

My friend Maloney, eighteen,
  Swears like a sentry,
Got into trouble two years back
  With the local gentry.

Parson and squire's sons
  Informed a copper.
The magistrate took one look at Maloney.
  Fixed him proper.

Talked of the crime of youth,
  The innocent victim.
Maloney never said a blind word
  To contradict him.

Maloney of Gun Street,
  Back of the Nuclear Mission,
Son of the town whore,
  Blamed television.

Justice, as usual, triumphed.
  Everyone felt fine.
Things went deader.
  Maloney went up the line.

Maloney learned one lesson:
  Never play the fool

With the products of especially a minor
    Public school.

Maloney lost a thing or two
    At that institution.
First shirt, second innocence,
    The old irresolution.

Found himself a girl-friend,
    Sharp suit, sharp collars,
Maloney on a moped,
    Pants full of dollars.

College boys on the corner
    In striped, strait blazers
Look at old Maloney,
    Eyes like razors.

You don't need talent, says Maloney.
    You don't need looks.
All I got you got, fellers.
    You can keep your thick books.

Parson got religion,
    Squire, in the end, the same.
The magistrate went over the wall.
    Life, said Maloney, 's a game.

Consider then the case of Maloney,
    College boys, parson, squire, beak.
Who was the victor and who was the victim?
    Speak.

R. S. Thomas

born 1913

It took a long time for R. S. Thomas's work to achieve recognition. His first book did not appear till 1946, and then it was not brought out by a large London publishing house. In 1952, his second book was noticed by the B.B.C. Critics, but his reputation was not established until the appearance of *Song at the Year's Turning*, which incorporates the bulk of the material from three previous collections. This has a preface by John Betjeman. Thomas, an Anglican priest with a parish in Wales, resembles his namesake Dylan Thomas not at all. It is permissible to detect a resemblance to Edward Thomas, however. In many respects a belated Georgian, he uses a slow meditative manner with great skill. Essentially this is the kind of 'country poetry' which has always appealed to English readers, and seems likely to go on doing so. As a country priest who is also a poet, R. S. Thomas has a long and distinguished ancestry.

The Welsh Hill Country

Too far for you to see
The fluke and the foot-rot and the fat maggot
Gnawing the skin from the small bones,
The sheep are grazing at Bwlch-y-Fedwen,
Arranged romantically in the usual manner
On a bleak background of bald stone.

Too far for you to see
The moss and the mould on the cold chimneys,
The nettles growing through the cracked doors,
The houses stand empty at Nant-yr-Eira,
There are holes in the roofs that are thatched with sunlight,
And the fields are reverting to the bare moor.

Too far, too far to see
The set of his eyes and the slow phthisis
Wasting his frame under the ripped coat,
There's a man still farming at Ty'n-y-Fawnog,

Contributing grimly to the accepted pattern,
The embryo music dead in his throat.

The Mixen

Yes, I forgot the mixen
Its crude colour and tart smell.
I described him fondly but not well
In showing his eyes blue as flowers,
His hair like the crow's wing,
His easy movements over the acres
Ploughed ready for the stars' sowing.
I sang him early in the fields
With dew embroidered, but forgot
The mixen clinging to his heel,
Its brand under the ripped coat,
The mixen slurring his strong speech.
I made him comely but too rich;
The mixen sours the dawn's gold.

The Country Clergy

I see them working in old rectories
By the sun's light, by candlelight,
Venerable men, their black cloth
A little dusty, a little green
With holy mildew. And yet their skulls,
Ripening over so many prayers,
Toppled into the same grave
With oafs and yokels. They left no books,
Memorial to their lonely thought
In grey parishes; rather they wrote
On men's hearts and in the minds
Of young children sublime words
Too soon forgotten. God in his time
Or out of time will correct this.

R. S. *Thomas*

Evans

Evans? Yes, many a time
I came down his bare flight
Of stairs into the gaunt kitchen
With its wood fire, where crickets sang
Accompaniment to the black kettle's
Whine, and so into the cold
Dark to smother in the thick tide
Of night that drifted about the walls
Of his stark farm on the hill ridge.

It was not the dark filling my eyes
And mouth appalled me; not even the drip
Of rain like blood from the one tree
Weather-tortured. It was the dark
Silting the veins of that sick man
I left stranded upon the vast
And lonely shore of his bleak bed.

PATRICIA BEER

born 1924

Patricia Beer comes from Devon, and quite a lot of her work concerns itself with her roots there. Essentially she is a poet who tries to say something individual within the bounds of an established tradition, and quite often succeeds in her aim. The two poems printed here are both about death and rebirth – characteristic themes. 'A Dream of Hanging' reveals a vein of slyly grotesque humour which appears elsewhere in her work.

Finis

Now he is being shot. The last page
Is a mere nail-tip away; he will surely die.
The first bullet jerks him into old age,

The second shows him a sight secretly.
But I, the reader, feel no surprise
Though he walks in spurts over the dry

Carpet to bed, for I recognize
What he is doing. It is his last food
He must gulp now, so down he lies

Pulling the bullets and the blood
In with him, curling up around them,
Hugging them tight to do him good.

Into each organ, into each limb
He pulls back strength. With his coiled breath
He lassoes what has run from him.

Drawn up like a tortoise on a path
He retracts everything. This is the end.
Yet it looks more like life than death.

A Dream of Hanging

He rang me up
In a dream,
My brother did.
He had been hanged
That morning,
Innocent,
And I had slept
Through the striking
Of the clock
While it had taken place,
Eight,
Just about time enough
For it to happen.
He spoke to me
On the telephone
That afternoon
To reassure me,
My dear brother
Who had killed nobody,
And I asked him,
Long distance,
What it had felt like
To be hanged.
'Oh, don't worry, lovey,' he said,
'When your time comes.
It tickled rather.'

Part three: The Movement

Movement poetry has been discussed *ad nauseam*: there is little new to add. As other critics and anthologists have done, I have taken as my criterion the inclusion of a writer in Robert Conquest's *New Lines* anthology of 1955. At this period, and despite the differences between, for example, D. J. Enright and the early Thom Gunn, the Movement was something stylistically cohesive and did represent a reaction against both modernism and internationalism. This said, one must take into account not only the protestations made by some of the poets at being thus forcibly yoked together, but the subsequent development of a number of them. If Larkin, Amis and Enright have remained substantially what they were, both Gunn and Davie have greatly altered, and in each case they have turned towards America. Gunn was one of the first British poets to use the syllabic metres which were already being used by some Americans; Davie at one time went almost entirely around the critical compass, and became a supporter of the American Black Mountain poets and an interpreter of Pound. It is perhaps worth noting that what Gunn and Davie have in common, besides this Americanism, is a philosophical bent; theirs has always been very much a poetry of ideas, which has possibly had something to do with their respective conversions.

PHILIP LARKIN

born 1922

On balance, Larkin is probably the most important poet to establish himself in England since the war. Ted Hughes has been as much discussed, but has not had nearly such a decisive effect on other writers. Even those poets who are most obviously influenced by Hughes, such as Ted Walker, turn out to owe something to Larkin as well. In his introduction to the new edition of *The North Ship*, Larkin has described how, shortly after the appearance of this volume, he exchanged the influence of W. B. Yeats for that of Thomas Hardy. It was a crucial decision, and it bore fruit almost ten years later with the publication of *The Less Deceived*: the signal for the Movement to begin. Larkin's scepticism, his skilful deflation of 'high emotion' fitted him perfectly for influence in those years. He found himself the spokesman of a whole new class, the Oxbridge meritocracy which was then emerging. English poetry was turning its back on modernism, was developing a suspicion of 'abroad'. Larkin took these reactions and made them respectable, by showing that the alternative tradition, that of Hardy and Edward Thomas, still had life in it. Larkin is a writer who understands perfectly the measure of his own gift, and seldom or never strays outside its limits. A subtle psychologist, an elegant but deliberately conventional technician, a man with an instinctive knowledge of the aspirations of a new and important class, an excellent critic of his own work, he made a position for himself which was never seriously challenged by the other poets of the fifties: Larkin is *the* characteristic voice of a whole generation. One's only quarrel might be with the attitudes which Larkin seemed to typify, rather than with the poetry itself.

Mr Bleaney

'This was Mr Bleaney's room. He stayed
The whole time he was at the Bodies, till
They moved him.' Flowered curtains, thin and frayed,
Fall to within five inches of the sill,

Whose window shows a strip of building land,
Tussocky, littered. 'Mr Bleaney took

My bit of garden properly in hand.'
Bed, upright chair, sixty-watt bulb, no hook

Behind the door, no room for books or bags –
'I'll take it.' So it happens that I lie
Where Mr Bleaney lay, and stub my fags
On the same saucer-souvenir, and try

Stuffing my ears with cotton-wool, to drown
The jabbering set he egged her on to buy.
I know his habits – what time he came down,
His preference for sauce to gravy, why

He kept on plugging at the four aways –
Likewise their yearly frame: the Frinton folk
Who put him up for summer holidays,
And Christmas at his sister's house in Stoke.

But if he stood and watched the frigid wind
Tousling the clouds, lay on the fusty bed
Telling himself that this was home, and grinned,
And shivered, without shaking off the dread

That how we live measures our own nature,
And at his age having no more to show
Than one hired box should make him pretty sure
He warranted no better, I don't know.

The Whitsun Weddings

That Whitsun, I was late getting away:
    Not till about
One-twenty on the sunlit Saturday
Did my three-quarters-empty train pull out,
All windows down, all cushions hot, all sense
Of being in a hurry gone. We ran
Behind the backs of houses, crossed a street
Of blinding windscreens, smelt the fish-dock; thence
The river's level drifting breadth began,
Where sky and Lincolnshire and water meet.

All afternoon, through the tall heat that slept
  For miles inland,
A slow and stopping curve southwards we kept.
Wide farms went by, short-shadowed cattle, and
Canals with floatings of industrial froth;
A hothouse flashed uniquely: hedges dipped
And rose: and now and then a smell of grass
Displaced the reek of buttoned carriage-cloth
Until the next town, new and nondescript,
Approached with acres of dismantled cars.

At first, I didn't notice what a noise
  The weddings made
Each station that we stopped at: sun destroys
The interest of what's happening in the shade,
And down the long cool platforms whoops and skirls
I took for porters larking with the mails,
And went on reading. Once we started, though,
We passed them, grinning and pomaded, girls
In parodies of fashion, heels and veils,
All posed irresolutely, watching us go,

As if out on the end of an event
  Waving good-bye
To something that survived it. Struck, I leant
More promptly out next time, more curiously,
And saw it all again in different terms:
The fathers with broad belts under their suits
And seamy foreheads; mothers loud and fat;
An uncle shouting smut; and then the perms,
The nylon gloves and jewellery-substitutes,
The lemons, mauves, and olive-ochres that

Marked off the girls unreally from the rest.
  Yes, from cafés
And banquet-halls up yards, and bunting-dressed
Coach-party annexes, the wedding-days
Were coming to an end. All down the line
Fresh couples climbed abroad: the rest stood round;
The last confetti and advice were thrown,
And, as we moved, each face seemed to define
Just what it saw departing: children frowned
At something dull; fathers had never known

Philip Larkin

Success so huge and wholly farcical;
   The women shared
The secret like a happy funeral;
While girls, gripping their handbags tighter, stared
At a religious wounding. Free at last,
And loaded with the sum of all they saw,
We hurried towards London, shuffling gouts of steam.
Now fields were building-plots, and poplars cast
Long shadows over major roads, and for
Some fifty minutes, that in time would seem

Just long enough to settle hats and say
   I nearly died,
A dozen marriages got under way.
They watched the landscape, sitting side by side
An Odeon went past, a cooling tower,
And someone running up to bowl – and none
Thought of the others they would never meet
Or how their lives would all contain this hour.
I thought of London spread out in the sun,
Its postal districts packed like squares of wheat:

There we were aimed. And as we raced across
   Bright knots of rail
Past standing Pullmans, walls of blackened moss
Came close, and it was nearly done, this frail
Travelling coincidence; and what it held
Stood ready to be loosed with all the power
That being changed can give. We slowed again,
And as the tightened brakes took hold, there swelled
A sense of falling, like an arrow-shower
Sent out of sight, somewhere becoming rain.

Going

There is an evening coming in
Across the fields, one never seen before,
That lights no lamps.

Silken it seems at a distance, yet
When it is drawn up over the knees and breast
It brings no comfort.

Where has the tree gone, that locked
Earth to the sky? What is under my hands,
That I cannot feel?

What loads my hands down?

Days

What are days for?
Days are where we live.
They come, they wake us
Time and time over.
They are to be happy in:
Where can we live but days?
Ah, solving that question
Brings the priest and the doctor
In their long coats
Running over the fields.

DONALD DAVIE

born 1922

Davie's career as a poet has gone hand in hand with his critical explorations. His book *Purity of Diction in English Verse* was, as he himself has since pointed out, almost the chief textbook of the Movement poets. It appeared in 1952. Other stages were marked by the publication of *Articulate Energy*, and *Ezra Pound: Poet as Sculptor*. In fact, Davie moved from his original neo-Augustan position, via the Russians, towards American modernism. Through all these shifts in position, his own work has retained certain characteristics unaltered. Technically very accomplished, its chief fault is that it tends to leave an impression of coldness, of being a poetry of will and reason. When the coldness is overcome, Davie can reveal himself as a fine lyrical poet.

Housekeeping

From thirty years back my grandmother with us boys
Picking the ash-grimed blackberries, pint on pint, is
Housekeeping Yorkshire's thrift, and yet the noise
Is taken up from Somerset in the nineties.

From homestead Autumns in the vale of Chard
Translated in youth past any hope of returning.
She toiled, my father a baby, through the hard
Fellside winters, to Barnsley, soused in the Dearne.

How the sound carries! Whatever the dried-out, lank
Sticks of poor trees could say of the slow slag stealing
More berries than we did, I hear her still down the bank
Slide, knickers in evidence, laughing, modestly squealing.

And I hear not only how homestead to small home echoes
Persistence of historic habit. Berries
Ask to be plucked, and attar pleases the rose.
Contentment cries from the distance. How it carries!

Green River

Green silk, or a shot silk, blue
Verging to green at the edges,
The river reflects the sky
Alas. I wish that its hue
Were the constant green of its sedges
Or the reeds it is floating by.

It reflects the entrances, dangers,
Exploits, vivid reversals
Of weather over the days.
But it learns to make these changes
By too many long rehearsals
Of overcasts and greys.

So let it take its station
Less mutably. Put it to school
Not to the sky but the land.
This endless transformation,
Because it is beautiful,
Let some of it somehow stand.

But seeing the streak of it quiver
There in the distance, my eye
Is astonished and unbelieving.
It exclaims to itself for ever:
This water is passing by!
It arrives, and it is leaving!

New York in August

(After Pasternak)

There came, for lack of sleep,
A crosspatch, drained-out look
On the old trees that keep
Scents of Schiedam and the Hook

In Flushing, as we picked out, past
Each memorized landmark,

Donald Davie

Our route to a somnolent breakfast.
Later, to Central Park,

UNO, and the Empire State.
A haven from the heat
Was the Planetarium. We got back late,
Buffeted, dragging our feet.

Clammy, electric, torrid,
The nights bring no relief
At the latitude of Madrid.
Never the stir of a leaf

Any night, as we went
Back, the children asleep,
To our bed in a loaned apartment,
Although I thought a deep

And savage cry from the park
Came once, as we flashed together
And the fan whirled in the dark,
For thunder, a break in the weather.

ELIZABETH JENNINGS

born 1926

Elizabeth Jennings once said of her association with the Movement
poets: 'I think it was positively unhelpful, because I tended to be grouped
and criticized rather than be grouped and praised.' On the same occasion
she pointed out that 'two big differences between myself and my con-
temporaries were that I was a woman and also a Roman Catholic, which
meant that I wanted to write about subjects which were simply unin-
teresting to most Movement poets: at least uninteresting to them in the
way that they were interesting to me.' In effect, she seemed from the
very beginning to be a more romantic, outgoing writer than those
whom she was grouped with. Perhaps as a result of this, she has had
a rough passage from the critics in recent years. Her themes are often
'confessional' – the walk 'from breakfast to madness', in Anne Sexton's
phrase – but the techniques she used, at least until recently, remained
rather prissily decorous. More recent experiments with free verse, and
even with prose-poetry, have not been really convincing. Miss Jennings
writes too much, so that the good poems have their impact muffled by
less accomplished versions of the same rather narrow range of themes.

Night Garden of the Asylum

An owl's call scrapes the stillness.
Curtains are barriers and behind them
The beds settle into neat rows.
Soon they'll be ruffled.

The garden knows nothing of illness.
Only it knows of the slow gleam
Of stars, the moon's distilling; it knows
Why the beds and lawns are levelled.

Then all is broken from its fullness.
A human cry cuts across a dream.
A wild hand squeezes an open rose.
We are in witchcraft, bedevilled.

Elizabeth Jennings

One Flesh

Lying apart now, each in a separate bed,
He with a book, keeping the light on late,
She like a girl dreaming of childhood,
All men elsewhere – it is as if they wait
Some new event: the book he holds unread,
Her eyes fixed on the shadows overhead,

Tossed up like flotsam from a former passion,
How cool they lie. They hardly ever touch,
Or if they do it is like a confession
Of having little feeling – or too much.
Chastity faces them, a destination
For which their whole lives were a preparation.

Strangely apart, yet strangely close together,
Silence between them like a thread to hold
And not wind in. And time itself's a feather
Touching them gently. Do they know they're old,
These two who are my father and my mother
Whose fire from which I came, has now grown cold?

D. J. ENRIGHT

born 1920

Enright could be rather gnomically described as 'the Lawrence Durrell of the Movement' – a traveller and observer with a wry wit. Unlike most Movement poetry, his work is technically rather loose, but the tone is certainly drier and less romantic than Durrell's. Enright seldom rises to great heights, and equally seldom writes a really bad poem.

In Memoriam

How clever they are, the Japanese, how clever!
The great department store, Takashimaya, on the
Ginza, near Maruzen Bookshop and British Council –
A sky-scraper swaying with every earth-tremor,
Bowing and scraping, but never falling (how clever!).
On the roof-garden of tall Takashimaya lives an
Elephant. How did he get there, that clever Japanese
Elephant? By lift? By helicopter? (How clever,
Either way.) And this young man who went there to teach
(Uncertificated, but they took him) in Tokyo,
This Englishman with a fine beard and a large and
(It seemed) healthy body.
                    And he married an orphan,
A Japanese orphan (illegitimate child of
A geisha – Japanese for 'a clever person' – and a
Number of customers), who spoke no English and
He spoke no Japanese. (But how clever they were!)
For a year they were married. She said, half in Japanese,
Half in English, wholly in truth: 'This is the first time
I have known happiness.' (The Japanese are a
Clever people, clever but sad.) 'They call it a
Lottery,' he wrote to me, 'I have made a lucky dip.'
(She was a Japanese orphan, brought up in a convent.)
At the end of that year he started to die.
They flew him to New York, for 2-million volt treatment

('Once a day,' he wrote, 'Enough to make you sick!')
And a number of operations. 'They say there's a
99% chance of a cure,' he wrote, 'Reversing
The odds, I suspect.' Flying back to his orphan,
He was removed from the plane at Honolulu and
Spent four days in a slummy hotel with no money or
Clothes. His passport was not in order. (Dying men
Are not always clever enough in thinking ahead.)
They operated again in Tokyo and again,
He was half a man, then no man, but the cancer
Throve on it. 'All I can say is,' he wrote in November,
'Takashimaya will damned well have to find
Another Father Christmas this year, that's all.'
(It was. He died a week later. I was still puzzling
How to reply.)
                    He would have died anywhere.
And he lived his last year in Japan, loved by a
Japanese orphan, teaching her the rudiments of
Happiness, and (without certificate) teaching
Japanese students. In the dungeons of learning, the
Concentration campuses, throbbing with ragged uniforms
And consumptive faces, in a land where the literacy
Rate is over 100%, and the magazines
Read each other in the crowded subways. And
He was there (clever of them!), he was there teaching.
Then she went back to her convent, the Japanese
Widow, having known a year's happiness with a
Large blue-eye red-bearded foreign devil, that's all.
There is a lot of cleverness in the world, but still
Not enough.

KINGSLEY AMIS

born 1922

Amis's poetry has more and more come to seem a kind of sideline. He is more essentially a novelist than a poet. His poems benefit, and suffer at the same time, from their lack of ambition. Crisp, witty, sardonic, they are comments in the margin of contemporary life.

The Last War

The first country to die was normal in the evening,
Ate a good but plain dinner, chatted with some friends
Over a glass, and went to bed soon after ten;
And in the morning was found disfigured and dead.
    That was a lucky one.

At breakfast the others heard about it, and kept
Their eyes on their plates. Who was guilty? No one knew,
But by lunch-time three more would never eat again.
The rest appealed for frankness, quietly cocked their guns,
    Declared 'This can't go on.'

They were right. Only the strongest turned up for tea:
The old ones with the big estates hadn't survived
The slobbering blindfold violence of the afternoon.
One killer or many? Was it a gang, or all-against-all?
    Somebody must have known.

But each of them sat there watching the others, until
Night came and found them anxious to get it over.
Then the lights went out. A few might have lived, even then;
Innocent, they thought (at first) it still mattered what
    You had or hadn't done.

They were wrong. One had been lenient with his servants;
Another ran an island brothel, but rarely left it;
The third owned a museum, the fourth a remarkable gun;
The name of a fifth was quite unknown, but in the end
    What was the difference? None.

Homicide, pacifist, crusader, cynic, gentile, jew
Staggered about moaning, shooting into the dark.
Next day, to tidy up as usual, the sun came in
When they and their ammunition were all used up,
     And found himself alone.

Upset, he looked them over, to separate, if he could,
The assassins from the victims, but every face
Had taken on the flat anonymity of pain;
And soon they'll all smell alike, he thought, and felt sick,
     And went to bed at noon.

Souvenirs

Photographs are dispensable.
The living, the still young,
Demand no such memorial.

Accusing letters still accuse,
Like the non-accusing.
No harm to be rid of those.

The mind will take surgery.
Though drink, resentment, self-
Defence impair the memory,

Something remains to be cut out.
God, car accident, stroke
Must do to remove it

For the body adjoins the limb.
Who, heart back to normal,
Could himself cut off his own arm?

A Point of Logic

Love is a finding-out:
Our walk to the bedroom
(Hand in hand, eye to eye)

Up a stair of marble
Or decently scrubbed boards,
As much as what we do
In our abandonment,
Teaches us who we are
And what we are, and what
Life itself is.

Therefore put out the light,
Lurch to the bare attic
Over buckets of waste
And labouring bodies;
Leave the door wide open
And fall on each other,
Clothes barely wrenched aside;
Stay only a minute,
Depart separately,
And use no names.

THOM GUNN

born 1929

Around 1960, it sometimes seemed as if all the poetry being written in England was being produced by a triple-headed creature called the 'Larkin-Hughes-Gunn'. Of this triumvirate, it is Gunn whose reputation has worn least well. The youngest of the Movement poets, he established himself with his first volume, *Fighting Terms*, which appeared in 1954. A mixture of the literary and the violent, this appealed both to restless youth and academic middle age (it is also a book which has since caused Gunn a great deal of unease, and he has made drastic revisions to the poems it contains). Afterwards Gunn went to America, and much of his work seems to be an attempt to come to terms with the nihilism of American life. Gunn's development has been a matter of fits and starts. His best poems have a compact philosophical elegance: 'The Annihilation of Nothing' is both influenced by, and worthy of, Rochester. Others seem strained and hollow, and his later collections show him to be a very uneven writer.

The Annihilation of Nothing

Nothing remained: Nothing, the wanton name
That nightly I rehearsed till led away
To a dark sleep, or sleep that held one dream.

In this a huge contagious absence lay,
More space than space, over the cloud and slime,
Defined but by the encroachments of its sway.

Stripped to indifference at the turns of time,
Whose end I knew, I woke without desire,
And welcomed zero as a paradigm.

But now it breaks – images burst with fire
Into the quiet sphere where I have bided,
Showing the landscape holding yet entire:

The power that I envisaged, that presided
Ultimate in its abstract devastations,
Is merely change, the atoms it divided

Complete, in ignorance, new combinations.
Only an infinite finitude I see
In those peculiar lovely variations.

It is despair that nothing cannot be
Flares in the mind and leaves a smoky mark
Of dread.
     Look upward. Neither firm nor free,

Purposeless matter hovers in the dark.

Considering the Snail

The snail pushes through a green
night, for the grass is heavy
with water and meets over
the bright path he makes, where rain
has darkened the earth's dark. He
moves in a wood of desire,

pale antlers barely stirring
as he hunts. I cannot tell
what power is at work, drenched there
with purpose, knowing nothing.
What is a snail's fury? All
I think is that if later

I parted the blades above
the tunnel and saw the thin
trail of broken white across
litter, I would never have
imagined the slow passion
to that deliberate progress.

My Sad Captains

One by one they appear in
the darkness: a few friends, and
a few with historical

names. How late they start to shine!
but before they fade they stand
perfectly embodied, all

the past lapping them like a
cloak of chaos. They were men
who, I thought, lived only to
renew the wasteful force they
spent with each hot convulsion.
They remind me, distant now.

True, they are not at rest yet,
but now that they are indeed
apart, winnowed from failures,
they withdraw to an orbit
and turn with disinterested
hard energy, like the stars.

Touch

You are already
asleep, I lower
myself in next to
you, my skin slightly
numb with the restraint
of habits, the patina of
self, the black frost
of outsideness, so that even
unclothed it is
a resilient chilly
hardness, a superficially
malleable, dead
rubbery texture.

You are a mound
of bedclothes, where the cat
in sleep braces
its paws against your
calf through the blankets,
and kneads each paw in turn.

Meanwhile and slowly
I feel a is it
my own warmth surfacing or
the ferment of your whole
body that in darkness beneath
the cover is stealing
bit by bit to break
down that chill.

      You turn and
hold me tightly, do
you know who
I am or am I
your mother or
the nearest human being to
hold on to in a
dreamed pogrom.

What I, now loosened,
sink into is an old
big place, it is
there already, for
you are already
there, and the cat
got there before you, yet
it is hard to locate.
What is more, the place is
not found but seeps
from our touch in
continuous creation, dark
enclosing cocoon round
ourselves alone, dark
wide realm where we
walk with everyone.

PART FOUR: EXPRESSIONISTS

Perhaps the heading I have chosen for this section, and the poets I have included in it, will alike seem unexpected. In fact, though the German Expressionist poets have probably had very little influence on English poetry, at this or any other time, a number of English poets in the post-war period seem to have had the same aims as writers such as Georg Trakl and Jakob van Hoddis. Ted Hughes's work, for example, has an expressionist violence, a tendency for the words to mime the action or feeling which is being described, even at the expense of structure. A. Alvarez's theory of 'extremist' art is essentially an expressionist one. Jon Silkin seems to link up with the tradition in a different way, through his admiration for Isaac Rosenberg, who of all the English poets of the First World War is the one who most resembles his opposite numbers in Germany.

Francis Berry

born 1915

A difficult, uneven, and therefore almost by definition neglected poet, Francis Berry is the very opposite of an 'academic' writer, though he teaches English at a university. Often clumsy, he can generate great intensity in his visions of the historical past, notably in his long narrative *Morant Bay*, an account of a Jamaican revolt which should be compared to William Styron's novel, *The Confessions of Nat Turner*. Berry's language is essentially mimetic, expressive language – language forced to become the event it describes. In his book, *Poetry and the Physical Voice*, he propounds a most interesting theory about the relationship between what the poet writes, and how the writer himself would actually speak what he has written. The two poems here are taken from Berry's most recent book, *Ghosts of Greenland*, which appeared as long ago as 1966, and concern themselves with the Nordic world, which seems to attract the poet by its ferocity. In 'Hvalsey', with its hideous vision of a burning for witchcraft, the speaker, by a typical conceit, is a ship. 'Vadstena' is perhaps the nearest an English writer has got to the intensity of Trakl, by whom it must surely be influenced.

Hvalsey

I didn't want to go there, I didn't, I was driven
Denying I wanted to go there, creaking out Damn
To the demons with my boards, rasping out N-o-o
With my ropes, rearing, romping, rattling, driven
South of Iceland (there's the Jökull Glacier), driven
(The horizon is heaving), driven and driving
Kap Farvel around, and up the west coast.

And there I stayed
Four years, and what I saw
– Main things that occurred –
Will now be said.
First, and O last, there was the burning, but we'll leave that.

Now I had carried a woman, and do you know
But this woman with her rambles over three years on the shore
Got married to a Greenlander, and this Greenlander
(It was this, and not the other way round, I am sure)
Was a giant of a man; and they married,
Married in Hvalsey Church, and the church bell tonged
Till my very tall lone mast ached, and the bell tanged
Because of the bitingly pale blue of the sky when they came out,
As though every tooth and nail, and every nerve and tail, of my
   hulk
Dinned and stung in delight and washed in dismay.
But that was alright.
But what was not alright
Was the burning, and that was my third year
Here.
      I don't like it. Will not like it
Ever.
       Well, they said that this Kolgrim
– Greenlander, yes, but black-browed, mean smile, thick hair –
Practised the Black Arts to get her so
– Get her SO, you understand, the wife of the second
Carpenter (that's all he was, that's all he was
Tinkering me, the said ship).
Well, they got him
For doing the Black Arts, and they did him –

Greenlander though he was, and she only an
Icelander – in this way . . .

But I can't go on, I must go on,
I am driven.
They got him, this Kolgrim, and they judged him
Not of Adultery, but of Black Arts
Guilty, and they burnt . . .

This year, after the marriage spoken of,
Fourth year.

And they burnt. Wood scarce in Greenland. And the bonfire
Attracted. And the sight. Attracted. And the screams
Attracted. Attracted, attracted, attracted, attracted more
More, more, more than the marriage
(And there were many, many were there a year or so
Earlier.)

And the woman, wife of the second
Carpenter (she wasn't worth it, that you do know),
She went hopping at the burning and, after hopping, mad,
Mad soon after.
     And leering.
                And dangerous.
But she died.

     These things I saw
During four years compulsory stay
At Hvalsey (Whale's Island), driven, driven there
Without my knowing, or my will, or my consent,
Anything.
     And now they say
Sheep stray into the roofless church of Hvalsey
And dirty on its altar.

Vadstena

Yes, I remember the name,
Vadstena; on that afternoon
The steamer drew up beside the quay,
Below the castle. It was July.

I disembarked. And everywhere and everywhere
There were roses, roses, roses, here
Upon the castle and on the convent stone,
And roses in the gardens of the wooden

Houses. St Bridget's *kloster*.
     And then the scream.
Rising and rising behind the bars
Of the convent, now the asylum, rose
That woman's scream, a sound of beating, soon

The roses shook in the sun as fists, and the sun
Shook like a colossal Mandarin rose, and there ran
Extraordinary grape shadows on the hot stone
Walls. Then stillness.
     Understand

That was Vadstena: a scream, a beating, rising
As a gigantic reeling stalk and the roses' fume
Swelling all of a sudden, till their odour
Colours, sickens, sounds.

TED HUGHES

born 1930

The most explosively individual poetic talent to appear in England since the war, Hughes immediately established a major reputation with the publication of his first book. His most characteristic gift is for writing about the natural world from the inside, as a being who knows that he is not divided from it. Hughes's work achieves its force through the way in which one image detonates another, so that the whole poem throbs with controlled violence. An important influence on the way in which he writes has been the reading in Middle English which he did as an undergraduate at Cambridge; he particularly admires *Sir Gawain and the Green Knight*. At one time hugely influential on other poets, Hughes is now a somewhat isolated though still greatly respected figure.

Wodwo[1]

What am I? Nosing here, turning leaves over
Following a faint stain on the air to the river's edge
I enter water. What am I to split
The glassy grain of water looking upward I see the bed
Of the river above me upside down very clear
What am I doing here in mid-air? Why do I find
this frog so interesting as I inspect its most secret
interior and make it my own? Do these weeds
know me and name me to each other have they
seen me before, do I fit in their world? I seem
separate from the ground and not rooted but dropped
out of nothing casually I've no threads
fastening me to anything I can go anywhere
I seem to have been given the freedom
of this place what am I then? And picking
bits of bark off this rotten stump gives me
no pleasure and it's no use so why do I do it

1. *Wodwo*: a 'wodwo' is a wood-demon.

me and doing that have coincided very queerly
But what shall I be called am I the first
have I an owner what shape am I what
shape am I am I huge if I go
to the end on this way past these trees and past these trees
till I get tired that's touching one wall of me
for the moment if I sit still how everything
stops to watch me I suppose I am the exact centre
but there's all this what is it roots
roots roots roots and here's the water
again very queer but I'll go on looking

Gog

I

I woke to a shout: 'I am Alpha and Omega.'
Rocks and a few trees trembled
Deep in their own country.
I ran and an absence bounded beside me.

The dog's god is a scrap dropped from the table.
The mouse's saviour is a ripe wheat grain.
Hearing the Messiah cry
My mouth widens in adoration.

How fat are the lichens!
They cushion themselves on the silence.
The air wants for nothing.
The dust, too, is replete.

What was my error? My skull has sealed it out.
My great bones are massed in me.
They pound on the earth, my song excites them.
I do not look at the rocks and stones, I am frightened of what
they see.

I listen to the song jarring my mouth
Where the skull-rooted teeth are in possession.
I am massive on earth. My feetbones beat on the earth
Over the sounds of motherly weeping . . .

Afterwards I drink at a pool quietly.
The horizon bears the rocks and trees away into twilight.
I lie down. I become darkness.

Darkness that all night sings and circles stamping.

II

The sun erupts. The moon is deader than a skull.
The grass-head waves day and night and will never know it
                                                       exists.
The stones are as they were. And the creatures of earth
Are mere rainfall rivulets, in flood or empty paths.
The atoms of saints' brains are swollen with the vast bubble of
                                               nothing.
Everywhere the dust is in power.

Then whose
Are these
Eyes,
     eyes and
Dance of wants,
Of offering?

Sun and moon, death and death,
Grass and stones, their quick peoples and the bright particles
Death and death and death –

Her mirrors.

III

Out through the dark archway of earth, under the ancient lintel
                                  overwritten with roots,
Out between the granite jambs, gallops the hooded horseman
                                    of iron.
Out of the wound-gash in the earth, the horseman mounts,
                          shaking his plumes clear of dark soil.
Out of the blood-dark womb, gallops bowed the horseman of
                                  iron.
The blood-crossed Knight, the Holy Warrior, hooded with iron,
                        the seraph of the bleak edge.
Gallops along the world's ridge in moonlight.

Through slits of iron his eyes search for the softness of the
                     throat, the navel, the armpit, the groin.
Bring him clear of the flung web and the coil that vaults from
                     the dust.

Through slits of iron, his eyes have found the helm of the
                     enemy, the grail,
The womb-wall of the dream that crouches there, greedier than
                     a foetus,
Suckling at the root-blood of the origins, the salt-milk drug of
                     the mothers.

Shield him from the dipped glance, flying in half light, that
                     tangles the heels,
The grooved kiss that swamps the eyes with darkness.
Bring him to the ruled slab, the octaves of order,
The law and mercy of number. Lift him
Out of the octopus maw and the eight lunatic limbs
Of the rocking, sinking cradle.
The unborn child beats on the womb-wall.
He will need to be strong
To follow his weapons towards the light.
Unlike Coriolanus, follow the blades right through Rome

And right through the smile
That is the judge's fury
That is the wailing child
That is the ribboned gift
That is the starved adder
That is the kiss in the dream
That is the nightmare pillow
That is the seal of resemblances
That is illusion
That is illusion

The rider of iron, on the horse shod with vaginas of iron,
Gallops over the womb that makes no claim, that is of stone.
His weapons glitter under the lights of heaven.
He follows his compass, the lance-blade, the gunsight, out
Against the fanged grail and tireless mouth
Whose cry breaks his sleep
Whose coil is under his ribs

Whose smile is in the belly of woman
Whose satiation is in the grave.

Out under the blood-dark archway, gallops bowed the horse-
man of iron.

Pibroch

The sea cries with its meaningless voice
Treating alike its dead and its living,
Probably bored with the appearance of heaven
After so many millions of nights without sleep,
Without purpose, without self-deception.

Stone likewise. A pebble is imprisoned
Like nothing in the Universe.
Created for black sleep. Or growing
Conscious of the sun's red spot occasionally,
Then dreaming it is the foetus of God.

Over the stone rushes the wind
Able to mingle with nothing,
Like the hearing of the blind stone itself.
Or turns, as if the stone's mind came feeling
A fantasy of directions.

Drinking the sea and eating the rock
A tree struggles to make leaves –
An old woman fallen from space
Unprepared for these conditions.
She hangs on, because her mind's gone completely.

Minute after minute, aeon after aeon,
Nothing lets up or develops.
And this is neither a bad variant nor a tryout.
This is where the staring angels go through.
This is where all the stars bow down.

Theology

No, the serpent did not
Seduce Eve to the apple.
All that's simply
Corruption of the facts.

Adam ate the apple.
Eve ate Adam.
The serpent ate Eve.
This is the dark intestine.

The serpent, meanwhile,
Sleeps his meal off in Paradise –
Smiling to hear
God's querulous calling.

Fifth Bedtime Story

Once upon a time there was a person
Almost a person
Somehow he could not quite see
Somehow he could not quite hear
He could not quite think
Somehow his body, for instance,
Was intermittent.
He could see the bread he cut
He could see the letters of words he read
He could see the wrinkles on handskin he looked at
Or one eye of a person
Or an ear, or a foot or the other foot
But somehow he could not quite see
Nevertheless the Grand Canyon spread wide open
Like a surgical operation for him
But somehow he had only half a face there
And somehow his legs were missing at the time
And though somebody was talking he could not hear
Though luckily his camera worked OK
The sea-bed lifted its privacy

And showed its most hidden fish thing
He stared he groped to feel
But his hands were silly hooves just at the crucial moment
And though his eyes worked
Half his head was jellyfish, nothing could connect
And the photographs were blurred
A great battleship broke in two with a boom
As if to welcome his glance
An earthquake shook the city onto its people
Just before he got there
With his rubber eye his clockwork ear
And the most beautiful girls
Laid their faces on his pillow, staring him out,
But somehow he was a tar-baby
Somehow somebody was pouring his brains into a bottle
Somehow he was already too late
And was a pile of pieces under a blanket
Somehow his eyes were in the wrong way round
He laughed he whispered but somehow he could not hear
He gripped and clawed but somehow his fingers would not
    catch
And when the sea-monster surfaced and stared at the rowboat
Somehow his eyes failed to click
And when he saw the man's head cleft with a hatchet
Somehow staring blank swallowed his whole face
Just at the crucial moment
Then disgorged it again whole
As if nothing had happened.
So he just went and ate what he could
And saw what he could and did what he could
Then sat down to write his autobiography

But somehow his arms had become just bits of wood
Somehow his guts were an old watch-chain
Somehow his feet were two old postcards
Somehow his head was a broken window-pane
'I give up,' he said. He gave up.

Creation had failed again.

SYLVIA PLATH

1932-63

The only poetic legend to rival that of Dylan Thomas in the post-war years in England has been that of Sylvia Plath. She was an American, born in Boston, who came to England on a Fulbright scholarship. She went to Cambridge, where she met Ted Hughes, who was a fellow student. They were married in 1956. Her first volume of verse, *The Colossus*, was widely praised, but it was the second, *Ariel*, published after her suicide in 1963, which established her reputation. A. E. Dyson, reviewing the book in *The Critical Quarterly*, remarked that the poems contained in it had 'impressed themselves on many readers with the force of myth'. M. L. Rosenthal, in his study of Plath's work in *The New Poets*, characterizes it as 'written out of a strange kind of terror, the calm centre of hysteria'. Most critics rank her with Robert Lowell as one of the chief poets of the 'confessional' school. To put all the emphasis on the emotional extremism of her late work is perhaps understandable, but it tends to distort certain important characteristics of her poetry. She was an obsessional writer, and the same images recur again and again throughout her work. The shore-bound spectator looking out at the formless, beckoning chaos of the sea is one of the most frequent.

Sylvia Plath seems in many ways more of an English writer than an American one, which is why I have included a selection of her poems here. Ted Hughes plainly had an important influence on her work, a point which is demonstrated by the first poem, which comes from a transitional phase, when she was only just moving towards her late style.

Blackberrying

Nobody in the lane, and nothing, nothing but blackberries,
Blackberries on either side, though on the right mainly,
A blackberry alley, going down in hooks, and a sea
Somewhere at the end of it, heaving. Blackberries
Big as the ball of my thumb, and dumb as eyes
Ebon in the hedges, fat
With blue-red juices. These they squander on my fingers.
I had not asked for such a blood sisterhood; they must love me.
They accommodate themselves to my milkbottle, flattening
their sides.

Overhead go the choughs in black, cacophonous flocks –
Bits of burnt paper wheeling in a blown sky.
Theirs is the only voice, protesting, protesting.
I do not think the sea will appear at all.
The high, green meadows are glowing, as if lit from within.
I come to one bush of berries so ripe it is a bush of flies,
Hanging their bluegreen bellies and their wing panes in a
                                        Chinese screen.
The honey-feast of the berries has stunned them; they believe
                                        in heaven.
One more hook and the berries and bushes end.

The only thing to come now is the sea.
From between two hills a sudden wind funnels at me,
Slapping its phantom laundry in my face.
These hills are too green and sweet to have tasted salt.
I follow the sheep path between them. A last hook brings me
To the hills' northern face, and the face is orange rock
That looks out on nothing, nothing but a great space
Of white and pewter lights, and a din like silversmiths
Beating and beating at an intractable metal.

Lady Lazarus

I have done it again.
One year in every ten
I manage it –

A sort of walking miracle, my skin
Bright as a Nazi lampshade,
My right foot

A paperweight,
My face a featureless, fine
Jew linen.

Peel off the napkin
O my enemy.
Do I terrify? –

The nose, the eye pits, the full set of teeth?
The sour breath
Will vanish in a day

Soon, soon the flesh
The grave cave ate will be
At home on me

And I a smiling woman.
I am only thirty.
And like the cat I have nine times to die.

This is Number Three.
What a trash
To annihilate each decade.

What a million filaments.
The peanut-crunching crowd
Shoves in to see

Them unwrap me hand and foot –
The big strip tease.
Gentlemen, ladies

These are my hands
My knees.
I may be skin and bone,

Nevertheless, I am the same, identical woman.
The first time it happened I was ten.
It was an accident.

The second time I meant
To last it out and not come back at all.
I rocked shut

As a seashell.
They had to call and call
And pick the worms off me like sticky pearls.

Dying
Is an art, like everything else.
I do it exceptionally well.

I do it so it feels like hell.
I do it so it feels real.
I guess you could say I've a call.

It's easy enough to do it in a cell.
It's easy enough to do it and stay put.
It's the theatrical

Comeback in broad day
To the same place, the same face, the same brute
Amused shout:

'A miracle!'
That knocks me out.
There is a charge

For the eyeing of my scars, there is a charge
For the hearing of my heart –
It really goes.

And there is a charge, a very large charge
For a word or a touch
Or a bit of blood

Or a piece of my hair or my clothes.
So, so, Herr Doktor.
So, Herr Enemy.

I am your opus,
I am your valuable,
The pure gold baby

That melts to a shriek.
I turn and burn.
Do not think I underestimate your great concern.

Ash, ash –
You poke and stir.
Flesh, bone, there is nothing there –

A cake of soap,
A wedding ring,
A gold filling.

Herr God, Herr Lucifer
Beware
Beware.

Out of the ash
I rise with my red hair
And I eat men like air.

Daddy

You do not do, you do not do
Any more, black shoe
In which I have lived like a foot
For thirty years, poor and white,
Barely daring to breathe or Achoo.

Daddy, I have had to kill you.
You died before I had time –
Marble-heavy, a bag full of God,
Ghastly statue with one grey toe
Big as a Frisco seal

And a head in the freakish Atlantic
Where it pours bean green over blue
In the waters off beautiful Nauset.
I used to pray to recover you.
Ach, du.

In the German tongue, in the Polish town
Scraped flat by the roller
Of wars, wars, wars.
But the name of the town is common.
My Polack friend

Says there are a dozen or two.
So I never could tell where you
Put your foot, your root,
I never could talk to you.
The tongue stuck in my jaw.

It stuck in a barb wire snare.
Ich, ich, ich, ich,
I could hardly speak.
I thought every German was you.
And the language obscene

An engine, an engine
Chuffing me off like a Jew.
A Jew to Dachau, Auschwitz, Belsen.
I began to talk like a Jew.
I think I may well be a Jew.

The snows of the Tyrol, the clear beer of Vienna
Are not very pure or true.
With my gypsy ancestress and my weird luck
And my Taroc pack and my Taroc pack
I may be a bit of a Jew.

I have always been scared of *you*,
With your Luftwaffe, your gobbledygoo.
And your neat moustache
And your Aryan eye, bright blue.
Panzer-man, panzer-man, O You –

Not God but a swastika
So black no sky could squeak through.
Every woman adores a Fascist,
The boot in the face, the brute
Brute heart of a brute like you.

You stand at the blackboard, daddy,
In the picture I have of you,
A cleft in your chin instead of your foot
But no less a devil for that, no not
Any less the black man who

Bit my pretty red heart in two.
I was ten when they buried you.
At twenty I tried to die
And get back, back, back to you.
I thought even the bones would do.

But they pulled me out of the sack,
And they stuck me together with glue.
And then I knew what to do.
I made a model of you,
A man in black with a Meinkampf look

And a love of the rack and the screw.
And I said I do, I do.
So daddy, I'm finally through.
The black telephone's off at the root,
The voices just can't worm through.

If I've killed one man, I've killed two –
The vampire who said he was you

And drank my blood for a year,
Seven years, if you want to know.
Daddy, you can lie back now.

There's a stake in your fat black heart
And the villagers never liked you.
They are dancing and stamping on you.
They always *knew* it was you.
Daddy, daddy, you bastard, I'm through.

A. ALVAREZ

born 1929

Alvarez was the most important critic and reviewer of modern poetry in England during the fifties and sixties. He was first of all associated with the Movement (and his poems of this period owe a debt to Empson), and later he became the advocate of the 'confessional' Americans: Robert Lowell, John Berryman and Sylvia Plath. His later poems, too few in number, have the spare, taut cleanness of style which he has always advocated.

Lost

My sleep falters and the good dreams:
The sky lit green, you reaching, reaching out
Through a bell of air. I stir.

The same wrist lies along my cheek;
My fingers touch it. The same head on my chest
Stirs. My arms round the same body;
And I feel the dead arms stir,
My fingers in the same dead hair.
The same belly, dead thighs stir.

The dream whirrs, cuts. The day blinks, stirs.
Hers. Not yours, my love. Hers.

Back

The night I came back from the hospital, scarcely
Knowing what had happened or when,
I went through the whole performance again in my dreams.
Three times – in a dance, in a chase and in something
Now lost – my body was seized and shaken
Till my jaw swung loose, my eyes were almost out

And my trunk was stunned and stretched with a vibration
Sharper than fear, closer than pain. It was death.
So I sweated under the sheets, afraid to sleep,
Though you breathed all night quietly enough by my side.

Was it the *tremor mortis*, the last dissolution
Known now in dreams, unknown in the pit itself
When I was gripped by the neck till my life shook
Like loosening teeth in my head? Yet I recall
Nothing of death but the puzzled look on your face,
Swimming towards me, weeping, clouded, uncertain,
As they took the tube from my arm
And plugged the strange world back in place.

Mourning and Melancholia

His face was blue, on his fingers
Flecks of green. 'This is my father',
I thought. Stiff and unwieldy
He stared out of my sleep. The parlourmaid
Smiled from the bed with his corpse,
Her chapped lips thin and welcoming.
In the next room her albino child
Kept shouting, shouting; I had to put him down
Like a blind puppy. 'Death from strangulation
By persons known ' I kept the clipping
In my breast-pocket where it burns and burns,
Stuck to my skin like phosphorus.

I wake up struggling, silent, undersea
Light and a single thrush
Is tuning up. You sleep, the baby sleeps,
The town is dead. Foxes are out on the Heath;
They sniff the air like knives.
A hawk turns slowly over Highgate, waiting.
This is the hidden life of London. Wild.

Three years back my father's corpse was burnt,
His ashes scattered. Now I breathe him in
With the grey morning air, in and out.

In out. My heart bumps steadily
Without pleasure. The air is thick with ash.
In out. I am cold and powerless. His face
Still pushes sadly into mine. He's disappointed.
I've let him down, he says. Now I'm cold like him.
Cold and untameable. Will have to be put down.

JON SILKIN

born 1930

Silkin has been one of the true 'independents' of the past three decades, and his work has followed a trajectory of its own, developing away from a rather heavily rhetorical style, which has a debt to Silkin's admiration for Isaac Rosenberg, towards something a great deal sparer. The 'Flower Poems', one of Silkin's best known sequences, clearly owe something to William Carlos Williams – see, for instance, Williams's poem 'The Crimson Cyclamen'.

Caring for Animals

I ask sometimes why these small animals
With bitter eyes, why we should care for them.

I question the sky, the serene blue water,
But it cannot say. It gives no answer.

And no answer releases in my head
A procession of grey shades patched and whimpering,

Dogs with clipped ears, wheezing cart horses
A fly without shadow and without thought.

Is it with these menaces to our vision
With this procession led by a man carrying wood

We must be concerned? The holy land, the rearing
Green island should be kindlier than this.

Yet the animals, our ghosts, need tending to.
Take in the whipped cat and the blinded owl;

Take up the man-trapped squirrel upon your shoulder.
Attend to the unnecessary beasts.

From growing mercy and a moderate love
Great love for the human animal occurs.

And your love grows. Your great love grows and grows.

Dandelion

Slugs nestle where the stem
Broken, bleeds milk.
The flower is eyeless: the sight is compelled
By small, coarse, sharp petals,
Like metal shreds. Formed,
They puncture, irregularly perforate
Their yellow, brutal glare.
And certainly want to
Devour the earth. With an ample movement
They are a foot high, as you look.
And coming back, they take hold
On pert domestic strains.
Others' lives are theirs. Between them
And domesticity,
Grass. They infest its weak land;
Fatten, hide slugs, infestate.
They look like plates; more closely
Like the first tryings, the machines, of nature
Riveted into her, successful.

A Bluebell

Most of them in the first tryings
Of nature, hang at angles,
Like lamps. These though
Look round, like young birds,
Poised on their stems. Closer,
In all their sweetness, malevolent. For there is
In the closed, blue flower, gas-coloured,
A seed-like dark green eye.
Carroway, grained, supple,
And watching; it is always there,
Fibrous, alerted,
Coarse grained enough to print
Out all your false delight
In 'sweet nature'. This is struggle.

The beetle exudes rot: the bee
Grapples the reluctant nectar
Coy, suppurating, and unresigned.
Buds print the human passion
Pure now not still immersed
In fighting wire worms.

A Daisy

Look unoriginal
Being numerous. They ask for attention
With that gradated yellow swelling
Of oily stamens. Petals focus them:
The eye-lashes grow wide.
Why should not one bring these to a funeral?
And at night, like children,
Without anxiety, their consciousness
Shut with white petals.
Blithe, individual.

The unwearying, small sunflower
Fills the grass
With versions of one eye.
A strength in the full look
Candid, solid, glad.
Domestic as milk.

In multitudes, wait,
Each, to be looked at, spoken to.
They do not wither;
Their going, a pressure
Of elate sympathy
Released from you.
Rich up to the last interval
With minute tubes of oil, pollen;
Utterly without scent, for the eye,
For the eye, simply. For the mind
And its invisible organ,
That feeling thing.

PART FIVE: THE GROUP

Unlike the Movement, the Group was a personal association of poets, who met weekly for discussions, first under the chairmanship of Philip Hobsbaum, and then under my own. These meetings began in the middle 1950s and were continued into the 1960s. A representative anthology (*A Group Anthology*) was published in 1963. Stylistically, the Group poets seem much less cohesive than the Movement ones. Perhaps the most characteristic, both in their aims and in the tone they adopt, are Martin Bell and the early Peter Porter. Essentially, what one finds in their work is the note of radical protest which one also finds in the dramatists who established themselves in the fifties, such as Osborne and Wesker. They are looser, more colloquial, more deliberately naturalistic than most of the poets of the Movement. On the other hand Peter Redgrove and David Wevill (who were contemporaries of Ted Hughes at Cambridge) can best be classified as expressionist writers, like those in the previous section, and expressionist, too, are the more violent examples of George MacBeth's early work. MacBeth, in fact, seems to have moved quite logically from an expressionist position to something resembling that of the Russian or Italian futurist poets.

PHILIP HOBSBAUM

born 1932

Having read English under Dr Leavis, Hobsbaum subsequently became
the leading spirit in a number of writers' workshops, which tried to
bring the tone and style of Leavis's seminars to the discussion of absol-
utely contemporary work. Hobsbaum founded the so-called 'Group' in
London in the mid fifties, as a revival of a similar organization which
had already existed among undergraduate poets at Cambridge. Another
influential discussion group was organized while he was teaching at
Queen's University, Belfast. Hobsbaum's own work represents one
aspect of the things the Group believed itself to stand for: clarity, natu-
ralism, a rejection of the tradition of Pound and Eliot in favour of that
of D. H. Lawrence and Wilfred Owen.

A Secret Sharer

'Tell me of the house where you were born
Near Tandragee – the field, the chicken-run,
The single shop more than a mile away,
The village even farther. Make me see
You waiting while your idiot neighbour pumps,
Your youth a murmur under Tilly lamps.
Did you walk out under the clear cold stars
To where the lights of Lisburn blur the skies
Or sit over the peat fire's acrid blaze,
Hair falling carelessly about your face
And think of me, or someone not unlike?'
The picture fades into the usual dark
That keeps us separate. You have your past,
I mine, trampled to city soot and dust –
So smile, and shake your head. Our lives were such,
Spent years apart, that thoughts can barely touch,
But bodies do much better. At a nod,
Without a word we slide into your bed
To clutch in a shared spasm. Once apart
I rise, rub myself down, bid you good night:

We shared a room, a bed, but not a life.
And so I leave and go home to my wife,
Whiling away in speech the hours that wane
Until my body talks to yours again.

Can I Fly Too?

You are a witch.
You taught me
To hear in the slurping of mud
The cry of the Ban Shee
To see in the life cycle of the caterpillar
The struggle of the soul
Towards immortality.
Take me.
You alone could turn the weight of years
Into release, ecstasy.

Ocarina

Oh and you seized the pierced stone in your hand
Breathing out such music, of no interval
Or known key
That the cells of my body recomposed
Into a strange land
Where you were indeed a witch
Long black hair, predator's eyes,
Nose of a hawk,
A black familiar
Purring in your hat –
Lady, I was afraid.

MARTIN BELL

1918–78

Martin Bell's work represents a strange coming-together of ideas and influences. He owed a debt to Eliot, and also to the poets who influenced Eliot, such as Laforgue. His ironies are very complex, and he uses rhetoric very skilfully for purposes of deflation. All of this might lead one to expect a kind of right-wing satirist. Instead, he is the representative of the generation which helped to win the Second World War, and then promptly turned Churchill out of office. As a writer, he was someone who matured very slowly. His earliest really characteristic poems belong to the middle and late fifties. As a result a great deal of experience and feeling tends to be packed into every poem, and he was a master of extremely rapid shifts of tone. His characteristic mode is the monologue – one spoken, not by an invented character, but by the poet himself. The idea of the mask plays an important part in the imagery of many of these poems, and Bell quotes Wallace Stevens's couplet as one of the three epigraphs to his volume of *Collected Poems*:

> To know that the balance does not quite rest,
> That the mask is strange, however like.

This provides as good a clue as any to the interpretation of his work.

The Enormous Comics

A Teacher to His Old School

Barnacled, in tattered pomp, go down
Still firing, battered admirals, still go down
With jutting jaw and tutting tooth and tongue,
Commanding order down cold corridors.

Superbly, O dyspeptic Hamlets,
Pause in the doorway, startle the Fourth Form
With rustlings of impatient inky cloaks –
Time and time again you go into your act.

Benevolent and shaven, county cricketers,
Heroes on fag-cards, lolling out of the frame,

Or smug and bun-faced, Happy Families,
Or swollen in shrill rage (Off With His Head!),

You lean huge areas into close-up
With cruel pampered lips like Edward G.
Robinson, or Tracy's anguished eyes,
And still remain the seediest of grandees.

Processioned hierarchically, larger than life,
Gigantic Guy Fawkes masks, great heads on stilts –
Your business was traditional, strictly articulated
Into timetables, only a few steps

From nightmare. Wild clowns will terrify
Wagging a wooden phallus at the crowd,
Raising a roar of response, of love and loathing –
Fat scapegoats with broad rosettes of learning.

I listened and made myself little, still as a mouse
Watching the growling pussies at their antics –
Now I see, in the back row of any classroom,
Sharp impatient eyes, weighing me up for the drop.

Large masks creak. Sir will tear a passion to tatters.
One must pray for unobstructed moments,
For chances to be useful,
Like theirs, old wretches, like theirs.

Letter to a Friend

Dear Russ, you're dead and dust. I didn't know.
I've heard it only at removes. For X
Who we detested, passed it on from Y,
For whom we had a jeering kind of fondness –
He read about it in the Old School Journal –
One way of keeping up.

'Organic disease' were the words. Which one?
Which painful monster had you when you died?
As good a life as me, I would have said –
You're one-up now, you smug old bastard:

'Christ, boy,' you say, I'm dead now.'
Stop dribbling bubbles of laughter round your pipe.

How many years since both of us owed letters?
Let's offer the usual excuses –
Marriage, of course, wives don't get on,
The housing-shortage, railway fares, etc.,
Weak putting-off, sheer bloody laziness.
We didn't want to say the way things went
Pissed on the hopes we entertained,
Naive, of course, but vivid and still pissed on –
The old gang born again in your careerists –
(Christ, boy, they're reading *The Times* now!)
As if we hadn't known all this before!

Gratitude, now, is what's appropriate.
How glad I am I've had your company!
After an adolescent's silly days
Of idle mornings, hypochondriac afternoons,
Thick skies that frowned and trees that swayed foreboding,
What evenings of relief have set me free!

Evenings of beer and talk, bezique, Tchaikovsky,
Hysterical evenings screeching at dull flicks,
And evenings when we gossiped into movement
The huge grotesque we knew, to keep us sane –
Hadji, Wokko, Nodger hardly knew themselves
And should we meet would start us off again.
'Christ, boy,' you say, 'Listen to this.'
Something new, I expect, about Taverner's sponges,
Drying, between the lying maps, in rows.
The sods today are duller and more utter,
But deadlier, deadlier still.

A formal ending I can't manage.
We've been solemn enough before, at Party meetings,
Constructive, eager, serious, ineffective . . .
'Yours fraternally,' then. And grin your inverted commas.
Help me to tell the truth and not feel dull.

PETER PORTER

born 1929

An Australian now permanently settled in England, Peter Porter was one of the few really gifted satirists to emerge in the 1960s. His early poems, packed with allusions, resemble those of the Elizabethan 'biting satirists' (who in turn modelled themselves on Juvenal) rather than the smooth verse of the Augustans. Since the 1960s his range has expanded, and he has created a considerable œuvre. The wide range of allusion is still there, but it is now linked to a new flexibility of tone and a greater poetic resonance. His moving *An Exequy* is a subtle updating of the famous poem by Bishop King.

Death in the Pergola Tea-Rooms

Snakes are hissing behind the misted glass.
Inside, there are tea urns of rubicund copper, chromium pipes
Pissing steam, a hot rattle of cups, British
Institutional Thickness. Under a covering of yellowing glass
Or old celluloid, cress-and-tomato, tongue-and-ham
Sandwiches shine complacently, skewered
By 1/6 a round. The wind spitefully lays the door shut
On a slow customer – ten pairs of eyes track
To his fairisle jersey; for a few seconds voices drop
Lower than the skirmishing of steam.
Outside by the river bank, the local doctor
Gets out of his '47 Vauxhall, sucking today's
Twentieth cigarette. He stops and throws it
Down in the mud of the howling orchard.
The orchard's crouching, half-back trees take the wind
On a pass from the poplars of the other bank,
Under the scooping wind, a conveyor-belt of wrinkles,
The buckled river cuts the cramping fields.
Just out of rattle reach and sound of cup clang,
The old rationalist is dying in the Pergola.
Two Labour Party friends and the doctor
Rearrange his woven rugs. The blood is roaring

In his head, the carcinoma commune, the fronde
Of pain rule in his brain – the barricades have broken
In his bowels – it is the rule of spasm, the terror sits.
He knows he is dying, he has a business of wills,
Must make a scaffolding for his wife with words,
Fit the flames in his head into the agenda.
Making up his mind now, he knows it is right
To take the body through committee meetings and campaign
rooms
To wear it and patch it like a good tweed; to come to
The fraying ends of its time, have to get the doctor
To staple up its seams just to keep the fingers
Pulling blankets up, stroking comfort on other fingers,
Patting the warm patch where the cat has been.
There is no God. It is winter, the windows sing
And stealthy sippers linger with their tea.
Now rushing a bare branch, the wind tips up
The baleful embroidery of cold drops
On a spider's web. Inside the old man's body
The draught is from an open furnace door – outside the room
Ignoring the doctor's mild professional face,
The carnival winter like the careful God
Lays on sap-cold rosetrees and sour flower beds
The cruel confusion of its disregard.

Madame de Merteuil on 'The Loss of an Eye'[1]

No letters. What's to become of an
Epistolary style it was no
Vanity to pride oneself on: chess
With a stupid curé, giving bad

1. *Madame de Merteuil on 'The Loss of an Eye'*: The Marquise de Merteuil is the villainess – or, rather, heroine – of *Les Liaisons Dangereuses* (1782), the remarkable epistolary novel in which Choderlos de Laclos (1741–1803) lays bare the corruption of French society under the *ancien régime*. She is successful in her enterprises throughout the book, but at the end of it the author rather arbitrarily punishes her with an attack of smallpox, which ruins her beauty and costs her the sight of one eye. The poet proposes a kind of coda to the events of the novel.

Advice about abortions to girls
With long chins whom no vice could ruin
Nor uxoriousness ever spoil.
Delphine has two kittens – how can I
Wheedle the cook's son to set his humpbacked
Tom on them? The tom is almost blind. We're two
Cerberus surveyors of the dark.
A young man called today, I recognized
The smell of boredom, the trap closing
In his eyes, a provincial appetite
For fame – the foxy diarist of love
Just waiting for old age to wax the world's
Ears with sententious aphorisms.
Sitting before a moral dish of nectarines,
I am pregnant again with self-love.
Crippled, sun stickying the socket
Of my dead eye, I choose *work*.
I can still plot the overthrow
Of a seminarist (a cut-price
Pascal with warts), plan the humbling of
A local Sévigné, wait calmly
For death to pay the courtesy of a call,
An old woman smelling lilac while her
Functionaries do evil in the sun.

The Great Poet Comes Here in Winter[1]

Frau Antonia is a cabbage:
If I were a grub I'd eat a hole in her.
Here they deliver the milk up a private path
Slippery as spit – her goddess' hands
Turn it to milk puddings. Below, little wind,
Steer in off this cardboard sea,

---

1. *The Great Poet Comes Here in Winter*: An 'allusion' to the career of
the German Symbolist poet Rainer Maria Rilke (1875–1926). Rilke fre-
quently stayed at the castle of Duino on the Adriatic, at the invitation
of his patroness, Princess Marie von Thurn und Taxis. His best-known
series of poems, the *Duino Elegies*, take their title from the place.

You are acclimatized like these veins
Warring on an inch of topsoil
You are agent of the Golden Republic,
So still blow for me – our flowers look one way,
If I were a good poet I would walk on the sea.

The sea is actually made of eyes.
Whether of drowned fishermen or of peasants
Accustomed to the hard bargains of the saints
I cannot say. Whether there will be
Any mail from Paris or even broccoli
For dinner is in doubt. My hat blew off the planet,
I knelt by the infinite sand of the stars
And prayed for all men. Being German, I have a lot of soul.
Nevertheless, why am I crying in this garden?
I refuse to die till fashion comes back to spats.

From this turret the Adriatic
Burns down the galley lanes to starved Ragusa,
How strange it can wash up condoms.
The world is coming unstitched at the seams.
All yesterday the weather was a taste
In my mouth, I saw the notes of Beethoven
Lying on the ground, from the horn
Of a gramophone I heard Crivelli's cucumbers
Crying out for paint. In the eyes of a stray bitch
Ribbed with hunger, heavy with young,
I saw the peneplain of all imagined
Misery, horizontal and wider than the world.
I gave her my unwrapped sugar. We said Mass
Together, she licking my fingers and me
Knowing how she would die, not glad to have lived.
She took her need away, I thought her selfish
But stronger than God and more beautiful company.

Fossil Gathering

Armed with hammers, we move along the cliff
Whose blue wall keeps a million million deaths;
The surf is low, the heat haze screens the stiff-

Backed searchers for imprisoned crystals. Blind.
Eyes of belemnites watch from narrow clefts,
Jurassic sun shines on them while they're mined.

The children look them up in paperbacks
And break an Ancient with impatient ease.
Sorted and cleaned, the fossils are in stacks,
Prepared and dressed for classrooms and jam jars –
At night in cupboards the reassembled seas
Break over England, straining for the stars.

A Little Guide in Colour tells us how
These creatures sank in their unconscious time,
That life in going leaves a husk the plough
Or amateur collector can displace,
That every feeling thing ascends from slime
To selfhood and in dying finds a face.

An Exequy

In wet May, in the months of change,
In a country you wouldn't visit, strange
Dreams pursue me in my sleep,
Black creatures of the upper deep –
Though you are five months dead, I see
You in guilt's iconography,
Dear Wife, lost beast, beleaguered child,
The stranded monster with the mild
Appearances, whom small waves tease,
(Andromeda upon her knees
In orthodox deliverance)
And you alone of pure substance,
The unformed form of life, the earth
Which Piero's brushes brought to birth
For all to greet as myth, a thing
Out of the box of imagining.
This introduction serves to sing
Your mortal death as Bishop King
Once hymned in tetrametric rhyme
His young wife, lost before her time;

Though he lived on for many years
His poem each day fed new tears
To that unreaching spot, her grave,
His lines a baroque architrave
The Sunday poor with bottled flowers
Would by-pass in their mourning hours,
Esteeming ragged natural life
('Most dearly loved, most gentle wife'),
Yet, looking back when at the gate
And seeing grief in formal state
Upon a sculpted angel group,
Were glad that men of god could stoop
To give the dead a public stance
And freeze them in their mortal dance.

The words and faces proper to
My misery are private – you
Would never share your heart with those
Whose only talent's to suppose,
Nor from your final childish bed
Raise a remote confessing head –
The channels of our lives are blocked,
The hand is stopped upon the clock,
No one can say why hearts will break
And marriages are all opaque:
A map of loss, some posted cards,
The living house reduced to shards,
The abstract hell of memory,
The pointlessness of poetry –
These are the instances which tell
Of something which I know full well,
I owe a death to you – one day
The time will come for me to pay
When your slim shape from photographs
Stands at my door and gently asks
If I have any work to do
Or will I come to bed with you.
O scala enigmatica,
I'll climb up to that attic where
The curtain of your life was drawn
Some time between despair and dawn –

I'll never know with what halt steps
You mounted to this plain eclipse
But each stair now will station me
A black responsibility
And point me to that shut-down room,
'This be your due appointed tomb.'

I think of us in Italy:
Gin-and-chianti-fuelled, we
Move in a trance through Paradise,
Feeding at last our starving eyes,
Two people of the English blindness
Doing each masterpiece the kindness
Of discovering it – from Baldovinetti
To Venice's most obscure jetty.
A true unfortunate traveller, I
Depend upon your nurse's eye
To pick the altars where no Grinner
Puts us off our tourists' dinner
And in hotels to bandy words
With Genevan girls and talking birds,
To wear your feet out following me
To night's end and true amity,
And call my rational fear of flying
A paradigm of Holy Dying –
And, oh my love, I wish you were
Once more with me, at night somewhere
In narrow streets applauding wines,
The moon above the Apennines
As large as logic and the stars,
Most middle-aged of avatars,
As bright as when they shone for truth
Upon untried and avid youth.

The rooms and days we wandered through
Shrink in my mind to one – there you
Lie quite absorbed by peace – the calm
Which life could not provide is balm
In death. Unseen by me, you look
Past bed and stairs and half-read book
Eternally upon your home,
The end of pain, the left alone.

I have no friend, or intercessor,
No psychopomp or true confessor
But only you who know my heart
In every cramped and devious part –
Then take my hand and lead me out,
The sky is overcast by doubt,
The time has come, I listen for
Your words of comfort at the door,
O guide me through the shoals of fear –
'Fürchte dich nicht, ich bin bei dir.'[1]

1. 'Don't be afraid, I am with you.' Pamina to Tamino in the Ordeal scene of Mozart's *Magic Flute*.

PETER REDGROVE

born 1932

Redgrove resembles Ted Hughes (his contemporary at Cambridge) perhaps more than he does any, of the poets of the Group, with whom he is here associated. Both of them are poets who concentrate on the use of dense, rich imagery. One might describe them both as being a little like the first generation German Expressionists, Trakl and Jakob van Hoddis. Redgrove is less disciplined than Hughes, and more grotesque: when unsuccessful, his poems are apt to become mere collections of images and effects. At their best, however, they have a muscular power.

The House in the Acorn

Ah, I thought just as he opened the door
That we all turned, for an instant, and looked away,
Checked ourselves suddenly, then he spoke:
'You're very good to come,' then,
Just for a moment his air thickened,
And he could not breathe, just for the moment.
'My son would have been glad that you came,'
He extended his thick hand, 'Here, all together –'
We are not ourselves or at our ease,
I thought, as we raised our glasses, sipped;
'Help yourselves, please. Please . . .'

'If anyone would care . . .' He stood by the table
Rapping his heavy nails in its polished glare,
'My son is upstairs, at the back of the house,
The nursery, if anyone . . .' I studied
Stocky hair-avenues along my hand-backs,
Wandered through grained plots dappled and sunlit;
'My son . . . sometimes I think they glimpse
Perhaps for a while through sealed lids a few faces
Bending in friendship before it all fades . . .' I nodded,
Slipped out, face averted,

And entered oak aisles; oaken treads
Mounted me up along oaken shafts, lifting me past
Tall silent room upon tall silent room:
Grained centuries of sunlight toppled to twilight
By chopping and fitting: time turned to timber
And the last oak enclosure with claws of bent oak
Where his white wisp cradled, instantaneous,
Hardly held by his home in its polished housetops.
A breath would have blown him; I held my breath
As I dipped to kiss . . .

Now the instant of this house rolls in my palm
And the company spins in its polished globe
And the drawing-room reels and the house recedes
(Pattering dome-grained out of the oak)
While, ah, as I open the door I hear their close laughter,
Cool earrings swing to the gliding whisper,
More apple-cup chugs from the stouted ewer.

The Half-Scissors

Humming water holds the high stars.
Meteors fall through the great fat icicles.
Spiders at rest from skinny leg-work
Lean heads forward on shaggy head-laces
All glittering from an askew moon in the sky:
One hinge snapped; a white door dislocated.
The night leans forward on this thin window;
Next door, tattered glass,
Wind twittering on jagged edges.
Doors beat like wings wishing to rise.
I lean forward to this thin fire.
A woman leaves – even the flames grow cool –
She is one hinge snapped, I am a half-scissors.

Peter Redgrove

Young Women with the Hair of Witches and No Modesty

('I Loved Ophelia!')

I have always loved water, and praised it.
I have often wished water would hold still.
Changes and glints bemuse a man terribly:
There is champagne and glimmer of mists;
Torrents, the distaffs of themselves, exalted, confused;
And snow splintering silently, skilfully, indifferently.
I have often wished water would hold still.
Now it does so, or ripples so, skilfully
In cross and doublecross, surcross and countercross.
A person lives in the darkness of it, watching gravely;

I used to see her straight and cool, considering the pond,
And as I approached she would turn gracefully
In her hair, its waves betraying her origin.
I told her that her thoughts issued in hair like consideration of
     water,
And if she laughed, that they would rain like spasms of weeping,
Or if she wept, then solemnly they held still,
And in the rain, the perfumes of it, and the blowing of it,
Confused, like hosts of people all shouting.
In such a world the bride walks through dressed as a waterfall,
And ripe grapes fall and splash smooth snow with jagged purple,
Young girls grow brown as acorns in their long climb towards
     oakhood,
And brown moths settle low down among ivories pale with
     love.
But she loosened her hair in a sudden tangle of contradictions,
In cross and doublecross, surcross and countercross,
And I was a shadow in the twilight of her late displeasure.
I asked water to stand still, now nothing else holds.

The Moon Disposes

(Perranporth Beach)

The mountainous sand-dunes with their gulls
Are all the same wind's moveables,
The wind's legs climb, recline,
Sit up gigantic, we wade
Such slithering pockets our legs are half the size,
There is an entrance pinched, a plain laid out,
An overshadowing of pleated forts.
We cannot see the sea, the sea-wind stings with sand,
We cannot see the moon that swims the wind,
The setting wave that started on the wind, pulls back.

Another slithering rim, we tumble whirling
A flying step to bed, better than harmless,
Here is someone's hoofprint on her hills
A broken ring with sheltering sides
She printed in the sand. A broken ring. We peer from play.

Hours late we walk among the strewn dead
Of this tide's sacrifice. There are strangled mussels:
The moon pulls back the lid, the wind unhinges them,
They choke on fans, they are bunched blue, black band.
The dead are beautiful, and give us life.
The setting wave recoils
In flocculence of blood-in-crystal,
It is medusa parched to hoofprints, broken bands,
Which are beautiful, and give us life.
The moon has stranded and the moon's air strangled
And the beauty of her dead dunes sent us up there
Which gave us life. Out at sea
Waves flee up the face of a far sea-rock, it is a pure white door
Flashing in the cliff-face opposite,
Great door, opening, closing, rumbling open, moonlike
Flying open on its close.

George MacBeth

born 1932

George MacBeth is arguably the most inventive and entertaining poet
now writing in England. In the strict sense of the term an experimen-
talist, he has included in nearly every collection of his work a section
of poems which are designed to extend the boundaries of the medium.
Though he has a reputation as a specialist in the outré and the out-
rageous, his poems cover an unexpectedly wide variety of themes. 'The
Bamboo Nightingale', the long poem printed here, shows his skill in
dealing with an ambitious topic. Unexpectedly for so strict a writer, it
seems to show the influence of Allen Ginsberg.

Owl

is my favourite. Who flies
like a nothing through the night,
who-whoing. Is a feather
duster in leafy corners ring-a-rosy-ing
boles of mice. Twice

you hear him call. Who
is he looking for? You hear
him hoovering over the floor
of the wood. O would you be gold
rings in the driving skull

if you could? Hooded and
vulnerable by the winter suns
owl looks. Is the grain of bark
in the dark. Round beaks are at
work in the pellety nest,

resting. Owl is an eye
in the barn. For a hole
in the trunk owl's blood
is to blame. Black talons in the
petrified fur! Cold walnut hands

on the case of the brain! In the reign
of the chicken owl comes like
a god. Is a goad in
the rain to the pink eyes,
dripping. For a meal in the day

flew, killed, on the moor. Six
mouths are the seed of his
arc in the season. Torn meat
from the sky. Owl lives
by the claws of his brain. On the branch

in the sever of the hand's
twigs owl is a backward look.
Flown wind in the skin. Fine
rain in the bones. Owl breaks
like the day. Am an owl, am an owl.

The Shell

Since the shell came and took you in its arms
   Whose body was fine bone
That walked in light beside a place of flowers,
    Why should your son
Years after the eclipse of those alarms
   Perplex this bitten stone
For some spent issue of the sea? Not one
Blue drop of drying blood I could call ours

In all that ocean that you were remains
   To move again. I come
Through darkness from a distance to your tomb
    And feel the swell
Where a dark flood goes headlong to the drains.
   I hear black hailstones drum
Like cold slugs on your skin. There is no bell
To tell what drowned king founders. Violets bloom

Where someone died. I dream that overhead
   I hear a bomber drone
And feel again stiff pumping of slow guns

Then the All Clear's
Voice break, and the long summing of the dead
  Below the siren's moan
Subdue the salt flood of all blood and tears
To a prolonged strained weeping sound that stuns.

I turn in anger. By whatever stars
  Clear out of drifting rack
This winter evening I revive my claim
      To what has gone
Beyond your dying fall. Through these cold bars
  I feel your breaking back
And live again your body falling on
That flood of stone where no white Saviour came

On Christian feet to lift you to the verge
  Or swans with wings of fire
Whose necks were arched in mourning. Black as coal
      I turn to go
Out of the graveyard. Headstone shadows merge
  And blur. I see the spire
Lift over corpses. And I sense the flow
Of death like honey to make all things whole.

The Bamboo Nightingale

A funeral-song to America, for her negro dead in Vietnam

I rise like a wooden bird from China. I sing
      from the echoing bellies of coolies
in the rice-fields. I mount on a curved gable
      in South Vietnam. I scream
across the Pacific to where you bask with your dolphins

in the riches of San Francisco. All down the coast
      your Golden Gate opens
to the poverty of Asia. I speak to the oranges
      rotting on trees. I address
the Bikini-strip of Sausalito, the beats

poising their chop-sticks. I make you the music
      of hunger and blood

crying for redress. America, listen. You have raided
    the inarticulate one time
too many. The reckoning comes. Below the pagodas

moulded in rain, your GI boots fill
    with the feet of centipedes. Your cowboy
politicians march on their stomachs into
    the supermarkets of mercy
without their credit-cards. Your dandy aviator[1]

posturing in leather gloves at his microphone
    inverts his torch each night
at the Hollywood Bowl of money. His witches' Sabbath
    sieg heils. And your army
of drafted ex-slaves fights out and across the ant-ridden

basin of the Mekong Delta watched over by the wings
    of helicopters. Out-generalled
by the Granddaughters of The Revolution, they die
    for the inalienable right
to six feet of Republican ground. At Forest Lawns

the suicide-fringe of your Upper Four Hundred are laid
    to rest in velvet. Your war
heroes are buried in a field commuters pack
    their abandoned Buicks by
a mile from the Pentagon. A shrouded crucifix

exploits the Passion. Each apache heart
    has a stake in it, the Old Glory
catches the throat. I see your packed quiver
    of machine-stitched chevrons, the
Redwood aisles are your coffin-timber. It is

the apocalypse of unequal rights. I hover
    with the eye of a newsreel camera
above the cortège of a black sergeant. My zoom
    lens pulls up his mother's
creased face into sweating ebony satin for

your moment of truth in *Life*. I caption her: *Jesus,*
    my boy was a white man

    1. *dandy aviator . . . sieg heils*: Air Vice-Marshal Ky once declared his
admiration for the late Adolf Hitler.

the day the reds nailed him. Remember that war
    when the limbs of your KIA airmen
formed up by fours again from their cold storage

in a Normandy abattoir. The Oxford hands
    reverently placed them back
in their air-cooled coffins, caring only what colour
    they were. America, here
The checkerboard squares of your white dream intermingle

in aerosol incense. Your soda-fountains are a-glitter
    with the nickel panoply
of the plastic Christian soldier. Even his screams
    are canned. You embark for crusades
against the marijuana-culture your fifth

column of Shanghai laundrymen in Buffalo
    smuggles in across the Great
Lakes. It is war to the needle against the yellow
    men the black men
are impressed to be targets for. The splinters of *Lightnings*

rust in the bones of North Korean villages
    nobody bombed except with
propaganda. O, exploding paper hurts
    only the graduate squaw
with her head in the schizophrenia of *Newsweek*. Truncheons

of Crazy Foam ooze from their cylinders
    in the All-white wigwams at Culver
City. Where is the doped brave with his hand
    burned in the embers of a New
Deal? The traffic cops in Alabama

bite on the bullet. Amphetamine is the mother
    of invention. O, come on,
America. The old con won't work
    any more. In the high-rise
incinerators of Austin Confessional Verse

can snipe itself to a Jewish cinder. Cry
    all the way to the bank while we cool
the Capone generation. The B-feature
    illusion is over. Your gangsters
have moved to the groin. Tonight is the massacre

in the under-trunk of·clover-leaves, the St Valentine's
     Day of the mobile gasoline
war. Vanzetti dies in the punctured sperm
     of your golden-armour-plated
Cadillacs. America, I smell your orgasms

in the copper exhausts of Mustangs. I taste your burned
     flesh in the sassy-flavour
of breakfast foods on WUOM. Your hypodermics
     have entered the marble temples
of Lincoln. In the scrapyards of Arlington

the Galaxie and the Continental are one
     tin. Its canisters
have unfolded their soup of blood in the clenched knuckles
     of the hard shoulder. Dip
your wheel into vomit, America. Spoon into flesh, the

cornflakes of Minnesota are deaf to the crackle
     of burning skin. I give you
the toast of Napalm. America, wring
     the brass neck of your melting-
pot. Hanoi is the cauldron of truth. Saigon is

the blazing Southern Cross of the Isolationist
     paradise. Ky is the killer
the Carl Sandburg village has no room
     in its penthouse for. America,
listen. The Goldwaterism that shelters your cold

executives in their minds of Samsonite
     has filtered the sun to a trickle
of ashes in light. Their mouths gape and scream
     for clay. Between them your body
they care about less than the clear glass in their eyes

is drained like a horse to make veal. Where now has the fury
     of dried blood gone? ask
the Macarthurite bronze gods in the fought-over beaches
     of conquered Iwojima
decorated by the sea. In the grey heart

of the University Section the heirs of Walt
     Whitman are a mile high
on the morning glory seeds of electrodes clipped

to the genitals. The great
American epic rocks in the spilled bowels

of Dillinger. The internal war-game
of Mah Jong continues
by the yolk of human eyes. The monks burn
into silence. There is no one to sweeten
the acid policy in the porcelain

of your L BJ Acropolis. Call it the Black
House, if you like. It looks
that way to the dark sergeant whose brains were charred
with the legacy in the headlines
of the *Times of Pecayune*. His eyes are closed

to the peacock of the American rainbow. His ears are deaf
to the buzzing of WASPS. His nose
is open to the stench of rotting corpses rising
out of the jungles of Hanoi
to corrupt the affluent. His mouth is twisted

with the sour flavour of black blood. His hands
are burned like an eskimo's
with the ice of not minding his business. America,
listen. This is the end
of the everlasting Charleston, the Wall Street crash

on the dollar merry-go-round, the dime hand-shake
in the golden soup-kitchens
of disillusion. I weep for the onion-domes
of the Kremlin. This is the bite
of iron. If you forget it your millionaires

will die in their XKEs for a brass thimble
of Curaçao. The days
of the sugar economy are over. The guerrillas walk down
your skyscrapers, beating
their steel breasts for the oiled virginskins

of Los Angeles. America, listen. Your body
moves like a moth in the beautiful
stage of emerging from metal. Her chrysalis
is the scrap-tide of iron. You advance
minute by minute towards the wheeled oblivion

of the killing-bottle. Take off your leopard-spot coat
    and bathe in the Yangtze river
with me tonight. There is no one to judge our battle
    except the future. I ask
for a striptease of guns. Lay aside your helmet and swim

for an hour in the moonlight. Perhaps beneath the willows
    in the evening cool of the water
some peaceful magic will happen. I ask you to move
    into the fluid of reason
below the lianas. I wait to bathe you in oil

or in blood. Answer me out of your prosperous iron
    in San Diego. Address
some message of sorrow to me in Saigon. Send
    your Pacific troubled with waves
of Oregon pity. Say that you hear and will come.

EDWARD LUCIE-SMITH

born 1933

The editor of this volume.

Looking at a Drawing

The line sets forth and
Wanders like a fox
Hunting. A blot falls
Here like a birdfoot.
This is like a man's
Steady striding round
The familiar paths
Of his own garden,
And this like the dragged
Belly of something
Wounded. The blood drops
Follow each other,
Hedgerow to hedgerow.
The mind follows that
Track. So many marks,
So many footprints
In the fields of snow.

Silence

Silence: one would willingly
Consume it, eat it like bread.
There is never enough. Now,
When we are silent, metal
Still rings upon shuddering
Metal; a door slams; a child
Cries; other lives surround us.

But remember, there is no
Silence within; the belly
Sighs, grumbles, and what is that
Loud knocking, that summoning?
A drum beats, a drum beats. Hear
Your own noisy machine, which
Is moving towards silence.

The Bruise

The ghost of your body
Clings implacably to
Mine. When you are absent
The air tastes of you, and
Last night the sheets had your
Texture. Then, when I looked
In this morning's mirror,
I found a bruise which had
Suddenly risen through
The milky flesh, a black
Star on the breast, surely
Not pinned there before (I
Count my wounds, and record
The number). How did it
Arrive? The ghost made it.
I turn, hearing you laugh.

Night Rain

The rain falls in strings, beads
To be counted. It wears
Out the night and the rock;
All things succumb to it.
I cannot tell if time
Is being washed away,
Or if this is time, made
Tangible as water.

My fever has returned,
Like an icy river.
In bed alone, I am
Dissolving. Flesh becomes
Like the wet sacks out there,
Abandoned in the dark
Of the garden, lapsing
Slowly into the earth.

DAVID WEVILL

born 1935

A Canadian poet, who belonged for some years to the English literary
world by residence and adoption, David Wevill writes poems in a style
which relates him to Peter Redgrove and Ted Hughes. Essentially, how-
ever, he is a quieter writer than either of these two. His difference from
the poets of the *New Lines* group can be summed up in his recorded
criticism of them: 'I think what is often lacking is what I can only call
intuition, the transforming quality of mind and the senses.' And essen-
tially his own poetry *is* sensuous, building itself up image by image,
rather than idea by idea.

My Father Sleeps

Who brought from the snow-wrecked
Hulk of winter his salvaged
Purpose; who came, blind but friendly
By these lines his mouth and his eyes
Have fixed; and without further talk
Taught me at last how to walk,
Until by his power I came
Out of innocence like the worm's flame
Into daylight. What practical need
His patience had, and anger bred
Of disillusionment, has gone with age.
I have this white-haired image,
Arrogant perhaps, and too much the hero
For our friendship's good: Lear, although
Afraid of words as of madness,
Of procrastination as of disease –
A lover of plain-spokenness –
Though not where it hurt, that he could understand.
If I trace the scars in my right hand
They tell me of purpose disobeyed,
Of old and factual truths my head
Cannot alter. And watching him thus

Sprawled like a crooked frame of clothes
In the sleep of sixty years, jaws firm,
Breathing through the obstacle of his nose
A stubborn air that is truth for him,
I confront my plainest self. And feel
In the slow hardening of my bones, a questioning
Depth that his pride could never reveal;
That in his sleep stirs its cruel beginning.

Groundhog

At the tip of my gun the goundhog sits
Hunched in the sun a hundred yards away.
At this range my Hornet's steel-lipped
Bullet could bleed him dry as a star,
As a rag in the pitching drought-drugged field.

Grasses waver and hide, I watch
His shadow's hare, quick at its burrow's
Mouth; the flinch of his rodent hump
Too far to see, like a piece of my eye put out.

No lead gift for a hawk this bead I draw.

Magnetic steel's the moment's only touch
Between us. Though his teeth and scent are sharp
They twitch no warning from the hot bright air.
And I cannot kill, but mark him, fat
As a neighbour safe in his rocking-chair.
Flat on my hips I lie in wait.
Earth beats with my heartbeat, and now
My body's jelly's hardened to take the blow
Of its triphammer weight at the soft exposed
Centre. Imagining it, I retreat –
Wait minutes as his black speck grows
Whiskering through the stalks of Indian corn
To confront me with 'Thou shalt not kill' –
A matter of temperament. No, his fate's
Inhuman, not mine. The riddle is why.

The riddle's this nerve that pecks at my hand.
Scissors to slice my aim's thread now would touch
Terror like a jumping nerve: Zero-urge,
Guiding my right hand and my eye –
Not the will's choice crying unmistakably No.

I fired because confusion made me think . . .

One spoilt instant's enough to be conqueror.

And now his brown blot melts to its darkest hole,
But I've beaten him there; in the dark, I feel him drop
Slithering past me, wet at the spot I touched.

Winter Homecoming

The airfield stretches its cantilever wings,
Its petrified flight of a gull . . .
Time is before me, blown by the solar wind
Lit by the sun's corona on the snow-sheeted glass.

It is daybreak, heart of winter.
The big jets listen, waiting for their flights.
I watch the blue-veined snowfields bleed with sunrise
Slowly turning my hands to catch,
Reflect, the cold light; asking myself

The way
The messiah comes.

Painfully he comes. Comes now,
As beyond the grey, wolf-shy pineforest,
The ice-shy villas of Montreal,
A million mirrors turn their heads
Watching this bird of departure, hearing his roar
Eventually even to the cross on the mountaintop –

He shakes the blood-pink snowfields,
His red light . . . green light flashes over the whole
Snow-tortured North –

Touching the snowshoe hare, the arctic fox,
Alarming the businessman sleeping his whisky off . . .

And I am coming to you this last time
Before the spreading sun has touched your eyes,
Passed on, and left no dawn where your eyes were.

PART SIX: INFLUENCES FROM ABROAD

Despite frequent criticisms of its provincialism (induced by a too exclusive concentration upon the work of writers such as Larkin and Amis), post-war British verse at one time showed a large measure of influence from abroad. The two principal sources of this have been Germany and the United States. Some poets were indeed born in Germany: Michael Hamburger and Karen Gershon are examples of this. Hamburger has been a prolific translator, and produced a notable anthology of modern German poetry, in collaboration with Christopher Middleton. Middleton and Matthew Mead (another translator from the German) seem to show the influence of Germany and America intermingled; Middleton also seems to have felt the impact of French surrealism. American influence was of two sorts: first there was that of the post-Poundian or 'Black Mountain' poets, perhaps most successfully absorbed and anglicized by Charles Tomlinson, but to be felt at least as strongly in the work of the poets grouped around Gael Turnbull's Migrant Press. Inevitably, there was also the influence of the Beats, seen most clearly in the work of the Liverpool poets, who appear in another section.

MICHAEL HAMBURGER

born 1924

Michael Hamburger was born in Germany, and has played an extremely active part in introducing modern German literature to English readers. His translations of Hölderlin and Hugo von Hofmannsthal are especially notable. Curiously enough, his own poetry remains more persistently 'English' in flavour than that of some of his collaborators, such as Christopher Middleton.

Travelling

I

Mountains, lakes. I have been here before
And on other mountains, wooded
Or rocky, smelling of thyme.
Lakes from whose beds they pulled
The giant catfish, for food,
Larger, deeper lakes that washed up
Dead carp and mussel shells, pearly or pink.
Forests where, after rain,
Salamanders lay, looped the dark mess with gold.
High up, in a glade,
Bells clanged, the cowherd boy
Was carving a pipe.
And I moved on, to learn
One of the million histories,
One weather, one dialect
Of herbs, one habitat
After migration, displacement,
With greedy lore to pounce
On a place and possess it,
With the mind's weapons, words,
While between land and water
Yellow vultures, mewing,
Looped empty air

Once filled with the hundred names
Of the nameless, or swooped
To the rocks, for carrion.

2

Enough now, of grabbing, holding,
The wars fought for peace,
Great loads of equipment lugged
To the borders of bogland, dumped,
So that empty-handed, empty-minded,
A few stragglers could stagger home.

And my baggage – those tags, the stickers
That brag of a Grand Hotel
Requisitioned for troops, then demolished,
Of a tropical island converted
Into a golf course;
The specimens, photographs, notes –
The heavier it grew, the less it was needed,
The longer it strayed, misdirected,
The less it was missed.

3

Mountains. A lake.
One of a famous number.
I see these birds, they dip over wavelets,
Looping, martins or swallows,
Their flight is enough.
The lake is enough,
To be here, forgetful,
In a boat, on water,
The famous dead have been here.
They saw and named what I see,
They went and forgot.

I climb a mountainside, soggy,
Then springy with heather.
The clouds are low,
The shaggy sheep have a name,
Old, less old than the breed
Less old than the rock

And I smell hot thyme
That grows in another country,
Through gaps in the Roman wall
A cold wind carries it here.

4

Through gaps in the mind,
Its fortifications, names:
Name that a Roman gave
To a camp on the moor
Where a sheep's jawbone lies
And buzzards, mewing, loop
Air between woods and water
Long empty of his gods;
Name of the yellow poppy
Drooping, after rain,
Or the flash, golden,
From wings in flight –
Greenfinch or yellowhammer –

Of this mountain, this lake. I move on.

The Jackdaws

Gone, I thought, had not heard them for years;
Gone like the nuthatch, the flycatcher,
Like the partridges from the bulldozed hill.
Now it was I who was going,
And they were back, or had never gone,
Chucking, bickering up on the elm's bare branches.

I forgot the changes, the chores,
Jackdaw's corpse in the water tank,
Jackdaw's nest, jackdaw's dry bones, dry feathers
Stuffed down the chimneys –
No longer mine to clear.
I heard them, I saw them again in the cold clean air
And, going, my tenure ended,
Brought in the harvest of three thousand weathers,
The soot, the silver, their hubbub on trees left behind.

CHRISTOPHER MIDDLETON

born 1926

Christopher Middleton is now a lecturer in German at the University of Texas, having previously taught at London University. His book *torse 3*, subtitled 'poems 1949–1961', met a warm welcome when it was published in 1962. It contained what is still his most accessible poetry. There had been two previous collections, both now disowned by the author. The epigraph to *torse 3* is a dictionary-definition which states the author's aims pretty clearly. A 'torse', it tells us, is 'a developable surface; a surface generated by a moving straight line which at every instant is turning, in some plane or other through it, about some point or other of its length'. For 'torse', Middleton means us to read 'poem'. Middleton is a sophisticated writer and an eclectic one: his work brings together influences from America, Germany and France. He is interested in the anti-logic of 'Pataphysics', for example, and, in collaboration with Michael Hamburger, he has edited an extremely important parallel text anthology of modern German verse. The rather removed precision of his work brings it close to that of Charles Tomlinson.

Climbing a Pebble

What did it mean (I ask myself), to climb a pebble.
From the head of a boy depends a very thin cloud.
A red speck shifting on the Roman Campagna.
This sea-rubbed pebble has no cleft for toes.

It is simple, the ant said (my Nares and Keats).
You start low down, with caution. You need not
Slash your soles for lime like medieval Swiss.
No, but with spread arms, easing up, imperceptibly
Colluding with the air's inverted avalanche.
This cushions, O, the aching spine.

A very thin cloud is falling from the sky.
A shot, a shifting robe of crimson,
Whiffs of powder on the wind –
The sidelong buffet slams. And still you cling,

Still easing upward; giant glades, they creaked and shone,
Fresh mown, now small below – you do not smell them.

And you begin to know what it can mean,
Climbing a pebble. The paradise bird
Drops, dies, with beak fixed in the ground.
An urchin made off with its cloudthin tail.
A cardinal, with footmen to load his fowling pieces,
Peppers Italian larks a glass held spellbound.

The glass was tied to an owl, the owl to a stick.
I struck the pebble, digging, as the sun went up.

Cabal of Cat and Mouse

He has a way, the cat, who sits
on the short grass in lamplight.
Him you could appreciate, and more –
how the musky night fits him,
like a glove; how he adapts down there,
below boughs, to his velvet arena.

His, for playing in. A shadow
plodding past his white paws
could be a swad of anything;
except that, as it bolts, he retrieves
and has tenderly couched it,
and must unroll alongside, loving.

His paws dab and pat at it; his
austere head swivels at an angle
to the barrel neck. Prone, he eyes
its minutest move; his haunch relaxing
parades tolerance, for the pose entreats
doubly to play – it is energy

involved, if you like, in a tacit exchange
of selves, as the cat flares up again,
and has seized what he seizes.
And acts proud, does a dance, for it is
his appetite puts all the mouse into a mouse;
the avid mouse, untameable,

bound by so being to concur
in his bones, with the procedure.
Even the end cannot cancel that.
The shift from play to kill, measured,
is not advertised. He has applied
a reserved gram of tooth power,

to raise this gibbering curt squeal
at last, and now glassily gazes down.
Plunged, barked as if punched,
and has axed his agitator. You heard
soon the headbones crunch; and you shrank,
the spine exploding like a tower in air.

Lenau's Dream[1]

Scares me mad, that dream;
wish I could tell my-
self I slept without

a dream! But what of
these tears pouring down
still, loud throb of heart?

Waking, I was done up.
My handkerchief wet
(had I just buried

someone?). Don't know how
I got hold of it,
and me fast asleep –

but they were there, the
visitors, evil,
I gave them my house

for their feast, then got
off to bed, while they
tore the place to bits,

1. *Lenau's Dream*: Nikolas Lenau (1802–50), Austrian poet. Died
insane, partly as the result of a protracted and disastrous love-affair.

the wild, fool ele-
mentals! Gone out now,
leaving their trail, these

tears and from tables
great wine pools dripping
slowly to the floor.

CHARLES TOMLINSON

born 1927

Tomlinson's work represents a kind of cultural crossroads. He has been influenced by the French Symbolists (as Donald Davie pointed out in the introduction to his first collection, *The Necklace*); he has made translations from the Spanish and the Russian; he has had considerable success in America, and certainly owes much to the American modernists, and particularly to William Carlos Williams and his disciples. Despite this, he is instantly recognizable as an English poet, with a very English sensibility.

Tramontana at Lerici

Today, should you let fall a glass it would
   Disintegrate, played off with such keenness
Against the cold's resonance (the sounds
   Hard, separate and distinct, dropping away
In a diminishing cadence) that you might swear
   This was the imitation of glass falling.

Leaf-dapples sharpen. Emboldened by this clarity
   The minds of artificers would turn prismatic,
Running on lace perforated in crisp wafers
   That could cut like steel. Constitutions,
Drafted under this fecund chill, would be annulled
   For the strictness of their equity, the moderation of their pity.

At evening, one is alarmed by such definition
   In as many lost greens as one will give glances to recover,
As many again which the landscape
   Absorbing into the steady dusk, condenses
From aquamarine to that slow indigo-pitch
   Where the light and twilight abandon themselves.

And the chill grows. In this air
   Unfit for politicians and romantics

Dark hardens from blue, effacing the windows:
    A tangible block, it will be no accessory
To that which does not concern it. One is ignored
    By so much cold suspended in so much night.

The Snow Fences

They are fencing the upland against
the drifts this wind, those clouds
would bury it under: brow and bone
know already that levelling zero
as you go, an aching skeleton,
in the breathtaking rareness of winter air.

Walking here, what do you see?
Little more, through wind-teased eyes,
than a black, iron tree
and, there, another, a straggle
of low and broken wall between, grass
sapped of its greenness, day going.

The farms are few: spread
as wide, perhaps, as when
the Saxons who found them, chose
these airy and woodless spaces
and froze here before they fed
the unsuperseded burial ground.

Ahead, the church's dead-white
limewash will dazzle the mind
as, dazed, you enter to escape:
despite the stillness here, the chill
of wash-light scarcely seems
less penetrant than the hill-top wind.

Between the graves, you find
a beheaded pigeon, the blood and grain
trailed from its bitten crop, as alien to all
the day's pallor as the raw
wounds of the earth, turned above
a fresh solitary burial.

A plaque of staining metal
distinguishes this grave among
an anonymity whose stones
the frosts have scaled, thrusting under
as if they grudged the ground
its ill-kept memorials.

The bitter darkness drives you
back valleywards, and again you bend
joint and tendon to encounter
the wind's force and leave behind
the nameless stones, the snow-shrouds
of a waste season: they are fencing
the upland against those years, those clouds.

The Fox

When I saw the fox, it was kneeling
in snow: there was nothing to confess
that, tipped on its broken forepaws
the thing was dead – save for its stillness.

A drift, confronting me, leaned down
across the hill-top field. The wind
had scarped it into a pennine wholly of snow, and
where did the hill go now?

There was no way round:
I drew booted legs
back out of it, took to my tracks again,
but already a million blown snow-motes were flowing and
    filling them in.

Domed at the summit, then tapering,
the drift still mocked
my mind as if the whole
fox-infested hill were the skull of a fox.

Scallops and dips
of pure pile rippled and shone, but what
should I do with such beauty
eyed by that?

It was like clambering between its white temples
as the crosswind tore
at one's knees, and each
missed step was a plunge at the hill's blinding interior.

A Given Grace

Two cups,
a given grace,
afloat and white
on the mahogany pool
of table. They unclench
the mind, filling it
with themselves.
Though common ware,
these rare reflections,
coolness of brown
so strengthens and refines
the burning of their white,
you would not wish
them other than they are –
you, who are challenged
and replenished by
those empty vessels.

MATTHEW MEAD

born 1924

Matthew Mead, who lives in Germany, is chiefly known for his brilliant translations of the poetry of the East German poet Johannes Bobrowski. His own work, like Christopher Middleton's, combines the influences of modern German poetry and of the Pound tradition – Middleton speaks of the way in which Mead combines 'the tradition of experimental form and European political themes'. Hugh Kenner has also praised his work.

Identities

II

Will you remember me Tatania
When your map of this country is folded,
When you see no more the low tower and the hills,
The humped bridge, the stream through the osier-holt?

We pause at the kissing-gate,
The spinney twists into evening;
The wind travels far Tatania
And you must follow.
When 'September' and 'remember' rhyme
Shall I rhyme them for a café translation?

The hills wait as always for the caressing eye,
The eager feet of glory or the warning beacon;
Over successive fields, breakers of hedge
Lift to a legacy of skyline:
Will you remember me Tatania
As I cling to these landmarks and scars
Which fade from your mind?

We stand here in the last of day,
The hills wait
The fields are a green sea.

And nearer the light fails
Changes and fades and our eyes
Clutch line of branch
Silhouette of leaf . . .

When Lazarus lies in his long tomb and dead leaves
Tremble in their forgetting dance,
Will you remember me Tatania?
Shall I come like a ghost to trouble joy?
Tatania, Tatania, what will you remember?
Here, with your lips on mine,
Who do you say I am?

Translator to Translated

I. M. Johannes Bobrowski

River, plain,
tree, the bird
in flight, habitation
and name, strange
to me, never strange
to you – the child's
eye, the soldier's
step, the known
threshold.
I crossed the plain
slowly, saw your fire
in the distance.
Have I set the tree
askew on your sky,
does your bird hover
strangely?
Love
translates
as love.
Her song sung
in a strange land.

An air that kills.

GAEL TURNBULL

born 1928

During the 1960s Gael Turnbull exercised a strong personal influence on the course taken by avant-garde poetry in England. His little Migrant Press provided a focus for the post-Poundian poets when these were entirely neglected and out of favour, and he was one of the principal links between the American Black Mountain poets and this country, long before writers such as Creeley or Olson got 'taken up' on either side of the Atlantic and extensively imitated. Turnbull was also the real rediscoverer of Bunting's work, and his set of duplicated notes, *An Arlespenny*, constituted the first serious critical attention that Bunting received in England after the war.

Homage to Jean Follain[1]

I think you must have written them on postcards, your poems,
    like something one sends home while visiting abroad;

or like woodcuts that one finds in an old book in the attic and
    stares at on a rainy day, forgetting supper, forgetting to
    switch on the light;

but not antique, though out of time, each fixed in its moment,
    like sycamore seeds spiralling down that never seem to
    reach the grass.

What became of the freak, the girl with animal fur, when the
    carnival moved on to the next village?

and the old souse, when he got home from the wineshop, did
    he beat his wife or did she beat him? did his daughter run
    away?

and that horseman coming home from a thirty years war, did
    the dogs know him? why should that one bird cry to an-
    nounce him from so far?

1. *Jean Follain*: (born 1903). Of all contemporary French poets, among the most pictorial. Turnbull's poem evokes Follain's characteristic imagery.

and the police, toiling day and night to manacle the world, did they finish the last link, or did their ink dry up? did their slide-rules crumble?

But you don't tell us, and perhaps you don't really know, as you drink autumn wine in the evening, leaning over the battlements of an imaginary tower, watching the unwearied insects hovering in the immaculate air.

George Fox,[1] From His Journals

Who had openings within
as he walked in the fields
(and saw a great crack through the earth)
  who went by eye across hedge and ditch toward the spires
  of the steeple-houses, until he came to Litchfield, and then
  barefoot in the market place, unable to contain, crying out,
and among friends
of much tenderness of conscience,
of a spirit by which all things might be judged
by waiting
for openings within which would answer each other
(and after that crack, a great smoke)
  and in a lousy stinking place, low in the ground, without
  even a bed, among thirty convicts, where he was kept al-
  most half a year, the excrement over the top of his shoes,
as he gathered his mind inward,
a living hope arose
(and after that smoke, a great shaking)
  but when he heard the bell toll to call people to the steeple-
  house, it struck at his life; for it was like a market-bell, to
  call them that the priest might sell his wares,
    such as fed upon words and fed one another with
    words until they had spoken themselves dry, and who raged
    when they were told, '*The man in leather breeches is here
. . .*'
a tender man
with some experience
of what had been opened to him.

1. *George Fox*: (1624–91), founder of the Society of Friends.

ROY FISHER

born 1930

Roy Fisher's work goes back beyond the modernism of America to the sources in Europe: he has at various times been described as 'a Cubist poet' and 'a 1905 Russian modernist'. These descriptions are accurate, in so far as they demonstrate an interest in simultaneity, and an affinity with certain kinds of Symbolist poetry.

The Hospital in Winter

A dark bell leadens the hour,
    the three-o'clock
light falls amber across a tower.

Below, green-railed within a wall
    of coral brick,
stretches the borough hospital

monstrous with smells that cover death,
    white gauze tongues,
cold-water-pipes of pain, glass breath,

porcelain, blood, black rubber tyres;
    and in the yards
plane trees and slant telephone wires.

On benches squat the afraid and cold
    hour after hour.
Chains of windows snarl with gold.

Far off, beyond the engine-sheds,
    motionless trucks
grow ponderous, their rotting reds

deepening towards night; from windows
    bathrobed men
watch the horizon flare as the light goes.

Smoke whispers across the town,
    high panes are bleak;
pink of coral sinks to brown;
a dark bell brings the dark down.

Interior I

Experimenting, experimenting,
    with long damp fingers twisting all the time and in the dusk
White like unlit electric bulbs she said
'This green goes with this purple,' the hands going,
The question pleased: 'Agree?'

Squatting beside a dark brown armchair just round from the
    fireplace, one hand on a coalscuttle the other prickling
    across the butchered remains of my hair,

I listen to the nylon snuffle in her poking hands,
Experimenting, experimenting.
'Old sexy-eyes,' is all I say.

So I have to put my face into her voice, a shiny, baize-lined
    canister that says all round me, staring in:
'I've tried tonight. This place!' Experimenting. And I:
'The wind off the wallpaper blows your hair bigger.'

Growing annoyed, I think, she clouds over, reminds me she's
    a guest, first time here, a comparative stranger however
    close; 'Doesn't *welcome* me.' She's not young of course;
Trying it, though, going on about the milk bottle, table leg,
The little things. Oh, a laugh somewhere. More words.
She knows I don't *live* here.

Only a little twilight is left washing around outside, her unease
    interfering with it as I watch.
Silence. Maybe some conversation. I begin:
'Perhaps you've had a child secretly sometime?'

'Hm?' she says, closed up. The fingers start again, exploring up
    and down and prodding, smoothing. Carefully
She asks, 'At least – why can't you have more walls?'
Really scared. I see she means it.

To comfort her I say how there's one wall each, they can't
    outnumber us, walls, lucky to have the one with the
    lightswitch, our situation's better than beyond the back
    yard, where indeed the earth seems to stop pretty abruptly
    and not restart;
Then she says, very finely:
'I can't look,' and 'Don't remind me,' and 'That blue gulf.'

So I ask her to let her fingers do the white things again and let
    her eyes look and her hair blow bigger, all in the dusk
    deeper and the coloured stuffs audible and odorous;
But she shuts her eyes big and mutters:
                    'And when the moon with horror –
                    And when the moon with horror –
                    And when the moon with horror –'

So I say, 'Comes blundering blind up the side tonight.'
She: 'We hear it bump and scrape.'
I: 'We hear it giggle.' Looks at me,
'And when the moon with horror,' she says.

Squatting beside a dark brown armchair just round from the
    fireplace, one hand on a coalscuttle the other prickling
    across the butchered remains of my hair,
'What have you been reading, then?' I ask her,
Experimenting, experimenting.

GEOFFREY HILL

born 1931

Geoffrey Hill is a powerful, difficult, learned writer – a true poet's poet.
He produced one or two of the best lyrics to have been written by an
Oxford undergraduate in this century, and then developed into a writer
so compressed and elliptical that sometimes it was difficult to avoid the
word 'costive'. More recently there has been a slight loosening – just
enough to liberate the real grandeur of his style, which can nevertheless
incorporate 'low' words and phrases to stunning effect.

In Piam Memoriam

I

Created purely from glass the saint stands,
Exposing his gifted quite empty hands
Like a conjurer about to begin,
A righteous man begging of righteous men.

II

In the sun lily-and-gold-coloured,
Filtering the cruder light, he has endured,
A feature for our regard; and will keep;
Of worldly purity the stained archetype.

III

The scummed pond twitches. The great holly-tree,
Emptied and shut, blows clear of wasting snow,
The common, puddled substance: beneath,
Like a revealed mineral, a new earth.

Geoffrey Hill

To the (Supposed) Patron

Prodigal of loves and barbecues,
Expert in the strangest faunas, at home
He considers the lilies, the rewards.
There is no substitute for a rich man.
At his first entering a new province
With new coin, music, the barest glancing
Of steel or gold suffices. There are many
Tremulous dreams secured under that head.
For his delight and his capacity
To absorb, freshly, the inside-succulence
Of untoughened sacrifice, his bronze agents
Speculate among convertible stones
And drink desert sand. That no mirage
Irritate his mild gaze, the lewd noonday
Is housed in cool places, and fountains
Salt the sparse haze. His flesh is made clean.
For the unfallen – the firstborn, or wise
Councillor – prepared vistas extend
As far as harvest; and idyllic death
Where fish at dawn ignite the powdery lake.

Ovid in the Third Reich

> non peccat, quaecumque potest peccasse negare,
> solaque famosam culpa professa facit.[1]

(Amores, III, xiv)

I love my work and my children. God
Is distant, difficult. Things happen.
Too near the ancient troughs of blood
Innocence is no earthly weapon.

I have learned one thing: not to look down
Too much upon the damned. They, in their sphere,
Harmonize strangely with the divine
Love. I, in mine, celebrate the love-choir.

1. She does not sin that can deny her sin – 'Tis only avowed
dishonour brings the fault.

Mercian Hymns VI

The princes of Mercia were badger and raven. Thrall to their freedom, I dug and hoarded. Orchards fruited above clefts. I drank from honeycombs of chill sandstone.

'A boy at odds in the house, lonely among brothers.' But I, who had none, fostered a strangeness; gave myself to unattainable toys.

Candles of gnarled resin, apple-branches, the tacky mistletoe. 'Look' they said and again 'look.' But I ran slowly; the landscape flowed away, back to its source.

In the schoolyard, in the cloakrooms, the children boasted their scars of dried snot; wrists and knees garnished with impetigo.

'Christmas Trees'

Bonhoeffer in his skylit cell
bleached by the flares' candescent fall,
pacing out his own citadel,

restores the broken themes of praise,
encourages our borrowed days,
by logic of his sacrifice.

Against wild reasons of the state
his words are quiet but not too quiet.
We hear too late or not too late.

Geoffrey Hill

From 'An Apology for the Revival of Christian Architecture in England'

11 IDYLLS OF THE KING

The pigeon purrs in the wood; the wood has gone;
dark leaves that flick to silver in the gust,
and the marsh-orchids and the heron's nest,
goldgrimy shafts and pillars of the sun.

Weightless magnificence upholds the past.
Cement recesses smell of fur and bone
and berries wrinkle in the badger-run
and wiry heath-fern scatters its fresh rust.

'O clap your hands' so that the dove takes flight,
bursts through the leaves with an untidy sound,
plunges its wings into the green twilight

above this long-sought and forsaken ground,
the half-built ruins of the new estate,
warheads of mushrooms round the filter-pond.

12 THE EVE OF ST MARK

Stroke the small silk with your whispering hands,
godmother; nod and nod from the half-gloom;
broochlight intermittent between the fronds,
the owl immortal in its crystal dome.

Along the mantelpiece veined lustres trill,
the clock discounts us with a telling chime.
Familiar ministrants, clerks-of-appeal,
burnish upon the threshold of the dream:

churchwardens in wing-collars bearing scrolls
of copyhold well-tinctured and well-tied.
Your photo-albums loved by the boy-king

preserve in sepia waterglass the souls
of distant cousins, virgin till they died,
and the lost delicate suitors who could sing.

KAREN GERSHON

born 1923

Of all the poets writing in English who have tried to deal with the theme of the German concentration camps, Karen Gershon is the most moving. She is one of the German Jewish children who were saved at the last moment from the Nazis, but whose parents were left behind to die. Of all the poets from abroad who have lived in England, she remains in a sense the most exiled. At one moment she even thinks of herself as 'exiled' in language: nevertheless, the influence of English poets, such as Wilfred Owen, has been important. In 1969, in search of 'native ground', she moved to Israel. Technically limited, and emotionally monotonous, her work still deserves a great deal more notice than it has so far received.

I Was Not There

The morning they set out from home
I was not there to comfort them
the dawn was innocent with snow
in mockery – it is not true
the dawn was neutral was immune
their shadows threaded it too soon
they were relieved that it had come
I was not there to comfort them

One told me that my father spent
a day in prison long ago
he did not tell me that he went
what difference does it make now
when he set out when he came home
I was not there to comfort him
and now I have no means to know
of what I was kept ignorant

Both my parents died in camps
I was not there to comfort them

I was not there they were alone
my mind refuses to conceive
the life the death they must have known
I must atone because I live
I could not have saved them from death
the ground is neutral underneath

Every child must leave its home
time gathers life impartially
I could have spared them nothing since
I was too young – it is not true
they might have lived to succour me
and none shall say in my defence
had I been there to comfort them
it would have made no difference

In the Jewish Cemetery

The dead Jews lie
divided by
the fate of their families
those with survivors have
flowers on their graves
the others have grass

One who is named
on her family's tomb
died in a camp
when she was twenty years old
I envied her as a child
and am ashamed

My mother's only son
died as he was born
him I also mourn
whatever he has been spared
counts as nothing compared
with what he might have done

My grandparents shall have
an evergreen grave
no flowers shall
divide them from those
whom no one now knows
I mourn them all

NATHANIEL TARN

born 1928

Tarn was educated both in England and in France, is a trained anthro-
pologist, and has travelled widely in Europe, Asia, and the Americas. He
now lives in the United States. This background gives his poetry a
cosmopolitan tone which is unusual in contemporary English poetry.

Last of the Chiefs

I speak from ignorance.
Who once learned much, but speaks from ignorance now.
Who trembled once with the load of such knowledge,
trembled and cried and gritted his teeth and gripped
with his fists the ends of the arms of his throne.

Who once distilled this island in his green intestines
like the whale distils her dung gone dry called ambergris –
a perfume for faraway races

who wrecked us.

Only here and there, like lightning before the rain's whips,
like a trench along the deep, a thought such as I had:

in the belly of the whale there is room for such an island.

I laugh. I come now. I clear space. My name, my very being
is that: I clear space. I pass over them with my thongs, laughing,
that have died fighting the island-bellied whale, not prevailed,
turned at last their steels against themselves, lie in spasms,
their cheek and chest muscles like rock. I pass over them,
smoke them, whip them, revive them, send them out again.

Wise wind singer with a forked tail like white lightning
and your black pin eye. Paradise tern on her tail-long hair.

I am thankful. I accept. I take your offerings of pork lard
and the myriad flowers of the scissored palm leaf. I take.

I accept. But above all I thank you for the breasts in heaven
of my daughters of the island which is Nukahiva of the
   Marquesas

that you know as Herman Melville's green garden, his Pacific.

Some say he beautified this green back yard.
I speak from ignorance. I remember little.

Markings

Un homme se possède par éclaircies, et même quand il se possède, il
ne s'atteint pas tout à fait. ANTONIN ARTAUD

My writing to forget
the thing I love
is but the signature
a root of fire
(that always seeks a home
but cannot find
a residence to let
and rise into)
must mark with to endure.
I sign with scent of breath,
with body rub,
against your willing flanks
so that remembrances
renew themselves till death,
project through history
intra-specific thanks
white skin by skin.
The game of win and lose
being but lick and sniff
we go as dogs progress
from sin to perfumed sin,
lifting a leg to trace
along your bare midriff
the sign of the true way.
Or when the doves digress
to build in bridal air
their parodies of grace

our feet race on below
with the black hound of hell
and resurrection's hare.
Where there's no stop and go
a thought may wet your face,
a breath arrest your stare.
Look: everything forgets
in this pure atmosphere –
before the sunshine sets
or the bright air can die,
it's time to make a start,
and mark in memory
these rituals of art.

PETER LEVI

born 1931

Of all the poets whom I have grouped together in this section, Peter Levi
is perhaps the most varied. His early work is, in a general sense, post-
Movement. It can sometimes be compared with that of Elizabeth
Jennings. Often, however, it seems an uneasy mixture of earlier literary
influences: Wordsworth and W. B. Yeats cohabit in one and the same
poem, and the tone varies wildly from stanza to stanza. In his more
recent work, there has been a gradual development towards a more
romantic and bardic stance.

Monologue Spoken by the Pet Canary of Pope Pius XII

Uccello cello cello
I love myself: it seems a dream sometimes
about the water spouting from tree-height,
and voices like a piece of looking-glass.
His shoulder had young pine-needles on it.
At night I used to wake when the big moon
swayed upward like a lighted playing-card,
and someone had uncombed the Great Hallel
with grimy fingers down the window-pane.
I am unable to read their faces
but the inscription like a neon sign
lights understanding in my thoughts and dreams.
The Spirit of God is gigantic:
white wings dripping aether bluer than air.
After I eat I plume myself bright yellow
Uccello cello cello
and hop about on his borrowed finger:
the jewel in the ring without a scratch
and the white silk and the gold thread are mine.
Oh yes, I hop about and love myself.
I do not understand humanity,

their emotions terrify me.
What I like in him is his company
and the long fingers of the Holy Ghost.

'To speak about the soul'

To speak about the soul.
I wake early. You don't sleep in summer.
In the morning a dead-eyed nightingale is still awake in you.
What has been done and suffered
with whatever is left to be suffered
is in the soul.
Oracles are given elsewhere. Their speech is associated with
    bronze.

In the early morning
you see women walking to the sanctuaries:
a light touch of sun on the whitewash:
a light touch of fire burning the oil.
You tell me nothing.
This is the desert I will write about.
The desert is not an island: the island is not enchanted: and the
    desert is no habitation for men.
The bird with the burnt eyes sang sweetest.
A desert further off
One small simple cloud. Heat at midday. A little constellated
    handwriting. Heat at midnight.
You never say.
To be woken by hearing
the voices of the enchanted birds
and the voices of disenchanted birds.

Say what is like a tree, like a river, like a mountain, a cloud over
    the sun?
My memory has been overshadowed
by that live light and by that dying light.

The soul is no more than human.

The rising sky is as wide as the desert.

HARRY GUEST

born 1932

Harry Guest, who now teaches French in Exeter, after lecturing at Yokohama National University, is probably the nearest English equivalent to a West Coast American poet such as Gary Snyder. Guest combines a delicate, rather romantic aestheticism with the influence of the French surrealists and, more distantly, of Pound.

Two Poems for O-Bon

(the Buddhist midsummer Festival of the Dead)

one

Clean the altars.
          Scour
the wood remembering
dead next of kin.
            Their ashes
are gathering energy, emit to love
remembered presences.
           Let
the temple-bell vibrate.

Clean the altars.
          Prepare
the past, a welcome for the past.

And, waiting, pray.

          The ghosts
enter the garden. Familiar
features take shape on the
lamplit leaves.

    A sad season (clean,
    the altars; longing so,
    the garden): chill
    inside drab heat.

Make
the whole house an expectation, greeting
the long-lost and the brief-loved.

Who, lightly, blur
the polished wood of the altars:
departing,
move like the faint
shadow of rain across the lanterns,
among us if they ever were
no more again.

two

Half-seen
smiles unmet like mist,
maybe the touch of a hand
resembles dew,
their footprints tentative
cobwebs on the grass.

Spectres
in air-conditioned
cinemas and, suddenly,
footless, shimmering on to the stage.
Tales of melancholy love,
revenge, the green flame
signifying presence.

Phantoms
hiding behind peonies,
dissolving to hard
bones the further side
of tombstones at rendezvous.

TOM RAWORTH

born 1940

Tom Raworth's work is obviously fairly heavily influenced by the American poets of the Black Mountain school, but also shows an elliptical quality which is reminiscent of Pierre Reverdy (1889–1960), a pioneer French modernist who wrote some of the few poems which can sensibly be described as 'Cubist'.

You Were Wearing Blue

the explosions are nearer this evening
the last train leaves for the south
at six   tomorrow
the announcements will be in a different language

i chew the end of a match
the tips of my finger and thumb are sticky

i will wait at the station and you
will send a note, i
will read it
              it will be raining

              our shadows in the electric light
when i was eight they taught me *real*
writing
          to join up the letters

listen you said i
preferred to look
     at the sea.   everything stops there are strange angles

only the boats spoil it
making you focus further

I Mean

all these americans here writing about america it's time to give
  something back, after all
our heroes were always the gangster the outlaw why
surprised you act like it
now, a place
the simplest man was always the most complex you gave me
the usual things, comics,
music, royal blue drape suits &
what *they* ever give me but unreadable books?

i don't know where i am now my face seems exposed
touching it   touching it

as i walk this evening no
tenderness   mad laughter from the rooms   what
do i know of my friends, they are always
showing small kind parts of themselves

no pacifist i am capable of murder
                the decision is not
this, but not
to sic on the official   the paid
extension of self   to react at the moment

oh, this ain't no town for a girl like dallas

jean peters to widmark 'how'd
you get to be this way?
how'd i get this way   things
happen, that's all'   but

we ain't never gonna say goodbye

follow me into the garden at night
i have my own orchestra

Inner Space

in an octagonal tower, five miles from the sea
he lives quietly with his books and doves
all walls are white, some days he wears
green spectacles, not reading

riffling the pages – low sounds of birds and their flying

holding to the use of familiar objects
in the light that is not quite

LEE HARWOOD

born 1939

Lee Harwood's work is a fascinating amalgam of different influences –
the romantic subjectivity of British poetry in the 1940s, the rather cold
experimentalism of the New York avant-garde, the wilfulness and high
spirits of the arch-Dadaist Tristan Tzara. He has translated Tzara and
compiled a bibliography of his work. But at the present moment (1984)
Harwood seems to represent a 'road not taken' in British verse.

When the Geography Was Fixed

for Marian

The distant hills are seen from the windows.
It is a quiet room, & the house is in a town
far from the capital.
The south-west province even now in spring
is warmer than the summer of the north.
The hills are set in their distance
from the town & that is where they'll stay.
At this time the colours are hard to name
since a whiteness infiltrates everything.
It could be dusk.
The memory & sound of chantings
is not so far away – it is only a matter
of the degree of veneer at that moment.
This is not always obvious & for many
undiscovered while their rhythm remains static.
It's all quite simple,
once past the door – & that's only a figure
of speech that's as clumsy as most symbols.
This formality is just a cover.
The hills & the rooms are both in
the white. The colours are here
inside us, I suppose. There's still a tower
on the skyline & it's getting more obscure.

When I say 'I love you' – that means
something. & what's in the past
I don't know anymore – it was all ice-skating.
In the water a thick red cloud
unfurls upwards; at times it's almost orange.
A thin thread links something & there are
fingers & objects of superstition
seriously involved in this.

The canvas is so bare
that it hardly exists – though the painting
is quite ready for the gallery opening.
The clear droplets of water sparkle
& the orange-red cloud hangs quite seductively.

There is only one woman in the gallery now
who knows what's really happening on the canvas –
but she knew that already, & she
also instinctively avoided all explanations.
She liked the picture & somehow the delicate
hues of her complexion were reflected in it.
She was very beautiful & it soon became
obvious to everyone that the whole show
was only put on to praise her beauty.
Each painting would catch one of the colours
to be found in her skin and then play with it.
Though some critics found this delicacy
too precious a conceit, the landscape
was undeniable in its firmness
& the power that vibrated from the
colours chosen & used so carefully.

During the whole gallery-opening a record of primitive red
indian chants was played – & this music
seemed to come from the very distant hills
seen in every painting – their distance was
no longer fixed & they came nearer.
But recognitions only came when all
the veneer was stripped off
& the inexplicable accepted in the whiteness.

Lee Harwood

The Final Painting

the white cloud passed over the land
there is sea always round the land
the sky is blue always above the cloud
the cloud in the blue continues to move
– nothing is limited by the canvas or frame –
the white cloud can be pictured like any
other clouds or like a fist of wool
or a white fur rose.
the white cloud passes a shadow across
the landscape and so there is a passing greyness.
The grey and the white both envelop
the watcher until he too is drawn into the picture
It is all a journey from a room through a door
down stairs and out into the street
The cloud could possess the house
the watchers have a mutual confidence
with the approaching string of white clouds
It is beyond spoken words what they are
silently mouthing to the sky
There was no mystery in this – only the firm
outline of people in overcoats on a hillside
and the line of clouds above them.
The sky is blue. The cloud white with touches
of grey – the rest – the landscape below –
can be left to the imagination.
The whole painting quietly dissolved itself
into its surrounding clouds.

TONY HARRISON

born 1937

Tony Harrison's work makes a startling contrast, not least because of its accessibility, to much of the poetry that appears in this section. Yet one must recognize that the presiding influence to be found in his poems is not that of any British writer, but of the American Robert Lowell, and especially of Lowell's *Life Studies*. The material is very different, but the tone of voice and even the technical strategies are the same. It is Lowell who resonates in a line such as 'My mind moves upon silence and *Aeneid VI*.'

Voortrekker

A spoor from a kraal. Then grass
greens the turd of the carnivore
gone all gums. So the sick Boer
lays on with the whip less.

Panic in him and round him
like a wind-flapped tilt –
only the sable sons of Ham
cram Death's dark veld.

Coupled together in God's span,
outnumbered many times over,
ox, dog, Hottentot, Caffre,
and just one Christian man.

Study

Best clock. Best carpet. Best three chairs.

For deaths, for Christmases, a houseless aunt,
for those too old or sick to manage stairs.

I try to whistle in it but I can't.

Uncle Joe came here to die. His gaping jaws
once plugged in to the power of his stammer
patterned the stuck plosive without pause
like a d-d-damascener's hammer.

Mi aunty's baby still. The dumbstruck mother,
The mirror, tortoise-shell-like celluloid
held to it, passed from one hand to another.
No babble, blubber, breath. The glass won't cloud.

The best clock's only wound for layings out
so the stillness isn't tapped at by its ticks.
The settee's shapeless underneath its shroud.

My mind moves upon silence and *Aeneid VI*.

Long Distance II

Though my mother was already two years dead
Dad kept her slippers warming by the gas,
put hot water bottles her side of the bed
and still went to renew her transport pass.

You couldn't just drop in. You had to phone.
He'd put you off an hour to give him time
to clear away her things and look alone
as though his still raw love were such a crime.

He couldn't risk my blight of disbelief
though sure that very soon he'd hear her key
scrape in the rusted lock and end his grief.
He *knew* she'd just popped out to get the tea.

I believe life ends with death, and that is all.
You haven't both gone shopping; just the same,
in my new black leather phone book there's your name
and the disconnected number I still call.

Clearing I

The ambulance, the hearse, the auctioneers
clear all the life of that loved house away.
The hard-earned treasures of some 50 years
sized up as junk, and shifted in a day.

A stammerer died here and I believe
this front room with such ghosts taught me my trade.
Now strangers chip the paintwork as they heave
the spotless piano that was never played.
The fingerprints they leave mam won't wipe clean
nor politely ask them first to wipe their boots,
nor coax her trampled soil patch back to green
after they've trodden down the pale spring shoots.

I'd hope my mother's spirit wouldn't chase
her scattered household, even if it could.
How could she bear it when she saw no face
stare back at her from that long polished wood?

GEORGE SZIRTES

born 1948

George Szirtes was born in Hungary and came to England after the Hungarian uprising of 1956. He seems to transfer some of the mysterious obliqueness of contemporary Eastern European poetry into purely English settings. He also suggests a more specific comparison. To me, the two poems printed here are curiously like Kafka's stories, in their mingling of the ordinary and the slightly askew.

North Wembley

The mongol boy makes friends over the fence,
his cat owns all the local mice.
From hosepipes squirts the Sunday carwash.
Tom and Joan are decorating.

There are trees, grass verges, a parking space,
and alleyways, alleyways by the dozen.
Khan is arguing with his wife.
The train whistles through an empty station.
Blackberries by the railway are quickly stripped.
Jewish boys practise the violin in dark but modern lounges.

Over the main road there is a Sporting Club
with pitches stretching out to distant hedges
from where, one summer night, a lazy rat
emerged and crossed, legally, over the zebra.

The Girls

A mosquito tipsy with blood, the children dozing.
Prams are curdling on the patio.
Here a high buzz of female conversation
Over cups of coffee, intelligent, worn young faces.

The house has a lot to answer for
But no one asks it to account for itself,
Instead they address themselves to the well of experience –
A long long throat before you hit the water,
The penny will be falling for years.

The room is charged with danger. At the bottom
Of the well there lives a toad
Clammy and neglected who forces them to speak.
Words bubble up, the toad is wounded.
They are thick with children.
Look what we have fished out of the water!
Each nurses a genius at her breast
Who sucks her dry. It is beautiful,
Sophisticated, dangerous, dull, charming.

PART SEVEN: POST-MOVEMENT

The poets I have included in this section seem for the most part to share the Movement commitment to the tradition of Hardy rather than that of Pound. There is also, as can be seen from the work of poets otherwise as different from one another as Anthony Thwaite and D. M. Thomas, an inclination to re-explore the heritage of Browning. This was also felt by several of the poets associated with the Group.

ANTHONY THWAITE

born 1930

Almost the type case of a poet who has been greatly influenced by the Movement without belonging to it, Thwaite is a writer whose work swings between a homage to Larkin, and something a good deal more expansive and romantic. 'Mr Cooper', for example, is a very accomplished poem, but almost precisely in Larkin's vein – compare Larkin's 'Mr Bleaney', which is also included in this anthology. The other two poems are taken from *The Stones of Emptiness*. Most of the poems in this collection were the product of a residence in Libya, and they suggest that Thwaite is in fact a poet more like Lawrence Durrell or Bernard Spencer than like any of those who were included in *New Lines* – the poems get their best effects from a savouring of heat, light and colour, and from an excited sense of the past.

Mr Cooper

Two nights in Manchester: nothing much to do,
One of them I spent partly in a pub,
Alone, quiet, listening to people who
Didn't know me. *So I told the bloody sub-*
Manager what he could do with it . . . Mr Payne
Covers this district – you'll have met before?
Caught short, I looked for the necessary door
And moved towards it; could hear, outside, the rain.

The usual place, with every surface smooth
To stop, I suppose, the aspirations of
The man with pencil stub and dreams of YOUTH
AGED 17. And then I saw, above
The stall, a card, a local jeweller's card
Engraved with name, JEWELLER AND WATCHMENDER
FOR FIFTY YEARS, address, telephone number.
I heard the rain falling in the yard.

The card was on a sort of shelf, just close
Enough to let me read this on the front.

Not, I'd have said, the sort of words to engross
Even the keenest reader, nothing to affront
The public decency of Manchester.
And yet I turned it over. On the back
Were just three words in rather smudgy black
Soft pencil: MR COOPER – DEAD. The year

Grew weakly green outside, in blackened trees,
Wet grass by statues. It was ten to ten
In March in Manchester. Now, ill at ease
And made unsure of sense and judgement when
Three words could throw me, I walked back into
The bar, where nothing much had happened since
I'd left. A man was trying to convince
Another man that somehow someone knew

Something that someone else had somehow done.
Two women sat and drank the lagers they
Were drinking when I'd gone. If anyone
Knew I was there, or had been, or might stay,
They didn't show it. *Good night,* I almost said,
Went out to find the rain had stopped, walked back
To my hotel, and felt the night, tall, black,
Above tall roofs. And Mr Cooper dead.

Butterflies in the Desert

Thrown together like leaves, but in a land
Where no leaves fall and trees wither to scrub,
Raised like the dust but fleshed as no dust is,
They impale themselves like martyrs on the glass,
Leaving their yellow stigmata. A hundred miles
And they form a screen between us and the sparse world.
At the end of the journey we see the juggernaut
Triumphant under their flattened wings, crushed fluids.
Innocent power destroys innocent power.
But who wins, when their bloody acid eats through chrome?
In the competition for martyrs, Donatus won,
But the stout churches of his heresy now stand
Ruined, emptied of virtue, choked with innocent sand.

Letters of Synesius[1]

Letter VI

Shut up here in our houses, then, as in a prison, we were to our regret
condemned to keep this long silence.

This autumn I felt the cold in my bones when
In the fountain of Apollo the frogs were spawning.
Persephone was faceless. Above the Jebel
The thunder grumbled.

Fortune was elsewhere, ministering her mercies,
Dispensing luck to barbarians and atheists.
We on the coast repaired the aqueducts
But the water failed us.

Then winter came and the highways flooded,
Keeping us chained to our useless harbours,
Pent in by storms, letting our cattle
Wander uncared for.

Somewhere in the east the administrators filed us
Under a pile of disregarded papers.
We were forgotten, except by the hungry
Collector of taxes.

The Governor sends me a gilt-edged invitation
To celebrate the fourteenth year of independence.
There I shall see the outlandish consuls-general
Talking dog-Latin.

My cultivated friend, please try to send me
Whatever new books the sophists have published:
I have read the reviews in the six-month-old journals
And feel a provincial.

'We traded in shrouds: people stopped dying.'
Fortune frustrates even our death-wish.

---

1. *Synesius*: (c. 370–c. 414). Born in Cyrene, he studied philosophy in
Alexandria under Hypatia, and afterwards in Athens. Later he was
bishop of Ptolemaïs in the Libyan Pentapolis. His letters offer a vivid
picture of the state of the Roman Empire in Africa during the period in
which he lived.

The infant mortality figures were lost by
The census department.

Remember me now to my old friends and colleagues,
Discussing the Trinity and aureate diction:
Think of me here, awaiting the fires of
The Austuriani.

See where they squat behind the escarpment,
Ignorant of metre, of faction and schism,
Destined by favourless Fortune to be the true
Heirs of the Kingdom.

ALAN BROWNJOHN

born 1931

Alan Brownjohn's work was included in *A Group Anthology*, but even then he did not seem a typical 'Group poet', even assuming that there was such a thing. The distinguishing mark of his work is scrupulousness. Brownjohn deals with certain very contemporary philosophical puzzles – the question of what is 'real', what 'possibly real', and what not real at all crops up again and again in his work. Yet there is emotional commitment, too. The poems that result from these concerns owe something to the Movement from the stylistic point of view, and yet, again, are recognizably different from the work which Robert Conquest chose for *New Lines*.

Office Party

We were throwing out small-talk
On the smoke-weary air,
When the girl with the squeaker
Came passing each chair.

She was wearing a white dress,
Her paper-hat was a blue
Crown with a red tassel,
And to every man who

Glanced up at her, she leant over
And blew down the hole,
So the squeaker inflated
And began to unroll.

She stopped them all talking
With this trickery,
And she didn't leave out anyone
Until she came to me.

I looked up and she met me
With a half-teasing eye
And she took a mild breath and
Went carefully by,

And with cold concentration
To the next man she went,
And squawked out the instrument
To its fullest extent.

And whether she passed me
Thinking that it would show
Too much favour to mock me
I never did know –

Or whether her withholding
Was her cruelty,
And it was that she despised me,
I couldn't quite see –

So it could have been discretion,
And it could have been disgust,
But it was quite unequivocal,
And suffer it I must:

All I know was: she passed me,
Which I did not expect
– And I'd never so craved for
Some crude disrespect.

The Space

Then why see it? This 'flat and ample
Space over which you walk at no one angle,
Led as by something very like your will?'

*You could go on with proper concerns. You
Are boiling tea, typing some letter, listening
To politics when it comes. Why let it, why let*

It come? – That pale, clean stretch
Stays small, and won't usurp the whole. So
I let it come. There is no harmful freedom.

*But where do you go across that space? Do you
See things, see anyone?* I don't go anywhere
But across it; taut and clear, though the wind leans at me.

Further, it might be a world, and not safe:
It might be stayed in. I keep it unfulfilled.
Its colour? Certain shadows, shades of green.

– And whoever she who walks there, and stands,
She won't tremble into definition, isn't
Like Fournier's girl, say, on the steps and real.

Then why let it come at all? Only, that to this
All common facts yearn to approximate,
While time strains to reach it. And it

Won't be otherwise, it refuses, and must
Return as plainly as before, nothing but
A kind of sober walking-space. – I see

You are not answered why, nor sense why I let it come.

For a Journey

House Field, Top Field, Oak Field, Third Field:
Though maps conclude their duties, the names trek on
Unseen across every county. Farmers call hillocks
And ponds and streams and lanes and rocks
By the first words to hand; a heavy, whittled-down
Simplicity meets the need, enough to help say
Where has yielded best, or the way they walked from home.

You can travel safely over land so named –
Where there is nowhere that could not somewhere
Be found in a memory which knows, and loves.
So watch then, all the more carefully, for
The point where the pattern ends: where mountains, even,
And swamps and forests and gaping bays acquire
The air of not needing ever to be spoken of.

Who knows what could become of you where
No one has understood the place with names?

TONY CONNOR

born 1930

Connor is one of the best of the naturalistic 'domestic' poets who have
abounded in England since the war. Perhaps this is because he has lived
much of his life in the north of England (he now lives and teaches in
America). He himself remarks on the 'moral ambiguity' of his 'apparent
simplicities', and suggests a comparison to Robert Frost.

A Child Half-Asleep

Stealthily parting the small-hours silence,
a hardly-embodied figment of his brain
comes down to sit with me
as I work late.
Flat-footed, as though his legs and feet
were still asleep.

On a stool,
staring into the fire,
his dummy dangling.

Fire ignites the small coals of his eyes;
it stares back through the holes
into his head, into the darkness.

I ask what woke him?

'A wolf dreamed me,' he says.

From *'Twelve Secret Poems'*

III

Dull headaches on dark afternoons
suggest the suburbs of Hell;
a city one's friends will never drive across,
where the telephone never rings.

There was something to think about . . .
a claim on insurance . . . China . . .
the rationalization of the Aircraft Industry . . .
or was it new shoes for the children?

One could pull down reputations
in the mind: Tiepolo tumbling;
Marvell going over with a shriek.
Bach and Shakespeare are not safe on a day like this.

Remember different women: those variations
on the one smell. Perhaps in Heaven
you could stay in bed forever
and never sicken of flesh or sleep.

Now the rain is beginning . . . orange lights
are flickering to life on the main road.
When the hidden sun sets so early
the appetite for subtleties is blunted, or disappears;

the mind hankers after final judgements,
crosses and ticks . . . ticks and crosses.
But soon the usual visitors will arrive,
those you dislike, you think, but can't be sure.

VI

There is a war going on.
Outside, gangs of youths
are looking for things to kill;
petals are smouldering in the garden.

You have been reading a book
for thirty-six years: a book about nothing:
you have four fine children
and a responsible position.

The old folk do not care about history,
but there is entertainment value
in world disorder;
they are glued to their television sets.

It is not as you thought it would be;
last week you scooped the pools,
and you are better looking
than you were as a young man.

The war is worrying, but you stay home;
your larder will outlast the worst,
your long poem only needs polishing,
there are no more best friends left to die.

Jon Stallworthy

born 1935

Neo-Augustanism and romanticism often seem to co-exist uneasily in Stallworthy's work. He shows the typical post-Movement hesitation between strict decorum and something altogether more rhetorical: he is an expert on Yeats, for instance, and Yeats's influence occasionally shows itself in his writing. His best poetry, however, has an ambiguity of tone which spans the incompatibles. The poet he most resembles at these moments seems to me to be John Crowe Ransom.

The Almond Tree

I

All the way to the hospital
the lights were green as peppermints.
Trees of black iron broke into leaf
ahead of me, as if
I were the lucky prince
in an enchanted wood
summoning summer with my whistle,
banishing winter with a nod.

Swung by the road from bend to bend,
I was aware that blood was running
down through the delta of my wrist
and under arches
of bright bone. Centuries,
continents it had crossed;
from an undisclosed beginning
spiralling to an unmapped end.

II

Crossing (at sixty) Magdalen Bridge
Let it be a son, said
the man in the driving mirror,
Let it be a son. The tower

held up its hand: the college
bells shook their blessing on his head.

III

I parked in an almond's
shadow blossom, for the tree
was waving, waving me
upstairs with a child's hands.

IV

Up
the spinal stair
and at the top
along
a bone-white corridor
the blood tide swung
me swung me to a room
whose walls shuddered
with the shuddering womb.
Under the sheet
wave after wave, wave
after wave beat
on the bone coast, bringing
ashore – whom?
         New-
minted, my bright farthing!
Coined by our love, stamped with
our images, how you
enrich us! Both
you make one. Welcome
to your white sheet,
my best poem!

V

At seven-thirty
the visitors' bell
scissored the calm
of the corridors.
The doctor walked with me
to the slicing doors.

His hand upon my arm,
his voice – *I have to tell*
you – set another bell
beating in my head:
your son is a mongol
the doctor said.

VI

How easily the word went in –
clean as a bullet
leaving no mark on the skin,
stopping the heart within it.

This was my first death.
The 'I' ascending on a slow
last thermal breath
studied the man below

as a pilot treading air might
the buckled shell of his plane –
boot, glove, and helmet
feeling no pain.

from the snapped wires' radiant ends.
Looking down from a thousand feet
I held four walls in the lens
of an eye; wall, window, the street

a torrent of windscreens, my own
car under its almond tree,
and the almond waving me down.
I wrestled against gravity,

but light was melting and the gulf
cracked open. Unfamiliar
the body of my late self
I carried to the car.

VII

The hospital – its heavy freight
lashed down ship-shape ward over ward –
steamed into night with some on board
soon to be lost if the desperate

charts were known. Others would come
altered to land or find the land
altered. At their voyage's end
some would be added to, some

diminished. In a numbered cot
my son sailed from me; never to come
ashore into my kingdom
speaking my language. Better not

look that way. The almond tree
was beautiful in labour. Blood-
dark, quickening, bud after bud
split, flower after flower shook free.

On the darkening wind a pale
face floated. Out of reach. Only when
the buds, all the buds, were broken
would the tree be in full sail.

In labour the tree was becoming
itself. I, too, rooted in earth
and ringed by darkness, from the death
of myself saw myself blossoming,

wrenched from the caul of my thirty
years' growing, fathered by my son,
unkindly in a kind season
by love shattered and set free.

VIII

You turn to the window for the first time.
I am called to the cot
to see your focus shift,
take tendril-hold on a shaft
of sun, explore its dusty surface, climb
to an eye you cannot

meet. You have a sickness they cannot heal,
the doctors say: locked in
your body you will remain.
Well, I have been locked in mine.
We will tunnel each other out. You seal
the covenant with a grin.

In the days we have known one another,
my little mongol love,
I have learnt more from your lips
than you will from mine perhaps:
I have learnt that to live is to suffer,
to suffer is to live.

DOM MORAES

born 1938

Moraes was born in India, and got some of his early education in accompanying his father (a newspaper editor) round the battlefields of the Korean War. Subsequently he went to Oxford, where he was a contemporary of John Fuller and Peter Levi. An extremely precocious writer, Moraes got off to a flying start by winning the Hawthornden Prize for his first book in 1957. Probably this early notice was no kindness to him, as he has had difficulty in breaking away from the fluent sentimentality of his first manner. Like many post-Movement poets, Moraes tempers Movement dryness with the rotundities of a more Keatsian style.

Craxton

Sunlight daubs my eye.
It is spring. A snail oils the sill.
My tulips are in good repair.
A thrush hops fiercely
Up the Everest of a rockery.
All the grass leans one way.

Spring. The breeze travels
Over the pools where the carp bask,
Disturbing them with reflections.
I watch from my desk.
They are as old as I am.
Wherever my daubed eye stares,
The blown fountains, the granite
Obelisks for dead gardeners,
Changing, remain the same.

It is the usual time.
A tray clashes at the door,
My man Craxton enters,
Tall in his black coat.
On the tray is the cup.

He waits for me to drink.
With a huge dry thumb
He shifts the bowl of ink
Towards me. 'Master, write.'
Now he is not here.
Slowly morning leaves me.
My humped hand idles.
The shadows spread widely
From the bases of the obelisks.
In a flurry of hopes the thrush
Chips the humped snail from the sill.
The wind chops down tulips.
What is this weather?
Autumn, and it is evening.

It is the usual time.
My man Craxton enters.
He ripples the plush curtains
To with a noise like fire.
His huge dry hand
Bandages mine. He lifts me.
The stairs creak as we climb.

He bathes me, he dresses me
In loose silk clothes.
He bestows me in silence
Between polished sheets.
He leaves me in darkness
Soon it will happen.
I do not want it.

It is the usual time.
My man Craxton enters.
So quietly I do not hear,
Tall in his black coat.
His huge dry hands
Carry up to my bed
A folded napkin on a tray,
A soupspoon, and a bowl of blood.

PETER DALE

born 1938

Dale is a poet who sticks pretty closely to the domestic 'Movement' themes, but there is an air of disquiet in his work which marks him off from Movement patness. His work reminds me of the early poems of Stephen Spender, a vulnerable and touching sensitivity which sometimes cannot communicate itself fully because of technical clumsiness.

Not Drinking Water

Home after years, tonight,
cleaning my teeth,
I taste the waters of childhood,
still unfluorided,
tangless, not tepid quite –
once an apple-slicing chill
by which all quenchings could be placed.

Suddenly minute fear, not noticing
the granary by the old mill pond
that used to dominate the sky round here –
dwarfed
a little beyond
some concrete block for storing flour.

I have tasted many waters,
mineralled, full of lime,
brine of the eyes,
the sweat on your brow,
hard and soft and somewhere bitter.
This taste I seem to forget.
I have been thirsty all my life.

Thrush

All day that thrush
divebombs the basking cat.
She must have nested in the nearby larches.
Soon she is bound to be caught,
head featherless already from its clutches.

Those silent claws
will knock her powerdive for six
once they've timed it right.

That cry
like the brake on a freight jolts me.
I'm sick of that bald ridiculous neck.

Dawnlight hatches her cheeks with shadow lashes.
Thinking I'm still asleep
she draws my fist to feel how well
her flesh is hummocked with child.
I let her, playing fast asleep,
and don't unclench my hand.

She claws my fingers
over her bared stomach.
They feel a bird
as though caught in the hand
tremble and flinch . . .

Gazing out of the window above my desk
    I start
as something plummets from the eaves
close to the glass in the dusk.
A tile,
I think,
tensed for the thud as it dives.

But a thrush mounts up in flight,
beats down the garden,
banks to miss the trees, and greys
into night without trace.

Still tense for the thud
I sit till quite late.

BRIAN JONES

born 1938

Brian Jones scored a notable success with his first small collection, *Poems*. The work it contained was in an extremely familiar idiom; a recording of the joy and the unease which lie beneath the surface of an apparently placid middle-class domesticity. The terms were narrow, but the poems themselves were sharply and honestly written, and Jones is certainly one of the very best practitioners of this overworked vein.

Husband to Wife: Party-Going

Turn where the stairs bend
In this other house; statued in other light,
Allow the host to ease you from your coat.
Stand where the stairs bend,
A formal distance from me, then descend
With delicacy conscious but not false
And take my arm, as if I were someone else.

Tonight, in a strange room
We will be strangers: let our eyes be blind
To all our customary stances –
Remark how well I'm groomed,
I will explore your subtly-voiced nuances
Where delicacy is conscious but not false,
And take your hand, as if you were someone else.

Home forgotten, rediscover
Among chirruping of voices, chink of glass,
Those simple needs that turned us into lovers,
How solitary was the wilderness
Until we met, took leave of hosts and guests,
And with delicate consciousness of what was false
Walked off together, as if there were no one else.

Sunday Outing

So the dog still yelps at the door
We slammed within an inch of his snout,
And the washing jerks unharvested,
Spoiling in the rain-laced wind
Five miles away in our backyard,
And the hag from below can make her stealthy climb,
Enter and pilfer as usual the rooms we forget to lock,
And perhaps the tap is running, the sink blocked,
Gas escaping, kitchen filling. Forget it. Watch
Through the windscreen (tick-tocked clear) the downs
Darkening with the rainy mist; let your flesh
Relax into the damp freedom (chuck that fag away);
Tell me (look this way damn you) tell me do you feel
An old design return? Do you recall hour after hour
Spent watching dusk or dawn inch up? What was your head
Vacant with then? Tell me, love, what did I speak of?
How did we manage without dogs and hags?

Runner

Steadily stepping first, I let the world
keep time beside me, watch it sidelong coolly,
my competitor – then, with a stretch of stride
I set the pace, and in the dazed
and jumping eyeball hedgerow spends itself,
unforms, and sprawls as shapeless
as any man whose flabby flesh I've mastered;
trees whirl, dizzy with pace, and the pumping heart
shakes the sky from blue complacency.

And here I ride on feet sprung with the will,
destroying rule of shape, the sway of custom,
while colours ribbon from the broken lines
of brick and trees. The brain
is hurled from platitude, the forced lungs
cry for the meagre air, organs of sense
are strained beyond their common catch, and

world
and tortured body
pulse into chaos. I unmake old realms.

Having to halt, I retch for breath
on a lonely road, and hear the blood
grow soft and usual. I feel stale threats
come up abreast and reassert
their normalcy, before whose arrogance
I straighten, fill my lungs, begin to stride.

D. M. THOMAS

born 1935

D. M. Thomas's reputation as a poet has now been overtaken by his reputation as a novelist, since the runaway success of his book *The White Hotel*. To me, his fiction seems to develop directly out of his poetry, and to be in fact indivisible from it: the sense of strangeness which he treats in a rather external way in some of his poems is effectively internalized in his fiction. But where his fiction is experimental, much of his poetry is technically rather conservative.

Missionary

A harsh entry I had of it, Grasud;
the tiny shuttle strained to its limits
by radiation-belts, dust-storms,
not to mention the pitiless heat which
hit it on plunging into the atmosphere
– its fire-shield clean vaporized; and then,
on landing, the utter cold and stillness
of a mountain-slope, cedar-trees and
what they call
snow. As I went numbly through the
routine I could do in my sleep –
mentalizing myself, smothering
my body and the shuttle in a
defensive neutrino-screen, hiding them
securely in the snow,
I looked up and, between the branches
of the cedars, could see
the mother-ship sliding away through
the dark, like an unfixed star, westwards
to its other destinations: that was
the worst moment of all, Grasud! I'd have
called it back! So lonely, such an alien
world they'd left me in. Goodbye, Lagash!

goodbye, Theremon! fare well! (But no
voice now even to make a gesture against
the silence.)
        Then the agonizingly slow
descent, towards the village,
my spirit dark, already missing
not only Theremon and Lagash, but
that other friend, my body's familiar
chemistry. By now I felt my
vaunted courage ebbing, Grasud; I think
those years of training
alone forced me to go on, into the village,
into the houses, inns, into
– after much vain searching – a ripened
womb; there superseding
(not without a pang) its foetus-spirit.
How black that airlock,
after the six suns of our own system,
I needn't tell you. Even space,
in recollection, seemed a blaze of
supernovas. But I settled to my task,
wrestling to get on terms with carbon
compounds fearsomely different from
the synthetic ones I'd practised in.
Of course, as I was born and the years
passed, it seemed as natural to go
on man's two legs as on our Vardian
limbs. But when these pains eased,
one far bitterer grew: my seeds were cast
on stony ground; the more
I exhorted,
– the more I spoke, obliquely, of
the many mansions of our Vardian
Commonwealth, and of the place
that could be theirs – the more it
seemed those simple, instinctive creatures
lied, stole, slandered, fornicated,
killed. . . . Grasud, how often, sick with
failure, only the words of Vrak
sustained me – 'a world lies in your hands.'
That was the time he

sent for the three of us when
all ears were ringing with the news of
the three life-planets found in
NDT 1065. If we had hopes,
we masked them. His words to us, for
all that's happened, I'll hoard always.
'Thoorin, Lagash, Theremon,' I hear him
saying, 'I'm sending *you* . . . you're young,
but this is what you've trained for, bio-
enlightenment. You've done well.'
And then – 'a world lies in your hands.'
So, Grasud, I toiled. In the end
I tried too hard; the time of space-
rendezvous was almost come. Anyway,
they killed me. I loved them, and they
killed me.
            Yes, it was hard,
as you can well imagine,
on the return-journey, to avoid feeling
the faintest warp of
jealousy, as Theremon and
Lagash talked with
the happy emissaries of their
planets. – What does Vrak say? He is
kind, promises – after this loathsome
rest – another
chance, though not of course on that
planet. My 'inability' (he avoids
the word failure) to raise them
ethically to the point where we could
safely announce ourselves, proves, he
says, there's no point trying again
for a few thousand years. Meanwhile,
he suggests, maybe some of my words
will start to bear fruit. . . . He is kind!
His last words were 'Forget about it,
Thoorin; enjoy your stay on
Atar.' Forget!
with the relaxed faces of my friends a
perpetual thorn!

BARRY COLE

born 1936

Barry Cole seems to belong neither to the 'experimental' nor fully to
the 'neo-Movement' wing. The reference seems to be directly to the
work of Robert Graves. Cole has a very tight, deliberately chastened
style, leavened by hints of the bizarre and the grotesque. These hints,
in turn, seem to link him to the young Scottish poet D. M. Black, with
whom he edited the little magazine *Extra Verse*.

The Domestic World in Winter

Two feet above the ground, I cross
Half of Africa before breakfast.
The morning and the afternoon
Are filled with swift surveyals of
The east and western hemispheres.
At night I spend some time at home.

This huge domesticity lets fall
A pattern of proportioned events:
The beer I spill no longer frets
My temper and the failure of
A friend to visit depresses
Nothing. I lift myself above

The world and watch as it unrolls
Beneath me. It is a fireside rug,
Material for me to work upon.
All is equal here, I permit no
Ruffling of my life until, at
Night, my frozen feet return to earth.

Reported Missing

Can you give me a precise description?
Said the policeman. Her lips, I told him,
Were soft. Could you give me, he said, pencil
Raised, a metaphor? Soft as an open mouth,
I said. Were there any noticeable
Peculiarities? he asked. Her hair hung
Heavily, I said. Any particular
Colour? he said. I told him I could recall
Little but its distinctive scent. What do
You mean, he asked, by distinctive? It had
The smell of woman's hair, I said. Where
Were you? he asked. Closer than I am to
Anyone at present, I said, level
With her mouth, level with her eyes. Her eyes?
He said, what about her eyes? There were two,
I said, both black. It has been established,
He said, that eyes cannot, outside common
Usage, be black; are you implying that
Violence was used? Only the gentle
Hammer blow of her kisses, the scent
Of her breath, the . . . Quite, said the policeman,
Standing, but I regret that we know of
No one answering to that description.

MILES BURROWS

born 1936

Miles Burrows, a doctor by profession, is one of the very few younger poets now writing in Britain who has been markedly influenced by Eliot. Significantly, it is the civilized, ironic Eliot of *Prufrock* which seems to attract him. His poem 'minipoet' takes a cool look at the Movement and its aftermath, and therefore very fittingly finds a place in this section. It is not, of course, exempt from the poetic vices which it satirizes.

minipoet

– slim, inexpensive, easy to discard
nippy rather than resonant, unpretentious.
we found them produced in increasing numbers
from oxford, home of pressed steel.
we remembered the days of the archpoet
comfortable if rather lumbering
extremely well upholstered.
still, the minipoet is basically safe.
not well equipped for (but who would think of)
leaving the highway, he is attuned
to the temporary surface, balanced,
reliable, yes, we have few regrets
for the archpoet, who either would not start
or starting stopped; was temperamental
wanted to show off, steamed up, was punctured:
we had to coax, persuade him he had wings
(we knew too well he hadn't, but had to get
the ramshackle show on the road somehow).
my grandmother remembers teams of leopards[1]
but most of us prefer the minipoet
for the sort of journeys we make nowadays.

1. *teams of leopards*: who traditionally draw the car of Dionysius.

KEN SMITH

born 1938

Ken Smith specifies his themes as being 'environment (hence nature),
domestic, human relations and human attitudes' – recognizably the post-
Movement range. What makes him individual is his attitude towards
language as a mode of enactment. He sees that the tone and style of a
poem are also in themselves a metaphor for what the poet is trying to
say.

Family Group

He also was a stormy day: a squat mountain man
smelling of sheep and the high pasture, stumping
through pinewoods, hunched and small, feeling
the weather on him. Work angled him.
Fingers were crooked with frost, stiffened.

Ploughing he would fix his eye on the hawthorn,
walking firm-booted, concerned for the furrow.
Horse and man in motion together, deliberate,
one foot put before the other, treading cut clay.
He would not see the bird perched on the plough.
He would not chase the plover limping over stubble.

He was my father who brought in wood and lit
the hissing lamp. And he would sit, quiet
as moor before the fire. She drew him
slowly out of silence. She had a coat
made from a blanket and wore boys' shoes.
She was small and had red hands, firm-boned,
and her hair was greying. The house was stone
and slate. It was her house, his home,
and their family, and they quarrelled often.

She churned butter, baked, and scrubbed floors,
and for forty years he laboured the raw earth
and rough weather. In winter we made mats

from rags with pegs. We guarded ourselves
and were close. We were poor and poorer banking
each pound saved. Each year passed slowly.

Now he lives in the glass world of his shop,
and time is grudged. Ham and tinned meat
and vegetables are his breathing day.
He works harder and is unhappy. She too
stoops through the labouring year, is greyer
and grumbles. Nothing gets made any more
but money that cannot be made. Nothing
means happiness. The light comes down wires,
water through tubes. All is expensive, paid.
Silence is gone from their lives, the city
has taken that poised energy. Violence
is articulate. The deliberate motion is gone
and he moves with pain through time that is work
that is cash. He will not notice the crashed
gull fallen in the storm, the grabbing sparrows.
She cannot ease him into speech, or be content
before the broody fire. She is in fashion now.
But seasons pass them without touching.
They will not feel the winter when it comes.

Eli's poem

I met a woman from the sea coast,
she took me aside in the bushes
and wrapped me around and said *we are alone
as the moon up there is with just two sides*.
I did what was to be done and came away with her.

Now I am with a crazy woman
who hurts herself with ashes and briars
running in the scrub. She takes blankets
and stuffs them under her skirt for a child.
She takes out the blanket and croons on it,
washes it, beats it with sticks till it cries
and tears it to pieces. Her lament
goes down the street on cut feet in the gravel.

She runs in a nightgown thinking she's the police
and charges anyone with ridiculous crimes
like wearing a hat sideways and walking wrong.
The people here know her and smile and say
yes they will come to the court to answer.
She writes everything down in her book.
In bed she's like trying to catch a hare.
She wants to sleep with me all night
till my back breaks, if I doze off
she wakes me crying for love.
I married a crazy woman for her brown hair.
At first I thought she was pregnant
but her blood runs, the doctor shakes his head at me.
I tell her your child is in the other country
and will not come here because of your frenzy.
She runs to the church crying she's evil,
the priest holds out his god's battered arms
and says *come child everyone's evil.*
I cool her with my breath, I cool her with water.
She's insatiable as the river, like winds
she has no place to go and runs
from whatever does not move. She's holding a wooden knife
and staring it down till it becomes pure menace
and I fear it myself. I sleep with her
because then I control her and know where she is,
but I don't know what runs in her.
Now she is out on the hill wailing
cutting her flesh on the stiff grass
where I go to her lamenting.

His lament

Was it all my effort
to release you, all I knew
but to give sound to your moving,
a white to your stark face.

Words I had spoken, pulled out
and held near to myself

I released then, their twistings
ran clear as milk from a jar.

I saw as you saw, shimmer
of the rising wave mirrored
in the cornfield, a thrush bone
splayed on the air's flesh.

I had walked this way, I
had not seen the spidery roots
of the grass, leaf-vein division,
map of my own blood.

Birds combed the estuary mud,
water threading their prints.
You sang an old song, I
saw you glance through the air's web,

I touched the thin bones.
You cried out as I entered you,
a gull's yelp, breath-borne, all
the years of my life crying.

You died, so scrawny you were.
You moved out of the light though
a shape of the light still,
and you stir in my bones now.

Douglas Dunn

born 1942

Born in Scotland, but associated with Hull through periods at the University there (which brought him the friendship of Philip Larkin, whose profession – librarianship – he shares), Douglas Dunn provides a very clear example of the way in which the Movement tradition continued to extend itself over a long period. Even more vividly than Larkin, Dunn feels himself to be an outsider – excluded both from any form of 'establishment' and from the working class which he described so vividly in *Terry Street*, his first collection of poems. Like his chief mentor, he is technically conservative, but very skilful in his handling of verse forms.

Men of Terry Street

They come in at night, leave in the early morning.
I hear their footsteps, the ticking of bicycle chains,
Sudden blasts of motorcycles, whimpering of vans.
Somehow I am either in bed, or the curtains are drawn.

This masculine invisibility makes gods of them,
A pantheon of boots and overalls.
But when you see them, home early from work
Or at their Sunday leisure, they are too tired

And bored to look long at comfortably.
It hurts to see their faces, too sad or too jovial.
They quicken their step at the smell of cooking,
They hold up their children and sing to them.

A Removal from Terry Street

On a squeaking cart, they push the usual stuff,
A mattress, bed ends, cups, carpets, chairs,
Four paperback westerns. Two whistling youths
In surplus US Army battle-jackets

Remove their sister's goods. Her husband
Follows, carrying on his shoulders the son
Whose mischief we are glad to see removed,
And pushing, of all things, a lawnmower.
There is no grass in Terry Street. The worms
Come up cracks in concrete yards in moonlight.
That man, I wish him well. I wish him grass.

Young Women in Rollers

Because it's wet, the afternoon is quiet.
Children pacified with sweets inside
Their small houses, stroke travelling cats
From the kingdom of dustbins and warm smells.

Young women come to visit their married friend.
Waiting for their hair to set beneath thin scarves,
They walk about in last year's fashions,
Stockingless, in coats and old shoes.

They look strong, white-legged creatures
With nothing to do but talk of what it is to love
And sing the words softly to the new tunes.
The type who burst each other's blackheads

In the street and look in handbag mirrors
While they walk, not talking of the weather;
Who call across the street they're not wearing knickers,
But blush when they pass you alone.

This time they see me at my window, among books,
A specimen under glass, being protected,
And laugh at me watching them.
They minuet to Mozart playing loudly

On the afternoon Third. They mock me thus,
They mime my softness. A landlord stares.
All he has worked for is being destroyed.
The slum rent-masters are at one with Pop.

The movements they imagine go with minuet
Stay patterned on the air. I can see soot,

It floats. The whiteness of their legs has changed
Into something that floats, become like cloth.

They disappear into the house they came to visit.
Out of the open door rush last year's hits,
The music they listen to, that takes up their time
In houses that are monuments to entertainment.

I want to be touched by them, know their lives,
Dance in my own style, learn something new.
At night, I even dream of ideal communities.
Why do they live where they live, the rich and the poor?

Tonight, when their hair is ready, after tea,
They'll slip through laws and the legs of policemen.
I won't be there, I'll be reading books elsewhere.
There are many worlds, there are many laws.

Witch-girl

For evermore, they said, that girl was lame
In hands and feet, and that, they said, was proof
The lightless Devil spelled her into horse,
Moulding her hands and feet in solid hoof.

Poor girl, her mother saddled her, then rode
Through Sutherland until the outraged Law
Attended to the giddy-ups of gossip,
Force-feeding both of them on Tolbooth straw.

Only her mother was condemned. A pious mob –
Citizens and presbyters – whinnied, neighed,
Clip-clopped, as, standing in their fear of God,
There too were men who watched but also pitied.

Cold day in Dornoch . . . Shivering, the witch
Relieved her freezing round that fire which burned
To burn her up. Crowds psalmed with horror.
She blistered in the tar and, screaming, burned.

They spoke in Dornoch how the horses mourned
And how that lame girl, wandering, was heard

Tearing at the grass; and how she sat and sang,
As if the Devil also made her bird;

And how she washed her lameness in the rivers
From Oykell to the Clyde and Tweed and Forth,
Notorious as something to be pitied,
A girl to look at but a beast in worth.

No one could see her but would think he saw
Hoof in her fumbling hands, her staggering gait.
They spurned her flowers, as if they'd grown from her;
They barbed their righteous charity with hate.

She hawked her flowers in Glasgow, by the Trongate;
In Edinburgh, selling flowers, she slept
Beside the braziers of the City Guard.
The earth and animals within her wept.

No one to help her; no one saw her die,
If she is dead. By Gryfe, by Deveron,
By Cree and Tay, I see her wash her lameness,
And hear her breathing in the wood and stone.

PART EIGHT: DISSENTERS

There has been a strong tradition of political and social dissent in the poetry written in England since the war. Though this appears in the work of poets represented in other sections (that of Jon Silkin, to name a conspicuous example) the two poets represented here would seem to most people the characteristic specimens of it. Both are skilled and exciting readers of their own work, and both have very big followings on the public performance circuit. In addition to this, Logue has made the poster-poem an instrument of statement which is peculiarly his own.

There is another reason, however, for labelling this section 'Dissenters', and that is the fact that neither poet falls into any established literary tradition. The one influence which they seem to have in common is that of Brecht, and in Mitchell's case this influence seems to be filtered through that of Auden.

CHRISTOPHER LOGUE

born 1926

Having learnt to write from Eliot, Pound, and Yeats, a stay of five years
in Paris opened Christopher Logue's work to the influence of foreign
poets like Brecht and Neruda. Returning to London in 1957 Logue wrote
plays for the Royal Court Theatre (*The Lily-White-Boys, The Trial of Cob
and Leach, Antigone*), pioneered poetry and jazz in this country, and, with
Adrian Mitchell, began non-specialist poetry readings. In 1958 he started
publishing his poems as posters. He wrote the songs for the
'Establishment' night-club and since 1962 he has written a fortnightly
column for *Private Eye*. His adaptations of sections of the *Iliad* are among
the most notable attempts made since the war at poetry on a large scale.

From Book XXI of Homer's Iliad

                                                        Then Achilles,
Leaving the tall enemy with eels at his white fat
And his tender kidneys infested with nibblers,
Pulled his spear out of the mud and waded off,
After the deadman's troop that beat upstream
For their dear lives; then, glimpsing Achilles' scarlet plume
Amongst the clubbed bullrushes, they ran and as they ran
The Greek got seven of them, swerved, eyeing his eighth, and
Ducked at him as Scamander bunched his sinews up,
And up, and further up, and further further still, until
A glistening stack of water, solid, white with sunlight,
Swayed like a giant bone over the circling humans,
Shuddered, and changed for speaking's sake into humanity.
And the stack of water was his chest; and the foaming
Head of it, his bearded face; and the roar of it –
Like weir-water – Scamander's voice:
'Indeed, Greek, with Heaven helping out, you work
Miraculous atrocities. Still, if God's Son
Has settled every Trojan head on you,
Why make my precincts the scupper for your dead inheritance?

Do them in the fields, Greek, or – or do them anywhere but here.
Thickened with carcasses my waters stiffen like a putrid syrup,
Downstream, the mouth cakes against standing blood-clots yet,
And yet, you massacre. Come, Greek, quit this loathsome
    rapture!'

                         Head back, Achilles cried:
'Good, River, good – and you shall have your way . . .
    presently.
When every living Trojan squats inside his city's wall.
When I have done with Hector, Hector with me, to death.'
                         And he bayed and leapt –
Bronze flame shattering like a divine beast –
Pity the Trojans!

                              So Scamander
Tried involving the Lord Apollo, thus:
                         'Lord, why the negligence?
Is this the way to keep your Father's word?
Time and again he said: Watch the Trojan flank
Till sundown comes, winds drop, shadows mix and lengthen,
War closes down for night, and nobody is out
Bar dogs and sentries.'

                              Hearing this,
The Greek jumped clear into the water, and Scamander
Went for him in hatred: curved back his undertow, and
Hunched like a snarling yellow bull drove the dead up,
And out, tossed by the water's snout on to the fields;
Yet those who lived he hid behind a gentle wave.
Around the Greek Scamander deepened. Wave clambered
Over wave to get at him, beating aside his studded shield so,
Both footholds gone, half toppled over by the bloodstained
    crud,
Achilles snatched for balance at an elm – ah! – its roots gave –
Wrenched out – splitting the bank, and tree and all
Crashed square across the river, leaves, splintered branches,
And dead birds blocking the fall. Then Achilles wanted out.
And scrambled through the root's lopsided crown, out of the
    ditch,
Off home.

    But the river Scamander had not done with him.

Forcing its bank, an avid lip of water slid
After him, to smother his Greek breath for Trojan victory.
Aoi! – but that Greek could run! – and put and kept
A spearthrow's lead between him and the quick,
Suck, quick, curve of the oncoming water,
Arms outstretched as if to haul himself along the air,
His shield – like the early moon – thudding against
His nape-neck and his ears, fast, fast
As the black winged hawk's full stoop he went –
And what is faster? – yet, Scamander was nigh on him,
Its hood of seething water poised over his shoulderblades.
Achilles was a quick man, yes, but the gods are quicker than
    men.
And easily Scamander's wet webbed claw stroked his ankles.

       You must imagine how a gardener prepares
       To let his stored rainwater out, along
       The fitted trench to nourish his best plants.
       Carefully, with a spade, he lifts the stone
       Gagging the throat of his trench, inch by inch,
       And, as the water flows, pebbles, dead grubs,
       Old bits of root and dusts are gathered and
       Swept along by the speed of it, until
       Singing among the plants, the bright water
       Overtakes its gardener and his control
       Is lost. Likewise Scamander took Achilles.

Each time he stood, looking to see which Part, or whether
Every Part of Heaven's Commonwealth was after him,
The big wave knocked him flat. Up, trying to outleap
The arch of it, Scamander lashed aslant and wrapped his knees
In a wet skirt, scouring the furrows so his toes got no grip.
And Achilles bit his tongue and shrieked: 'Father . . .'
Into the empty sky '. . . will Heaven help me? No?
Not one of you? Later, who cares? But now? Not now. Not
    this . . .'
Why did my lying mother promise death
Should enter me imaged as Lord Apollo's metal arrowheads?
Or Hector, my best enemy, call Hector for a big hit
Over Helen's creditors, and I'll go brave.
Or else my death is waste.
Trapped like a pig-boy beneath dirty water.

                    In Heaven, two heard him:
First, the woman Prince, Athena; and with her came
Fishwaisted Poseidon, Lord of the Home Sea.
And dressed as common soldiers they came strolling by,
And held his hand, and comforted him, with:
'Stick, my friend, stick. Swallow the scare for now.
We're with you and, what's more, God knows it, so
Stick. This visitation means one thing – no River
Will put you down. Scamander? . . . He'll subside. And soon.
Now child, do this: Keep after him no matter what.
Keep coming, till – I use your own fine words –
Every living Trojan squats inside his city's wall
And Hector's dead. You'll win. We promise it.'

   So the Greek, strong for himself, pushed by, thigh deep,
Towards the higher fields, through water
Bobbing with armoured corpses. Sunlight glittered
Off the intricate visions etched into breastplates
By Trojan silversmiths, and Trojan flesh
Bloomed over the rims of them, leather toggles sunk
To the bone. Picking his knees up, Achilles, now
Punting aside a deadman, now swimming a stroke or two,
Remembered God's best word and struck
Like a mad thing at the river. He beat it
With the palm of his free hand, sliced at it,
At the whorled ligaments of water, yes, sliced at them, Ah! –
There, there – there, and – *there* – such hatred,
Scamander had not thought, the woman Prince,
Scamander had not thought, and now, slice, slice,
Scamander could not hold the Greek! Yet,
Would not quit, bent, like a sharp-crested hyoid bone,
And sucking Achilles to his midst, called out:
'Simois, let's join to finish off this Greek – What's that?
Two against one, you say? Yes. Or Troy is ash,
For our soldiers cannot hold him. Quick, and help, come
Spanned out as a gigantic wave, foot up to peak
A single glinting concave welt, smooth, but fanged
Back in the tumultuous throat of it, with big
Flinty stones, clubbed pumice, trees, and all
Topped by an epaulette of mucid scurf to throttle,
Mash each bone, and shred the flesh and drown away

The impudent who plays at God.
Listen, Simois . . . Nothing can help him now.
Strength, looks – nothing. Why, that heavy armour, how
It will settle quietly, quietly, in ooze,
And his fine white body, aye, slimy and coiled up
I'll suck it down a long stone flue,
And his fellow Greeks will get not one bone back,
And without a barrow to be dug can save their breath
For games.'

                   And the water's diamond head
Shut over Achilles, locked round his waist
Film after film of sopping froth, then
Heaved him sideways up while multitudinous crests
Bubbled around his face, blocked his nostrils with the blood
He shed an hour before.

                 Then Hera, Heaven's queen,
Looked over the cloudy battlements of Paradise
And saw it all and saw the Greek was done and cursed
    Scamander,
Turned to Hephaestus her son, balanced on a silver crutch
And playing with a bag of flames, who, when his mother
Beckoned with her head, came close and listened:
'Little Cripple, would you fight Scamander for me?
Yes?' – rumpling his hair – 'You must be quick or' –
Giving him a kiss – 'Achilles will be dead. So,
Do it with fire, son; an enormous fire, while' –
Twisting his ear a bit – 'I fetch the white south wind to thrust
Your hot nitre among the Trojan dead, and you must
Weld Scamander wet to bank – now! But . . .
Wait. Little One, don't be talked out of it, eh?
More Gods are threatened than struck, Scamander's promises
Are bought. Now, off with you, and one last thing –
Sear him, Hephaestus, till you hear me shout!'

                   And the Fire God
From a carroty fuse no bigger than his thumb,
Raised a burning fan as wide as Troy,
And brushed the plain with it until,
Scamander's glinting width was parched
And the smoke stopped sunlight.

                    Then the garnet-coloured bricks
Coped with whitestone parapets that were Troy's wall,
Loomed in smoky light, like a dark wicket bounding
The fire's destruction.
Troy's plain was charred and all in cinders
The dead Trojans and their gear. Yet Heaven's Queen
Did not call her son, and the Cripple
Turned on the beaten river.

                                Flame ate the elms,
Sad-willow, clover, tamarisk and galingale – the lot.
Rushes and the green, green lotus beds crinkled – wet dust,
The eels and the pike began to broil.
Last of all, Scamander's back writhed like a burning poultice,
Then, reared up, into a face on fire:
'How can I fight you, Cripple? Flames in my throat,
My waters griddled by hot lacquer! Quit – and I'll quit.
As for Troy and Trojans – let 'em burn. Are not we Gods
Above the quarrels of mere humans?'

                You must imagine how the water
                For boiling down the fat of a juicy pig
                After the women pour it in a cauldron,
                Seethes and lifts as the kindling takes
                And the iron sits in a flamy nest.
                Likewise Hephaestus fixed Scamander.

  So the wretched River God called to Heaven:
'Queen, why does your boy pick on me?
What of the other Gods who side with Troy?
I promise to leave off if *he* leaves off. What's more
I swear to turn away when Troy is burnt by Greeks.'

                    So she called the Cripple off.
And between the echoing banks
  Scamander
Rushed gently over his accustomed way.

ADRIAN MITCHELL

born 1932

Mitchell is perhaps the best-known 'protest poet' in England, and is therefore, in one sense, an English counterpart to the Beats. However, there are marked differences. As the two poems printed here show, he is not really interested in the idea of the immediate, uncensored response to a moment of inspiration, but is, rather, a social poet, who tries to make himself the mouthpiece for the feelings of many. The contrast in styles was very marked when Mitchell read with Ginsberg, Corso and Ferlinghetti at the Albert Hall in 1965. His career forms an interesting compendium of influences. He belongs to the same Oxford generation as Anthony Thwaite, George MacBeth and Geoffrey Hill, and is represented with them in *Oxford Poetry 1954* and *1955*, and was subsequently published in a Fantasy pamphlet. He was also represented in *A Group Anthology*. Later, he made the verse adaptation for Peter Brook's production of Peter Weiss's *Marat/Sade*. Brecht and early Auden are perhaps more clearly present in his recent work than Allen Ginsberg.

Nostalgia – Now Threepence Off

Where are they now, the heroes of furry-paged books and comics brighter than life which packed my inklined desk in days when BOP meant Boys' Own Paper, where are they anyway?

Where is Percy F. Westerman? Where are H. L. Gee and Arthur Mee? Where is Edgar Rice (The Warlord of Mars) Burroughs, the Bumper Fun Book and the Wag's Handbook? Where is the Wonder Book of Reptiles? Where the hell is The Boy's Book of Bacteriological Warfare?

Where are the Beacon Readers? Did Ro-ver, that tireless hound, devour his mon-o-syll-ab-ic-all-y correct family? Did Little Black Sambo and Epaminondas dig the last sit-in?

Did Peter Rabbit get his when myxomatosis came round the second time, did the Flopsy Bunnies stiffen to a standstill, grow bug-eyed, fly-covered and then disintegrate?

Where is G. A. Henty and his historical lads – Wolfgang the Hittite, Armpit the Young Viking, Cyril who lived in Sodom?

Where are their uncorrupted bodies and Empire-building brains,
England needs them, the *Sunday Times* says so.

There is news from Strewelpeter mob. Johnny-Head-In-Air
spends his days reporting flying saucers, the telephone receiver
never cools from the heat of his hand. Little Harriet, who played
with matches, still burns, but not with fire. The Scissor-man is
everywhere.

Barbar the Elephant turned the jungle into a garden city. But
things went wrong. John and Susan, Titty and Roger, became
unaccountably afraid of water, sold their dinghies, all married
each other, live in a bombed-out cinema on surgical spirits and
weeds of all kinds.

Snow White was in the *News of the World* – Virgin Lived With
Seven Midgets, Court Told. And in the psychiatric ward an old
woman dribbles as she mumbles about a family of human bears,
they ate porridge, yes Miss Goldilocks of course they did.

Hans Brinker vainly whirled his silver skates round his head
as the jackboots of Emil and the Detectives invaded his Resist-
ance Cellar.

Some failed. Desperate Dan and Meddlesome Matty and
Strang the Terrible and Korky the Cat killed themselves with
free gifts in a back room at the Peter Pan Club because they were
impotent, like us. Their audience, the senile Chums of Red
Circle School, still wearing for reasons of loyalty and lust the
tatters of their uniforms, voted that exhibition a super wheeze.

Some succeeded. Tom Sawyer's heart has cooled, his ingen-
uity flowers at Cape Canaveral.

But they are all trodden on, the old familiar faces, so at the
rising of the sun and the going down of the ditto I remember
I remember the house where I was taught to play up play up
and play the game though nobody told me what the game was,
but we know now, don't we, we know what the game is, but
lives of great men all remind us we can make our lives sublime
and departing leave behind us arseprints on the sands of time,
but the tide's come up, the castles are washed down, where are
they now, where are they, where the deep shelters? There are
no deep shelters. Biggles may drop it, Worrals of the Wraf may
press the button. So, Billy and Bessie Bunter, prepare for the
last and cosmic Yarooh and throw away the Man-Tan. The sky
will soon be full of suns.

To Whom It May Concern

I was run over by the truth one day,
Ever since the accident I've walked this way
    So stick my legs in plaster
    Tell me lies about Vietnam.

Heard the alarm clock screaming with pain,
Couldn't find myself so I went back to sleep again
    So fill my ears with silver
    Stick my legs in plaster
    Tell me lies about Vietnam.

Every time I shut my eyes all I see is flames.
Made a marble phone book and I carved all the names
    So coat my eyes with butter
    Fill my ears with silver
    Stick my legs in plaster
    Tell me lies about Vietnam.

I smell something burning, hope it's just my brains.
They're only dropping peppermints and daisy-chains
    So stuff my nose with garlic
    Coat my eyes with butter
    Fill my ears with silver
    Stick my legs in plaster
    Tell me lies about Vietnam.

Where were you at the time of the crime?
Down by the Cenotaph drinking slime
    So chain my tongue with whisky
    Stuff my nose with garlic
    Coat my eyes with butter
    Fill my ears with silver
    Stick my legs in plaster
    Tell me lies about Vietnam.

You put your bombers in, you put your conscience out,
You take the human being and you twist it all about
    So scrub my skin with women
    Chain my tongue with whisky
    Stuff my nose with garlic

Adrian Mitchell

Coat my eyes with butter
Fill my ears with silver
Stick my legs in plaster
Tell me lies about Vietnam.

PART NINE: SCOTLAND

In this section, I have made the perhaps controversial decision to omit all poetry in Scots except that of Robert Garioch. The reason is simple; the Lallans written by most Scottish practitioners is, of course, the artificial language invented by MacDiarmid, and abandoned by him in favour of English as early as the middle thirties. It would be foolish to deny the merit of *The Drunk Man Looks at a Thistle*: the difficulty is that no subsequent writer has succeeded in adding much (if anything at all) to MacDiarmid's achievement. Today, Scottish poets seem for the most part to write in standard English. I make an exception in the case of Garioch because he seems to me to be writing, not a literary language, but the actual speech of Edinburgh, or one version of it. For the rest, MacDiarmid remains the central figure in contemporary poetry in Scotland, and most positions must be charted in relation to him. The exception is Concrete Poetry, especially that written by Ian Hamilton Finlay – the opposition between the poets flared up when MacDiarmid issued his savage pamphlet *The Ugly Birds Without Wings* in 1962. It is perhaps too easy to say that Hamilton Finlay is internationalist where MacDiarmid is nationalist, a purist where MacDiarmid's inclination is to cram in everything, relevant or irrelevant. In fact, both are representative of the openness of Scottish culture; the way in which Scotland remains open to new ideas which get no hearing in England. The difference is that Hamilton Finlay wants to be on an equal footing with colleagues in Germany, in Brazil, in the United States or Italy, while MacDiarmid wanted to maintain a proud distinctiveness. In addition, one believes in the absolute quality of art, and the other (as a good Marxist) that all art must be 'social art'.

ROBERT GARIOCH

born 1909

For reasons I have already explained in the introduction to this section, Garioch is the only poet writing in Scots who is represented here. With Garioch, Scots seems not an artificial literary language, but a natural, and indeed racy, mode of speech, the equivalent of the nineteenth-century Roman dialect poet Belli, whom he has translated so brilliantly.

I'm Neutral

Last nicht in Scotland Street I met a man
that gruppit my lapel – a kinna foreign
cratur he seemed; he tellt me. There's a war on
atween the Lang-nebs and the Big-heid Clan.

I wasna fasht, I took him for a moron,
naething byordnar, but he said, Ye're wan
of thae lang-nebbit folk, and if I can,
I'm gaunnae pash ye doun and rype your sporran.

Says he, I'll get a medal for this job;
we're watchan ye, we ken fine what ye're at,
ye're with us or agin us, shut your gob.

He gied a clout that knockit aff my hat,
bawlan, A fecht! Come on, the Big-heid Mob!
Aweill, I caa'd him owre, and that was that.

Lang-nebs: long-noses. *byordnar*: out of the ordinary. *pash*: knock. *fecht*: fight.

Robert Garioch

In Princes Street Gairdens

Doun by the baundstaund, by the ice-cream barrie,
there is a sait that says, Wilma Is Fab.
Sit doun aside me here and gieze your gab,
jist you and me, a dou, and a wee cock-sparrie.

Up in the street, shop-folk sairve and harrie;
weill-daean tredsmen sclate and pent and snab
and jyne and plaister. We never let dab
sae lang as we can jink the strait-and-narrie.

A sculptured growp, classical and symbolic,
staunds by the path, maist beautiful to see:
National Savings, out for a bit frolic,

peys echt per cent til Thrift and Industry,
but dour Inflatioun, a diabolic
dou, has owrecam, and duin Thrift in the ee.

gieze your gab: have a chat. *sclate and pent and snab:* slate and paint and
cobble. *let dab:* let fly.

NORMAN MACCAIG

born 1910

MacCaig has long enjoyed the slightly galling tribute of being thought 'second only to MacDiarmid' among modern Scottish poets. In fact, he and MacDiarmid seem to me to be far apart in temperament. MacCaig is not an innovator; he makes skilful use of established forms. When he shifts to free verse, however, the result can be a bit thin.

Nude in a Fountain

Clip-clop go water-drops and bridles ring –
Or, visually, a gauze of water, blown
About and falling and blown about, discloses
Pudicity herself in shameless stone,
In an unlikely world of shells and roses.

On shaven grass a summer's litter lies
Of paper bags and people. One o'clock
Booms on the leaves with which the trees are quilted
And wades away through air, making it rock
On flowerbeds that have blazed and dazed and wilted.

Light perches, preening, on the handle of a pram
And gasps on paths and runs along a rail
And whitely, brightly in a soft diffusion
Veils and unveils the naked figure, pale
As marble in her stone and stilled confusion.

And nothing moves except one dog that runs,
A red rag in a black rag, round and round
And that long helmet-plume of water waving,
In which the four elements, hoisted from the ground,
Become this grace, the form of their enslaving.

Meeting and marrying in the midmost air
Is mineral assurance of them all;
White doldrum on blue sky; a pose of meaning

Whose pose is what is explicit; a miracle
Made, and made bearable, by the water's screening.

The drops sigh, singing, and, still sighing, sing
Gently a leaning song. She makes no sound.
They veil her, not with shadows, but with brightness;
Till, gleam within a glitter, they expound
What a tall shadow is when it is whiteness.

A perpetual modification of itself
Going on around her is her; her hand is curled
Round more than a stone breast; and she discloses
The more than likely in an unlikely world
Of dogs and people and stone shells and roses.

Fetching Cows

The black one, last as usual, swings her head
And coils a black tongue round a grass-tuft. I
Watch her soft weight come down, her split feet spread.

In front, the others swing and slouch; they roll
Their great Greek eyes and breathe out milky gusts
From muzzles black and shiny as wet coal.

The collie trots, bored, at my heels, then plops
Into the ditch. The sea makes a tired sound
That's always stopping though it never stops.

A haycart squats prickeared against the sky.
Hay breath and milk breath. Far out in the West
The wrecked sun founders though its colours fly.

The collie's bored. There's nothing to control . . .
The black cow is two native carriers
Bringing its belly home, slung from a pole.

Interruption to a Journey

The hare we had run over
Bounced about the road
On the springing curve
Of its spine.

Cornfields breathed in the darkness.
We were going through the darkness and
The breathing cornfields from one
Important place to another.

We broke the hare's neck
And made that place, for a moment,
The most important place there was,
Where a bowstring was cut
And a bow broken for ever
That had shot itself through so many
Darknesses and cornfields.

It was left in that landscape.
It left us in another.

GEORGE MACKAY BROWN

born 1921

The Orcadian poet George Mackay Brown produces work of entirely individual flavour – juxtaposed statements, often without connectives, build up brick by brick the picture of a primitive world, where no distinction is made between what is contemporary, and what is already history. As the poet himself put it in the 'Prologue' to his first collection:

> For the islands I sing
> and for a few friends,
> not to foster means
> or be midwife to ends.

Ikey on the People of Helya

Rognvald who stalks round Corse with his stick
I do not love.
His dog has a loud sharp mouth.
The wood of his door is very hard.
Once, tangled in his barbed wire
(I was paying respects to his hens, stroking a wing)
He laid his stick on me.
That was out of a hard forest also.

Mansie at Quoy is a biddable man..
Ask for water, he gives you rum.
I strip his scarecrow April by April.
Ask for a scattering of straw in his byre
He lays you down
Under a quilt as long and light as heaven.
Then only his raging woman spoils our peace.

Gray the fisherman is no trouble now
Who quoted me the vagrancy laws
In a voice slippery as seaweed under the kirkyard.
I rigged his boat with the seven curses.

Occasionally still, for encouragement,
I put the knife in his net.

Though she has black peats and a yellow hill
And fifty silken cattle
I do not go near Merran and her cats.
Rather break a crust on a tombstone.
Her great-great-grandmother
Wore the red coat[1] at Gallowsha.

The thousand rabbits of Hollandshay
Keep Simpson's corn short,
Whereby comes much cruelty, gas and gunshot.
Tonight I have lit a small fire.
I have stained my knife red.
I have peeled a round turnip
And I pray the Lord
To preserve those nine hundred and ninety-nine innocents.

Finally in Folscroft lives Jeems,
Tailor and undertaker, a crosser of limbs,
One tape for the living and the dead.
He brings a needle to my rags in winter,
And he guards, against my stillness,
The seven white boards
I got from the Danish wreck one winter.

The Hawk

On Sunday the hawk fell on Bigging
  And a chicken screamed
  Lost in its own little snowstorm.
And on Monday he fell on the moor
  And the Field Club
  Raised a hundred silent prisms.
And on Tuesday he fell on the hill
  And the happy lamb
  Never knew why the loud collie straddled him

---

1. *wore the red coat*: was burnt as a witch.

And on Wednesday he fell on a bush
  And the blackbird
  Laid by his little flute for the last time
And on Thursday he fell on Cleat
  And peerie Tom's rabbit
  Swung in a single arc from shore to hill.
And on Friday he fell on a ditch
  But the rampant rat,
  That eye and that tooth, quenched his flame.
And on Saturday he fell on Bigging
  And Jock lowered his gun
  And nailed a small wing over the corn.

EDWIN MORGAN

born 1920

Hugely prolific and inventive, Edwin Morgan has produced many different kinds of poetry. He is, together with Ian Hamilton Finlay, one of the few considerable British figures in the international Concrete Poetry movement, though Concrete Poetry forms only part of his production. He is also one of the few contemporary poets to be really interested in scientific ideas. He has, for example, written on the creative and critical potentialities of computers. It was his variousness, one suspects, which helped to slow down the rate at which recognition came to him.

From the Domain of Arnheim

And so that all these ages, these years
we cast behind us, like the smoke-clouds
dragged back into vacancy when the rocket springs –

The domain of Arnheim was all snow, but we were there.
We saw a yellow light thrown on the icefield
from the huts by the pines, and laughter came up
floating from a white corrie
miles away, clearly.
We moved on down, arm in arm.
I know you would have thought it was a dream
but we were there. And those were trumpets –
tremendous round the rocks –
while they were burning fires of trash and mammoths' bones.
They sang naked, and kissed in the smoke.
A child, or one of their animals, was crying.
Young men blew the ice crystals off their drums.
We came down among them, but of course
they could see nothing, on their time-scale.
Yet they sensed us, stopped, looked up – even into our eyes.
To them we were a displacement of the air,
a sudden chill, yet we had no power
over their fear. If one of them had been dying

he would have died. The crying
came from one just born: that was the cause
of the song. We saw it now. What had we stopped
but joy?
I know you felt
the same dismay, you gripped my arm, they were waiting
for what they knew of us to pass.
A sweating trumpeter took
a brand from the fire with a shout and threw it
where our bodies would have been –
we felt nothing but his courage.
And so they would deal with every imagined power
seen or unseen.
There are no gods in the domain of Arnheim.

We signalled to the ship; got back;
our lives and days returned to us, but
haunted by deeper souvenirs than any rocks or seeds.
From time the souvenirs are deeds.

Opening the Cage

14 variations on 14 words

I have nothing to say and I am saying it and that is poetry.

JOHN CAGE

I have to say poetry and is that nothing and am I saying it
I am and I have poetry to say and is that nothing saying it
I am nothing and I have poetry to say and that is saying it
I that am saying poetry have nothing and it is I and to say
And I say that I am to have poetry and saying it is nothing
I am poetry and nothing and saying it is to say that I have
To have nothing is poetry and I am saying that and I say it
Poetry is saying I have nothing and I am to say that and it
Saying nothing I am poetry and I have to say that and it is
It is and I am and I have poetry saying say that to nothing
It is saying poetry to nothing and I say I have and am that
Poetry is saying I have it and I am nothing and to say that
And that nothing is poetry I am saying and I have to say it
Saying poetry is nothing and to that I say I am and have it

Pomander

pomander
open pomander
open poem and her
open poem and him
open poem and hymn
hymn and hymen leander
high man pen meander
o pen poem me and her
pen me poem me and him
om mane padme hum
pad me home panda hand
open up o holy panhandler
ample panda pen or bamboo pond
ponder a bonny poem pomander opener
open banned peon penman hum and banter
open hymn and pompom band and panda hamper
o i am a pen open man or happener
i am open manner happener
happy are we open
poem and a pom
poem and a panda
poem and aplomb

Ian Hamilton Finlay

born 1925

Ian Hamilton Finlay is the most important figure in the British Concrete Poetry movement, and one of the most playfully inventive of current poets. This inventiveness also characterizes that part of his work (an important one) which is not concrete. Unfortunately, much of his work needs to be seen in the special formats which he himself designs for it, and the effect of the poems which need to be read in a particular rhythm, turning page after page, would be lost here, as would that of those which rely on illustrative material for part of their meaning. There is no collected edition of Hamilton Finlay's work, for obvious reasons, and it is to be found in a large number of books and pamphlets, many of them published by his own Wild Hawthorn Press. His work has also more and more tended to proliferate into forms which belong in an art gallery or sculpture garden rather than on a bookshelf, and in recent years his most spectacular appearances have been in art exhibitions, and not in bookshops or libraries.

Orkney Lyrics

(One)

Peedie Mary Considers the Sun

The peedie sun is not so tall
He walks on golden stilts
Across, across, across the water
But I have darker hair.

(Two)

The English Colonel Explains an Orkney Boat

The boat swims full of air.
You see, it has a point at both
Ends, sir, somewhat
As lemons. I'm explaining

The hollowness is amazing. That's
The way a boat
Floats.

(*Three*)

Mansie Considers Peedie Mary

Peedie Alice Mary is
My cousin, so we cannot kiss.
And yet I love my cousin fair:
She wears her seaboots with such an air.

(*Four*)

Mansie Considers the Sea in the Manner of Hugh MacDiarmid

The sea, I think, is lazy,
It just obeys the moon
– All the same I remember what Engels said:
'Freedom is the consciousness of necessity.'

(*Five*)

Folk Song for Poor Peedie Mary

Peedie Mary
Bought a posh
Big machine
To do her wash.

Peedie Mary
Stands and greets.
Where dost thoo
Put in the peats?

Silly peedie
Mary thoo
Puts the peats
Below, baloo.

Peedie Mary
Greets the more.

What did the posh paint
Come off for?

(*Six*)

John Sharkey is Pleased to Be in Sourin at Evening

How beautiful, how beautiful, the mill
– Wheel is not turning though the waters spill
Their single tress. The whole old mill
Leans to the West, the breast.

Stones for Gardens

I.   THE WATER'S BREAST
and ripples

2.   ONE (ORANGE) ARM
OF THE WORLD'S OLDEST WINDMILL
autumn

3.   THE CLOUD'S ANCHOR
swallow

4.   THE BOAT'S
inseparable ripples

Green Waters[1]

Green Waters
Blue Spray
Grayfish

1. 'Green Waters' etc: fishing trawlers of Aberdeen, Milford Haven, and other fishing ports.

Anna T
Karen B
Netta Croan

Constant Star
Daystar
Starwood

Starlit Waters
Moonlit Waters
Drift

IAIN CRICHTON SMITH

born 1928

Iain Crichton Smith also writes in Gaelic – something which seems to
have left no very notable traces on his work. He writes poems in stan-
dard English, with no conspicuous technical mannerisms. He is, in fact,
much the kind of writer that R. S. Thomas is, living remote (in Oban)
from literary London, and pursuing a private meditation in his verse.

Old Woman

Your thorned back
heavily under the creel
you steadily stamped the rising daffodil.

Your set mouth
forgives no-one, not even God's justice
perpetually drowning law with grace.

Your cold eyes
watched your drunken husband come
unsteadily from Sodom home.

Your grained hands
dandled full and sinful cradles.
You built for your children stone walls.

Your yellow hair
burned slowly in a scarf of grey
wildly falling like the mountain spray.

Finally you're alone
among the unforgiving brass,
the slow silences, the sinful glass.

Who never learned,
not even ageing, to forgive
our poor journey and our common grave

while the free daffodils
wave in the valleys and on the hills
the deer look down with their instinctive skills,

and the huge sea
in which your brothers drowned sings slow
over the headland and the peevish crow.

The Departing Island

Strange to see it – how as we lean over
this vague rail, the island goes away
into its loved light grown suddenly foreign:
how the ship slides outward like a cold ray
from a sun turned cloudy, and rough land draws down
into an abstract sea its arranged star.

Strange how it's like a dream when two waves past,
and the engine's hum puts villages out of mind
or shakes them together in a waving fashion.
The lights stream northward down a wolfish wind.
A pacing passenger wears the air of one
whom tender arms and fleshly hands embraced.

It's the island that goes away, not we who leave it.
Like an unbearable thought it sinks beyond
assiduous reasoning light and wringing hands,
or, as a flower roots deep into the ground,
it works its darkness into the gay winds
that blow about us in a later spirit.

Farewell

We were gone from each other
not that I was happy
in this country
nor not happy
when your chair was empty

which you had filled (rounded)
not as a theory
but as a fruit ripening
ripening towards harvest

in another country
where some evening you'll see
in another chair
by your autumn nursery

a sky barred and ruled
with a red cloud above
and perhaps think of me
late late in that world
where your round cornstacks are.

D. M. Black

born 1941

D. M. Black has a talent for bizarre narratives and allegories, expressed
in a highly original language which seems to owe little to any other poet.
He is one of the few poets of his generation who has an immediately
recognizable tone.

The Educators

In their
limousines the
teachers come: by
hundreds. O the
square is
blackened with dark suits, with grave
scholastic faces. They
wait to be summoned.
                              These are the
educators, the
father-figures. O you could
warm with love for the firm lips, the
responsible foreheads. Their
ties are strongly set, between their collars. They
pass with dignity the exasperation of waiting.

A
bell rings. They turn. On the
wide steps my
dwarf is standing, both hands raised. He
cackles with laughter. Welcome, he cries, welcome
to our elaborate Palace. It is indeed. He
is tumbling in cartwheels over the steps. The
teachers turn to each other their grave faces.

With
a single grab they have him up by the shoulders. They
dismantle him. Limbs, O

limbs and delicate organs, limbs and
guts, eyes, the tongue, the
lobes of the brain, glands; tonsils, several
eyes, limbs, the tongue,
a kidney, pants, livers, more
kidneys, limbs, the tongue
pass from hand to hand, in their serious hands. He is
utterly gone. Wide
crumbling steps.

They
return to their cars. They
drive off smoothly, without disorder;
watching the road.

From the Privy Council

Delicacy was never enormously
My style. All my favourite girls
Walked at five miles an hour or ate haggis,
Or swam like punts. I myself,
Though not of primeval clumsiness, would often
Crack tumblers in my attention to their content
Or bruise with my embrace some tittering nymph.
It was accidental only – I have little
Sadistic enthusiasm – yet when the time came
And they sent me to the Consultant on Careers,
Executioner was the immediate decision.
My nature is a quiet, conforming thing,
I like to be advised, and am not arrogant:
I agreed:
They stripped me of my suit, shored off my hair
And shaved a gleaming scalp onto my skull;
Clad me in fitting hides,
Hid my poignant features with a black mask,
And led me the very first day to the public platform.
I had to assist only: the carriage of carcases
Is a heavy job, and not for a spent headsman.

Later they let me handle the small hatchet
For cutting off hands and so forth – what is called hackwork
Merely; but I earned the prize for proficiency
And the end of my first year brought total promotion:
Hangman and headsman for the metropolitan burgh
Of Aberfinley. I had a black band
Printed on all my note-paper. Every morning
I hectored my hatchetmen into a spruce turn-out,
Insisted on a keen edge to all their axes.
My jurisdiction spilled
Over the county border – half Scotland's assassins
Dragged their victims into the benign realm
Where I held sway;
And the trade was gripped in the rigours of unemployment
Outside my scope. There was one solution:
The London parliament passed an urgent Act
Creating a new sinecure: Hangman
And headsman in the Royal Chamber – the post
To be of Cabinet rank, and in the Privy Council.
How many lepers and foundling-hospitals
Have cause to bless me now! On the Privy Council
My stately head is much admired, and the opulent grace
With which I swing my kindly turnip watch.
And here you will find the origin of the tired joke
About passing from executive to admin.

Prayer

Clarity, once
more, the uncluttered! May even the gross
colicky lout lumbering under the plane-trees,
(track-suited) in
misty October
               thin;
and a dawn be clear in which he
will walk marvellously
on a springing downs. O clean and
dewy air! And a sea not distant.

Let the dew make him a dancer
for a formal time:
gratifying a plain aspiration,
for all week he has cleaned out kennels, and covered poodles
    in lather.

ALAN BOLD

born 1942

MacDiarmid's Marxist dialectic finds an energetic disciple in Alan Bold. Bold is an enemy of modernism – or at least of concrete poetry, abstract painting and dodecaphonic music. His best poetry has a harsh plainness which eschews overtones.

June 1967 at Buchenwald

The stillness of death all round the camp was uncanny and intolerable.

Bruno Apitz, *Naked Among Wolves*

This is the way in. The words
Wrought in iron on the gate:
JEDEM DAS SEINE. Everybody
Gets what he deserves.

The bare drab rubble of the place.
The dull damp stone. The rain.
The emptiness. The human lack.
JEDEM DAS SEINE. JEDEM DAS SEINE.
Everybody gets what he deserves.

It all forms itself
Into one word: Buchenwald.
And those who know and those
Born after that war but living
In its shadow, shiver at the words.
Everybody gets what he deserves.

It is so quiet now. So
Still that it makes an absence.
At the silence of the metal leads
We can almost hear again the voices,
The moaning of the cattle that were men.
Ahead, acres of abandoned gravel.
Everybody gets what he deserves.

Wood, beech wood, song
Of birds. The sky, the usual sky.
A stretch of trees. A sumptuous sheet
Of colours dragging through the raindrops.
Drizzle loosening the small stones
We stand on. Stone buildings. Doors. Dark.
A dead tree leaning in the rain.
Everybody gets what he deserves.

Cold, numb cold. Despair
And no despair. The very worst
Of men against the very best.
A joy in brutality from lack
Of feeling for the other. The greatest
Evil, racialism. A man, the greatest good.
Much more than a biological beast.
An aggregate of atoms. Much more.
Everybody gets what he deserves.

And it could happen again
And they could hang like broken carcases
And they could scream in terror without light
And they could count the strokes that split their skin
And they could smoulder under cigarettes
And they could suffer and bear every blow
And they could starve and live for death
And they could live for hope alone
And it could happen again.
Everybody gets what he deserves.

We must condemn our arrogant
Assumption that we are immune as well
As apathetic. We let it happen.
History is always more comfortable
Than the implications of the present.
We outrage our own advance as beings
By being merely men. The miracle
Is the miracle of matter. Mind
Knows this, but sordid, cruel and ignorant
Tradition makes the world a verbal shell.
Everybody gets what he deserves.

Words are fallible. They cannot do
More than hint at torment. Let us
Do justice to words. No premiss is ever
Absolute; so certain that enormous wreckage
Of flesh follows it syllogistically
In the name of mere consistency. In the end
All means stand condemned. In a cosmic
Context human life is short. The future
Is not made, but waits to be created.
Everybody gets what he deserves.

There is the viciously vicarious in us
All. The pleasure in chance misfortune
That lets us patronize or helps to lose
Our limitations for an instant.
It is that, that struggle for survival
I accuse. Let us not forget
Buchenwald is not a word. Its
Meaning is defined with every day.
Everybody gets what he deserves.

Now it is newsprint, and heavy headlines
And looking with a camera's eyes.
Now for many it is only irritating
While for others it is absolutely deadly.
No one is free while some are not free.
While the world is ruled by precedent
It remains a monstrous chance irrelevance.
Everybody gets what he deserves.

We turn away. We always do.
It's what we turn into that matters.
From the invisible barracks of Buchenwald
Where only an unsteady horizon
Remains. The dead cannot complain.
They never do. But we, we live.
Everybody gets what he deserves.

That which once united man
Now drives him apart. We are not helpless
Creatures crashing onwards irresistibly to doom.
There is time for everything and time to choose

For everything. We are that time, that choice.
Everybody gets what he deserves.

This happened near the core
Of a world's culture. This
Occurred among higher things.
This was a philosophical conclusion.
Everybody gets what he deserves.

The bare drab rubble of the place.
The dull damp stone. The rain.
The emptiness. The human lack.

PART TEN: THE LIVERPOOL POETS

Liverpool is one of the places, together with Northern Ireland, where poetry has developed a strong local identity. It was the 'pop' element in Liverpool poetry which first attracted attention; it was stressed in my own anthology *The Liverpool Scene*. And in a broad sense the popular appeal of the leading Liverpool writers – Henri, McGough and Brian Patten – has proven remarkably durable. Audiences still flock to their readings; their poetry still sells in large quantity in paperback. But there is another element in their work which needs to be stressed, and that is its commitment to modern art. It is only in Liverpool that some attempt has been made to re-enact the coming-together of poets and painters (Picasso and Apollinaire; Marinetti and Boccioni; Mayakovsky and the Russian Futurists) which first gave birth to modern art. It is for this reason that I have added to this group of poets of Liverpool origin Jeff Nuttall, who was always in any case closely allied to their way of thinking, and who now runs the Liverpool College of Art.

ADRIAN HENRI

born 1932

Adrian Henri is the theoretician of the Liverpool group – a poet-painter who is trying to relate what he writes to his experience of modern art. He remarks, for example, that poetry, as a medium of communication, is more direct and less ambiguous than the visual arts, but that 'even the worst painter when he exhibits a painting now relates himself to the whole twentieth-century tradition in the arts whether he wants to or not, his work implicitly states where he stands in relation to it.' That is, Henri is by intention a modernist, and this is probably more important in assessing what he does than a knowledge of his involvement in the pop scene.

Tonight at Noon[1]

Tonight at noon
Supermarkets will advertise 3d EXTRA on everything
Tonight at noon
Children from happy families will be sent to live in a home
Elephants will tell each other human jokes
America will declare peace on Russia
World War I generals will sell poppies in the streets on
    November 11th.
The first daffodils of autumn will appear
When the leaves fall upwards to the trees

Tonight at noon
Pigeons will hunt cats through city backyards
Hitler will tell us to fight on the beaches and on the landing
    fields
A tunnel full of water will be built under Liverpool
Pigs will be sighted flying in formation over Woolton
and Nelson will not only get his eye back but his arm as well

    1. The title of this poem is taken from an L.P. by Charles Mingus, 'Tonight at Noon', Atlantic 1416.

White Americans will demonstrate for equal rights
in front of the Black House
and the Monster has just created Dr Frankenstein

Girls in bikinis are moonbathing
Folksongs are being sung by real folk
Artgalleries are closed to people over 21
Poets get their poems in the Top 20.
Politicians are elected to insane asylums
There's jobs for everyone and nobody wants them
In back alleys everywhere teenage lovers are kissing
in broad daylight
In forgotten graveyards everywhere the dead will quietly
bury the living
and
You will tell me you love me
Tonight at noon

The Entry of Christ into Liverpool[1]

City morning. dandelionseeds blowing from wasteground.
smell of overgrown privethedges. children's voices
in the distance. sounds from the river.
round the corner into Myrtle St. Saturdaymorning shoppers
headscarves. shoppingbaskets. dogs.

then
  down the hill
      THE SOUND OF TRUMPETS
      cheering and shouting in the distance
        children running
         icecream vans
     flags breaking out over buildings
      black and red green and yellow
      Union Jacks   Red Ensigns

1. Henri has painted a large picture of this subject, intended as a trib-
ute to James Ensor's 'The Entry of Christ into Brussels'. Ensor
(1860–1949) is a hallucinatory artist some of whose imagery foreshadows
the surrealists. He was fascinated by the imagery of masks.

LONG LIVE SOCIALISM
stretched against the blue sky
over St George's hall

Now the procession
THE MARCHING DRUMS
hideous masked Breughel faces of old ladies in the crowd
yellow masks of girls in curlers and headscarves
smelling of factories
Masks   Masks   Masks
red masks   purple masks   pink masks

crushing surging carrying me along

down the hill past the Philharmonic The Labour Exchange
excited feet crushing the geraniums in St Luke's Gardens
placards   banners   posters
Keep Britain White
End the War in Vietnam
God Bless Our Pope
Billboards hoardings drawings on pavements
words painted on the road
STOP   GO   HALT
the sounds of pipes and drums down the street
little girls in yellow and orange dresses paper flowers
embroidered banners
Loyal Sons of King William Lodge, Bootle
Masks more Masks crowding in off buses
standing on walls   climbing fences
familiar faces among the crowd
faces of my friends   the shades of Pierre Bonnard and
Guillaume Apollinaire
Jarry cycling carefully through the crowd. A black cat
picking her way underfoot
posters
signs
gleaming salads
COLMANS MUSTARD
J. Ensor, Fabriqueur de Masques
HAIL JESUS, KING OF THE JEWS
straining forward to catch a glimpse through the crowd
red hair   white robe   grey donkey
familiar face

trafficlights   zebracrossings
GUIN
GUINN
GUINNESS IS
white bird dying unnoticed in a corner
splattered feathers
blood running merged with the neonsigns
in a puddle
GUINNESS IS GOOD
GUINNESS IS GOOD FOR
Masks   Masks   Masks   Masks   Masks
GUINESS IS GOOD FOR YOU
brassbands cheering   loudspeakers blaring
clatter of police horses
ALL POWER TO THE CONSTITUENT
ASSEMBLY[1]
masks cheering glittering teeth
daffodils trodden underfoot
BUTCHERS OF JERUSALEM
banners cheering   drunks stumbling and singing
masks
masks
masks
evening
thin sickle moon
pale blue sky
flecked with bright orange clouds
streamers newspapers discarded paper hats
blown slowly back up the hill by the evening wind
dustmen with big brooms sweeping the gutters
last of the crowds waiting at bus-stops
giggling schoolgirls   quiet businessmen
me
walking home
empty chip-papers drifting round my feet.

---

1. *All Power To The Constituent Assembly* – a quotation from Anselm
Hollo's translation of 'The Twelve' by the Russian Symbolist poet
Aleksandr Blok (1880–1921). The subject of 'The Twelve' is a dozen
Revolutionary soldiers marching across St Petersburg. At the end of the
poem, Christ is revealed as their leader.

HENRY GRAHAM

born 1930

Graham is also a painter, and has worked as a jazz-musician. To this extent he is typical of the Liverpool environment. He is perhaps untypical in having little interest in 'pop' materials.

Cat Poem

A soprano sings. The poem
limps on. The cat yawns. It feels
the air with the fine
wires on its nose. It yearns
to wear away the white
marble of milk it commands
morning and evening; while I
wander on my hands
through the stars, burning
my fingers. The soprano sings.
A cold wind blows through the holes
in the poem, I shiver. The cat
moves a long curved dagger
and carefully pierces my skin.
Distant red supernovas appear
amongst the negative spaces
of the poem; an island universe
dots an i, Henry's comet crosses
a t. The cat sings, the soprano
yawns, I bleed. The poem
limps from the page, and drags
its weary way to the saucer
of milk, and drowns itself.

Henry Graham

Two Gardens

I

There is a black bird with eyes
like the surface of a lake,
making fun of a grieving child.
The eyes of the child contain
the sky, the clouds and vast spaces.
The child always has the last laugh.

2

I sliced a worm in half yesterday
and then went away. This morning
when I looked out, I watched
a child attempting to glue
the wriggling ends together.

ROGER MCGOUGH

born 1937

McGough was a member of the satirical pop group The Scaffold, and
has written sketches, one-act plays and one full-length play as well as
poems and the 'mini-novel' *Frinck*. His poetry is very much 'perform-
ance poetry', with a penchant for puns and spoonerisms which is remi-
niscent of e.e. cummings. At its best it has outstanding neatness and
elegance: McGough has the concern for 'style' and 'stylishness' which
is very much part of the British pop-music scene. Of all the so-called
'pop' poets, he is probably the one who comes closest to what the music
is about.

Let Me Die a Youngman's Death

Let me die a youngman's death
not a clean & inbetween
the sheets holywater death
not a famous-last-words
peaceful out of breath death

When I'm 73
& in constant good tumour
may I be mown down at dawn
by a bright red sports car
on my way home
from an allnight party

Or when I'm 91
with silver hair
& sitting in a barber's chair
may rival gangsters
with hamfisted tommyguns burst in
& give me a short back & insides

Or when I'm 104
& banned from the Cavern
may my mistress

catching me in bed with her daughter
& fearing her son
cut me up into little pieces
& throw away every piece but one

Let me die a youngman's death
not a free from sin tiptoe in
candle wax & waning death
not a curtains drawn by angels borne
'what a nice way to go' death

From 'summer with monika': 39

monika the teathings are taking over!
the cups are as big as bubblecars
they throttle round the room
tinopeners skate on the greasy plates
by the light of the silvery moon
the biscuits are having a knees-up
they're necking in our breadbin
thats jazz you hear from the saltcellars
but they don't let nonmembers in
the eggspoons had our eggs for breakfast
the saucebottle's asleep in our bed
i overheard the knives and forks
'it won't be long' they said
'it won't be long' they said

BRIAN PATTEN

born 1946

The youngest of the Liverpool poets, and in many ways the most tra-
ditional in his aims. Patten says that what he wants to write is 'lyric, the
hard lyric', and he feels that 'poetry is a private thing in itself . . . it's
nothing to do with educating or saying anything'. In fact, it's clear that
he is deliberately trying to revive the full-blooded romantic mode.

Little Johnny's Confession

This morning
    being rather young and foolish
    I borrowed a machinegun my father
    had left hidden since the war, went out,
    and eliminated a number of small enemies.
    Since then I have not returned home.

This morning
    swarms of police with trackerdogs
    wander about the city
    with my description printed
    on their minds, asking:
    'Have you seen him?
    He is seven years old,
    likes Pluto, Mighty Mouse
    and Biffo the Bear,
    have you seen him, anywhere?'

This morning
    sitting alone in a strange playground
    muttering you've blundered, you've blundered
    over and over to myself
    I work out my next move
    but cannot move.
    The trackerdogs will sniff me out,
    they have my lollypops.

Brian Patten

Into My Mirror Has Walked

Into my mirror has walked
A woman who will not talk
Of love or of its subsidiaries,
But who stands there,
Pleased by her own silence.
The weather has worn into her
All seasons known to me,
In one breast she holds
Evidence of forests,
In the other, of seas.

I will ask her nothing yet
Would ask so much
If she gave a sign –

Her shape is common enough,
Enough shape to love.
But what keeps me here
Is what glows beyond her.

I think at times
A boy's body
Would be as easy
To read light into,
I think sometimes
My own might do.

It is Always the Same Image

It is always the same image;
of you wandering naked out from autumn rivers,
your body steaming, covered with rain,
blue and grey drops fall from you,
when you speak
leaves fall and disintegrate.

It is always the image of your breasts,
full of the violence of seaplants

that quiver when touched; fish
mate beneath you; your body blue, your
shadow following,
both seen like ghosts from distant promenades
by a fearful audience.

The same image
but now a lake surrounded by ferns,
and just visible through the mist
a thousand lovers following you naked
leaving no traces in the corners of dawn.

JEFF NUTTALL

born 1933

It seems appropriate that Jeff Nuttall has now gravitated to Liverpool. He resembles some of the Liverpool poets in being a painter and ex-jazz musician. He has since been a leading experimentalist in the field of multi-media. He is perhaps best known for the 'People Shows' which he staged at the Arts Laboratory in Drury Lane. He was also the editor of one of the best known of British avant-grade duplicated magazines, *My Own Mag*. Nuttall has summed up his own experience of the post-war British avant-garde in a critical book, *Bomb Culture*.

Insomnia

Shall I do it, get up?
Curl like a hurt furred animal?
Shall I curl like an early embryo
All hairy, simian, gone wrong?
Curl up out there, out of the bed,
Red, raw bitten under my itch of a pelt,
All huddled up, all curled on my side?
Out of the bed and over there
Like an idiot, but I'm not an idiot,
Just a late, shamed, withered beast
Who'd whimper there on the bedroom boards,
Whimper love,
Whimper all the limp last love away
And sleep.

'When it had all been told'

When it had all been told
(Afternoon was a virgin
Drunk and sleeping in the overloaded trees)

When the bitter core was bared
(Distant road was a mumbling cordon of hornets
    winking their chrome)

When the long-dead dramas were interred,
(Sky was empty as an Easter tomb)

The still unburied body of love
(Earth was cool with the fragrance of mould)

Was certified dead as a nail
(The trees caught birds on their twigs)

He wanted to tell her
(Occasional breezes dictating dictating)

How, now his life was an absence,
(Sky was the absence of Earth)

Then his death
(A dead oak gesticulated)

Could perhaps be a plenitude
(Treasure of buttercup heads)

To offer her still, should
(Grass was veined at the root in brown)

He come to her down through the last thick cream of summer
(Light was sweet on her tongue)

The blood of his broken head
(Headache was heavy as heat)

As ribbons for her
(Shadow lace) unwoven wedding gown.

PART ELEVEN: BELFAST

The Northern Irish phenomenon has been the most striking event in British poetry during the last decade and a half. In purely literary terms, the work of these poets is rooted in that of the Movement and the Group. It owes much to the fact that Philip Hobsbaum taught for a period at the Queen's University, Belfast, and ran a discussion group there which was attended by (among others) Seamus Heaney, Derek Mahon and Michael Longley. But it is political and social circumstances which seem to have given the Northern Irish poets their real impetus – they found a subject (the condition of Ireland) and a way to write about it. Belfast seems to be the one place in the British Isles where poetry has been able to take on some of the centrality it has in Russia, and indeed throughout Eastern Europe, and it has done so for not dissimilar reasons.

Seamus Heaney

born 1939

The first to establish himself of the Northern Irish poets, and still the best known, Seamus Heaney now occupies the central position in British verse which was once accorded to Ted Hughes. He is the yardstick against which other poets, of the same generation or younger, must measure their own success. In his earlier work some influences were visible – both Hughes and Larkin played their part. This now seems much less significant than the way in which he has evolved his own stratagems, his own metaphors for the condition of Ireland.

Death of a Naturalist

All year the flax-dam festered in the heart
Of the townland; green and heavy headed
Flax had rotted there, weighted down by huge sods.
Daily it sweltered in the punishing sun.
Bubbles gargled delicately, bluebottles
Wove a strong gauze of sound around the smell.
There were dragon-flies, spotted butterflies,
But best of all was the warm thick slobber
Of frogspawn that grew like clotted water
In the shade of the banks. Here, every spring
I would fill jampotfuls of the jellied
Specks to range on window-sills at home,
On shelves at school, and wait and watch until
The fattening dots burst into nimble-
Swimming tadpoles. Miss Walls would tell us how
The daddy frog was called a bullfrog
And how he croaked and how the mammy frog
Laid hundreds of little eggs and this was
Frogspawn. You could tell the weather by frogs too
For they were yellow in the sun and brown
In rain.

Then one hot day when fields were rank
With cowdung in the grass the angry frogs
Invaded the flax-dam; I ducked through hedges
To a coarse croaking that I had not heard
Before. The air was thick with a bass chorus.
Right down the dam gross-bellied frogs were cocked
On sods; their loose necks pulsed like sails. Some hopped:
The slap and plop were obscene threats. Some sat
Poised like mud grenades, their blunt heads farting.
I sickened, turned, and ran. The great slime kings
Were gathered there for vengeance and I knew
That if I dipped my hand the spawn would clutch it.

The Barn

Threshed corn lay piled like grit of ivory
Or solid as cement in two-lugged sacks.
The musty dark hoarded an armoury
Of farmyard implements, harness, plough-socks.

The floor was mouse-grey, smooth, chilly concrete.
There were no windows, just two narrow shafts
Of gilded motes, crossing, from air-holes slit
High in each gable. The one door meant no draughts

All summer when the zinc burned like an oven.
A scythe's edge, a clean spade, a pitch-fork's prongs:
Slowly bright objects formed when you went in.
Then you felt cobwebs clogging up your lungs

And scuttled fast into the sunlit yard.
And into nights when bats were on the wing
Over the rafters of sleep, where bright eyes stared
From piles of grain in corners, fierce, unblinking.

The dark gulfed like a roof-space. I was chaff
To be pecked up when birds shot through the air-slits.
I lay face-down to shun the fear above.
The two-lugged sacks moved in like great blind rats.

Punishment

I can feel the tug
of the halter at the nape
of her neck, the wind
on her naked front.

It blows her nipples
to amber beads,
it shakes the frail rigging
of her ribs.

I can see her drowned
body in the bog,
the weighing stone,
the floating rods and boughs.

Under which at first
she was a barked sapling
that is dug up
oak-bone, brain-firkin:

her shaved head
like a stubble of black corn,
her blindfold a soiled bandage,
her noose a ring

to store
the memories of love.
Little adulteress,
before they punished you

you were flaxen-haired,
undernourished, and your
tar-black face was beautiful.
My poor scapegoat,

I almost love you
but would have cast, I know,
the stones of silence.
I am the artful voyeur

of your brain's exposed
and darkened combs,

your muscles' webbing
and all your numbered bones:

I who have stood dumb
when your betraying sisters,
cauled in tar,
wept by the railings,

who would connive
in civilized outrage
yet understand the exact
and tribal, intimate revenge.

Anahorish

My 'place of clear water',
the first hill in the world
where springs washed into
the shiny grass

and darkened cobbles
in the bed of the lane.
Anahorish, soft gradient
of consonant, vowel-meadow,

after-image of lamps
swung through the yards
on winter evenings.
With pails and barrows

those mound-dwellers
go waist-deep in mist
to break the light ice
at wells and dunghills.

The Backward Look

A stagger in air
as if a language
failed, a sleight
of wing.

A snipe's bleat is fleeing
its nesting ground
into dialect,
into variants,

transliterations whirr
on the nature reserves –
little goat of the air,
of the evening,

little goat of the frost.
It is his tail-feathers
drumming elegies
in the slipstream

of wild goose
and yellow bittern
as he corkscrews away
into the vaults

that we live off, his flight
through the sniper's eyrie,
over twilit earthworks
and wall-steads,

disappearing among
gleanings and leavings
in the combs
of a fieldworker's archive.

Aisling[1]

He courted her
With a decadent sweet art
Like the wind's vowel
Blowing through the hazels:

'Are you Diana . . .?'
And was he Actaeon,
His high lament
The stag's exhausted belling?

   1. 'a vision'

Derek Mahon

born 1941

Of all the poets whose work was included in the first edition of this
book, it is Derek Mahon who seems to have made the greatest strides.
His ear is marvellously exact, and his gift for combining music and
meaning is remarkable. It is clear that he has learned a great deal in recent
years from the study of Auden's lyrics.

My Wicked Uncle

It was my first funeral.
Some loss of status as a nephew since
Dictates that I recall
My numbness, my grandfather's hesitance,
My five aunts busy in the hall.

I found him closeted with living souls –
Coffined to perfection in the bedroom.
Death had deprived him of his mustache,
His thick horn-rimmed spectacles,
The easy corners of his salesman dash
(Those things by which I have remembered him)
And sundered him behind unnatural gauze.
His hair was badly parted on the right
As if for Sunday school. That night
I saw my uncle as he really was.

The narrative he dispensed was mostly
Wicked avuncular fantasy –
He went in for waistcoats and haircream.
But something about him
Demanded that you picture the surprise
Of the chairman of the board, when to
'What will you have with your whiskey?' my uncle replies –
'Another whiskey, please.'

Once he was jailed in New York
Twice on the same day –
The crookedest chief steward in the Head Line.
And once (he affected communism)
He brought the whole crew out on strike
In protest at the loss of a day's pay
Crossing the international date line.

They buried him slowly above the sea,
The young Presbyterian minister
Rumpled and windy in the sea air.
A most absorbing ceremony –
Ashes to ashes, dust to dust.
I saw sheep huddled in the long wet grass
Of the golf-course, and the empty freighters
Sailing for ever down Belfast Lough
In a fine rain, their sirens going,
As the gradual graph of my uncle's life and
Times dipped precipitately
Into the bowels of Carnmoney Cemetery.

His teenage kids are growing horns and claws –
More wicked already than ever my uncle was.

An Unborn Child

I have already come to the verge of
Departure. A month or so and
I shall be vacating this familiar room.
Its fabric fits me almost like a glove
While leaving latitude for a free hand.
I begin to put on the manners of the world,
Sensing the splitting light above
My head, where in the silence I lie curled.

Certain mysteries are relayed to me
Through the dark network of my mother's body
While she sits sewing the white shrouds
Of my apotheosis. I know the twisted

Derek Mahon

Kitten that lies there sunning itself
Under the bare bulb, the clouds
Of goldfish mooning around upon the shelf –
In me these data are already vested.

I feel them in my bones – bones which embrace
Nothing, for I am completely egocentric.
The pandemonium of encumbrances
Which will absorb me, mind and senses –
Intricacies of the box and the rat-race –
I imagine only. Though they linger and,
Like fingers, stretch until the knuckles crack,
They cannot dwarf the dimensions of my hand.

I must compose myself in the nerve-centre
Of this metropolis, and not fidget –
Although sometimes at night, when the city
Has gone to sleep, I keep in touch with it
Listening to the warm red water
Racing in the sewers of my mother's body –
Or the moths, soft as eyelids, or the rain
Wiping its wet wings on the window-pane.

And sometimes too, in the small hours of the morning
When the dead filament has ceased to ring –
After the goldfish are dissolved in darkness
And the kitten has gathered itself up into a ball
Between the groceries and the sewing,
I slip the trappings of my harness
To range these hollows in discreet rehearsal
And, battering at the concavity of my caul,

Produce in my mouth the words I WANT TO LIVE –
This is my first protest, and shall be my last.
As I am innocent, everything I do
Or say is couched in the affirmative.
I want to see, hear, touch and taste
These things with which I am to be encumbered.
Perhaps I need not worry – give
Or take a day or two, my days are numbered.

Rage for Order

Somewhere beyond the scorched gable end and the burnt-out
   buses
     there is a poet indulging
       his wretched rage for order –
or not as the case may be; for his
     is a dying art,
    an eddy of semantic scruples
       in an unstructurable sea.

     He is far from his people,
and the fitful glare of his high window is as
       nothing to our scattered glass.

His posture is grandiloquent and deprecating, like this,
     his diet ashes,
his talk of justice and his mother
      the rhetorical device
    of an etiolated emperor –
Nero if you prefer, no mother there.

     '. . . and this in the face of love,
       death, and the wages of the poor . . .'

If he is silent, it is the silence of enforced humility;
     if anxious to be heard, it is the anxiety
       of a last word
when the drums start; for his is a dying art.

Now watch me as I make history. Watch as I tear down
     to build up with a desperate love,
       knowing it cannot be
    long now till I have need of his
       desperate ironies.

In the Aran Islands

He is earthed to his girl, one hand fastened
In hers, and with his free hand listens,
An earphone, to his own rendition,

Singing the darkness into the light.
I close the pub door gently and step out
Into the yard, and the song goes out
And a gull creaks off from the corrugated
Iron roof of an outhouse, over the ocean,
Circling now with a hoarse inchoate
Screaming the boned fields of its vision.
God, that was the way to do it,
Hand-clasping, echo-prolonging poet!

Scorched with a fearful admiration
Walking over the nacreous sand,
I dream myself to that tradition,
Fifty winters off the land –
One hand to an ear for the vibration,
The far wires, the reverberation
Down light-years of the imagination
And, in the other hand, your hand.

The long glow leaps from the dark soil, however –
No marshlight holds a candle to this.
Unearthly still in its white weather
A crack-voiced rock-marauder, scavenger, fierce
Friend to no slant fields or the sea either,
Folds back over the forming waters.

Derry Morning

The mist clears and the cavities
Glow black in the rubbled city's
Broken mouth. An early crone,
Muse of a fitful revolution
Wasted by the fray, she sees
Her *aisling* falter in the breeze,
Her oak-grove vision hesitate
By empty wharf and city gate.

Here it began, and here at least
If fades into the finite past
Or seems to: clattering shadows whop

Mechanically over pub and shop.
A strangely pastoral silence rules
The shining roofs and murmuring schools;
For this is how the centuries work –
Two steps forward, one step back.

Hard to believe this tranquil place,
Its desolation almost peace,
Was recently a boom-town wild
With expectation, each unscheduled
Incident a measurable
Tremor on the Richter Scale
Of world events, each vibrant scene
Translated to the drizzling screen.

What of the change envisioned here,
The quantum leap from fear to fire?
Smoke from a thousand chimneys strains
One way beneath the returning rains
That shroud the bomb-sites, while the fog
Of time receives the ideologue.
A Russian freighter bound for home
Mourns to the city in its gloom.

The Woods

Two years we spent
down there, in a quaint
outbuilding bright with recent paint.

A green retreat,
secluded and sedate,
part of a once great estate,

it watched our old
bone-shaker as it growled
with guests and groceries through heat and cold,

and heard you tocsin
meal-times with a spoon
while I sat working in the sun.

Derek Mahon

Above the yard
an old clock had expired
the night Lenin arrived in Petrograd.

Bourbons and Romanovs
had removed their gloves
in the drawing-rooms and alcoves

of the manor house;
but these illustrious
ghosts never imposed on us.

Enough that the pond
steamed, the apples ripened,
the conkers on the gravel opened.

Ragwort and hemlock,
cinquefoil and ladysmock
throve in the shadows at the back;

beneath the trees
foxgloves and wood-anemones
looked up with tearful metamorphic eyes.

We woke the rooks
on narrow, winding walks
familiar from the story books,

or visited
a disused garden shed
where gas-masks from the war decayed;

and we knew peace
splintering the thin ice
on the bath-tub drinking-trough for cows.

But how could we
survive indefinitely
so far from the city and the sea?

Finding, at last,
too creamy for our taste
the fat profusion of that feast,

we travelled on
to doubt and speculation,
our birthright and our proper portion.

Another light
than ours convenes the mute
attention of those woods tonight –

while we, released
from that pale paradise,
ponder the darkness in another place.

MICHAEL LONGLEY

born 1939

Michael Longley sees himself as a 'conservative' poet, and has stated as much in one of his poems. In particular, his work shows the effect of a careful study of the seventeenth-century Metaphysicals. But there is also a strangeness which is unlike theirs – a feeling that the world is being seen from a slightly skewed perspective. This makes Longley's best work memorable. It is perhaps most striking of all when it also has roots in experiences most people eventually share, such as the death of parents.

In Memoriam

My father, let no similes eclipse
Where crosses like some forest simplified
Sink roots into my mind; the slow sands
Of your history delay till through your eyes
I read you like a book. Before you died,
Re-enlisting with all the broken soldiers
You bent beneath your rucksack, near collapse,
In anecdote rehearsed and summarized
These words I write in memory. Let yours
And other heartbreaks play into my hands.

Now I see in close-up, in my mind's eye,
The cracked and splintered dead for pity's sake
Each dismal evening predecease the sun,
You, looking death and nightmare in the face
With your kilt, harmonica and gun,
Grow older in a flash, but none the wiser
(Who, following the wrong queue at The Palace,
Have joined the London Scottish by mistake),
Your nineteen years uncertain if and why
Belgium put the kibosh on the Kaiser.

Between the corpses and the soup canteens
You swooned away, watching your future spill.

But, as it was, your proper funeral urn
Had mercifully smashed to smithereens,
To shrapnel shards that sliced your testicle.
That instant I, your most unlikely son,
In No Man's Land was surely left for dead,
Blotted out from your far horizon.
As your voice now is locked inside my head,
I yet was held secure, waiting my turn.

Finally, that lousy war was over.
Stranded in France and in need of proof
You hunted down experimental lovers,
Persuading chorus girls and countesses:
This, father, the last confidence you spoke.
In my twentieth year your old wounds woke
As cancer. Lodging under the same roof
Death was a visitor who hung about,
Strewing the house with pills and bandages,
Till he chose to put your spirit out.

Though they overslept the sequence of events
Which ended with the ambulance outside,
You lingering in the hall, your bowels on fire,
Tears in your eyes, and all your medals spent,
I summon girls who packed at last and went
Underground with you. Their souls again on hire,
Now those lost wives as recreated brides
Take shape before me, materialize.
On the verge of light and happy legend
They lift their skirts like blinds across your eyes.

Ash Keys

Ghosts of hedgers and ditchers,
The ash trees rattling keys
Above tangles of hawthorn
And bramble, alder and gorse,

Would keep me from pacing
Commonage, long perspectives

357

And conversations, a field
That touches the horizon.

I am herding cattle there
As a boy, as the old man
Following in his footsteps
Who begins the task again,

As though there'd never been
In some interim or hollow
Wives and children, milk
And buttermilk, market days.

Far from the perimeter
Of watercress and berries,
In the middle of the field
I stand talking to myself,

While the ash keys scatter
And the gates creak open
And the barbed wire rusts
To hay-ropes strung with thorns.

The Third Light

The sexton is opening up the grave,
Lining with mossy cushions and couch grass
This shaft of light, entrance to the earth
Where I kneel to marry you again,
My elbows in darkness as I explore
From my draughty attic your last bedroom.
Then I vanish into the roof space.

I have handed over to him your pain
And your preference for Cyprus sherry,
Your spry quotations from the *Daily Mail*
With its crossword solved in ink, your limp
And pills, your scatter of cigarette butts
And last-minute humorous spring-cleaning
Of a corner of a shelf in his cupboard.

You spent his medals like a currency,
Always refusing the third light, afraid
Of the snipers who would extinguish it.
Waiting to scramble hand in hand with him
Out of the shell hole, did you imagine
A Woodbine passing to and fro, a face
That stabilizes like a smoke ring?

PAUL MULDOON

born 1951

Paul Muldoon belongs to a younger generation than that of Seamus
Heaney, Derek Mahon and Michael Longley, and the difference in age
is marked by a difference in tone. His poems are highly polished but also
aggressive – he uses his skills with words and metre to spring surprises
on the reader, not always pleasant ones. There is also, as other critics
have pointed out, a strange and rather eerie feeling of distance in his
work, of the poet going away suddenly and leaving behind him a
question rather than a solution, as the farmer Brownlee does in the
beautiful lyric 'Why Brownlee Left'.

Why Brownlee Left

Why Brownlee left, and where he went,
Is a mystery even now.
For if a man should have been content
It was him; two acres of barley.
One of potatoes, four bullocks,
A milker, a slated farmhouse.
He was last seen going out to plough
On a March morning, bright and early.

By noon Brownlee was famous;
They had found all abandoned, with
The last rig unbroken, his pair of black
Horses, like man and wife,
Shifting their weight from foot to
Foot, and gazing into the future.

Anseo

When the Master was calling the roll
At the primary school in Collegelands,

You were meant to call back *Anseo*
And raise your hand
As your name occurred.
Anseo, meaning here, here and now,
All present and correct,
Was the first word of Irish I spoke.
The last name on the ledger
Belonged to Joseph Mary Plunkett Ward
And was followed, as often as not,
By silence, knowing looks,
A nod and a wink, the Master's droll
'And where's our little Ward-of-court?'

I remember the first time he came back
The Master had sent him out
Along the hedges
To weigh up for himself and cut
A stick with which he would be beaten.
After a while, nothing was spoken;
He would arrive as a matter of course
With an ash-plant, a salley-rod.
Or, finally, the hazel-wand
He had whittled down to a whip-lash,
Its twist of red and yellow lacquers
Sanded and polished,
And altogether so delicately wrought
That he had engraved his initials on it.

I last met Joseph Mary Plunkett Ward
In a pub just over the Irish border.
He was living in the open,
In a secret camp
On the other side of the mountain.
He was fighting for Ireland,
Making things happen.
And he told me, Joe Ward,
Of how he had risen through the ranks
To Quartermaster, Commandant:
How every morning at parade
His volunteers would call back *Anseo*
And raise their hands
As their names occurred.

Glanders

When you happened to sprain your wrist or ankle
you made your way to the local shaman,
if 'shaman' is the word for Larry Toal,
who was so at ease with himself, so tranquil,

a cloud of smoke would graze on his thatch
like the cow in the cautionary tale,
while a tether of smoke curled down his chimney
and the end of the tether was attached

to Larry's ankle or to Larry's wrist.
He would conjure up a poultice of soot and spit
and flannel-talk, how he had a soft spot

for the mud of Flanders,
how he came within that of the cure for glanders
from a Suffolkman who suddenly went west.

The Frog

Comes to mind as another small upheaval
amongst the rubble.
His eye matches exactly the bubble
in my spirit-level.
I set aside hammer and chisel
and take him on the trowel.

The entire population of Ireland
springs from a pair left to stand
overnight in a pond
in the gardens of Trinity College,
two bottles of wine left there to chill
after the Act of Union.

There is, surely, in this story
a moral. A moral for our times.
What if I put him to my head
and squeezed it out of him,
like the juice of freshly squeezed limes,
or a lemon sorbet?

TOM PAULIN

born 1949

Tom Paulin was not born in Northern Ireland, but he was brought up there. Though he now no longer lives there its problems seem to haunt him, and this is the reason why I have placed his work in this section. 'To the Linen Hall', which is one of his most impressive poems, seems to be not merely a comment on Ireland's troubles, but a prescription for curing them through a change of attitudes.

Under Creon

Rhododendrons growing wild below a mountain
and no long high wall or trees either;
a humped road, bone-dry, with no one –
passing one lough and then another
where water-lilies glazed, primed like traps.

A neapish hour, I searched out gaps
in that imperial shrub: a free voice sang
dissenting green, and syllables spoke
holm oaks by a salt shore, their dark tangs
glistening like Nisus in a night attack.

The daylight gods were never in this place
and I had pressed beyond my usual dusk
to find a cadence for the dead: McCracken,
Hope, the northern starlight, a death mask
and the levelled grave that Biggar traced;

like an epic arming in an olive grove
this was a stringent grief and a form of love.
Maybe one day I'll get the hang of it
and find joy, not justice, in a snapped connection,
that Jacobin oath on the black mountain.

Tom Paulin

To the Linen Hall

After extremity
art turns social
and it's more than fashion
to voice the word *we*.
The epic yawp
hangs like an echo
of the big bang,
though now we tell children
to shun that original –
primal light, soaked green,
the slob mud
and a salt tang.
There is a ban
on philosophies of blood,
a terse demand
for arts and skills
to be understood,
and a common flow
into the new academy
which rules with a chill,
strenuous and insistent,
enforced formality.
Here we have a form
and a control
that is our own,
and on the stone steps
of that eighteenth-century,
reasoned library
we catch the classic spore
of Gibbon and new *ceps*,
the busts and statues
that might be stored
under the squares.
Our shaping brightness
is a style and discipline
that finds its tongue
in the woody desk-dawns
of fretting scholars

who pray, invisibly,
to taste the true vine
and hum gently
in holy sweetness.

MEDBH MCGUCKIAN

born 1950

More romantic in tone than her male colleagues, more wilful also in the way she constructs her poems, Medbh McGuckian seems deliberately to have turned her back on the political preoccupations which underlie so much verse from Northern Ireland, even when these preoccupations are not directly expressed. She is clearly the least mature of the writers included in this section, and it will be interesting to see how her work develops.

The Aphrodisiac

She gave it out as if it were
A marriage or a birth, some other
Interesting family event, that she
Had finished sleeping with him, that
Her lover was her friend. It was his heart
She wanted, the bright key to his study,
Not the menacings of love. So he is
Banished to his estates, to live
Like a man in a glasshouse; she has taken to
A little cap of fine white lace
In the mornings, feeds her baby
In a garden you could visit blindfold
For its scent alone:
                              But though a ray of grace
Has fallen, all her books seem as frumpish
As the last year's gambling game, when she
Would dress in pink taffeta, and drive
A blue phaeton, or in blue, and drive
A pink one, with her black hair supported
By a diamond comb, floating about
Without panniers. How his most
Caressing look, his husky whisper suffocates her,
This almost perfect power of knowing

More than a kept woman. The between-maid
Tells me this is not the only secret staircase.
Rumour has it she's taken to rouge again.

The Sun-Trap

Our lean-to greenhouse lends
Quite a sun-trap in the mornings,
Where I page you from this sickly Irish weather.
And the hygroscope says 'orchid',
Though in winter it stays blue,
Unless placed between the window and the storm-sash.

I am touched by even the strange gesture
Of rain stopping, your penetration
Of my mask of 'bon viveur', my crested notepaper,
My lined envelopes. From your last letter
I construed at least the word
For kisses, if not quite a kindred spirit.

But my night has been chequered
By toothache, and your reference
To the magically fertile German girl
Who sleeps in the bunk above you
At the workcamp. She seems
To me quite flirtatious

Though you say she's the sort of girl
You'd rather have as a daughter –
Which reminds me of my cousin once-removed,
And the near-tragedy
Of our long pony-trekking weekend . . .
You find it odd I should resurrect him

Just when I seemed
To be losing the urge to discuss him?
My wholesome curiosity in corpses?
Miles from anywhere, if you could learn
From other people's letters to me,
We might talk like human beings are supposed to.

Medbh McGuckian

Gentians

In my alpine house, the slavery I pay
My wilful gentians! exploring all their pleats
And tucks as though they had something precious
Deep inside, that beard of camel-hair
In the throat. I watch them
Ease their heads so slowly
Through their thumbhole necklines, till they sit
Like tailors in their earth shoes,
Their watery husbands' knots. No insects
Visit them, nor do their ovaries swell,
Yet every night in Tibet their seeds
Are membraned by the snow, their roots
Are bathed by the passage of melt-water,
They tease like sullen spinsters
The dewfall of summer limes.

PART TWELVE: UNIVERSITY WITS

The title of this final section is necessarily something of a catch-all. Though its degree of factual accuracy, as applied to the eight poets included here, is of course variable, it does seem to me that it helps to pinpoint things they have in common – though not all of them share all the qualities I list. They are sophisticated and well-educated, but tend to wear these characteristics lightly. They are sceptical. They are interested in witty and surprising verbal effects. Though capable of a kind of moral indignation which marks them as 'liberals' in a political sense, they are cautious – even gingerly so – in their approach to the modernist tradition. In terms of the current politics of the British literary world, most of them rank as insiders rather than outsiders. Essentially their work seems to me to illustrate the extreme tenacity of the poetic ideals originally set up by the Movement, though they have succeeded in shedding the Movement's typical dourness. They are not merely individually skilful, but typical of their country and their time – in their real virtues and occasional limitations.

JOHN FULLER

born 1937

John Fuller appeared in the first edition of this anthology among the post-Movement writers. Indeed, I said of him then that he seemed 'to represent the second generation of the Movement almost perfectly'. Since then he has grown considerably in stature, chiefly because he has discovered more and more about the real nature of his own gift. Essentially he is a writer who is at his best and most original when saying serious things in a light way. His concern for technical elegance and his ruthless skill in pricking all forms of poetic pretentiousness have had a considerable effect on poets of his own age or younger than himself. Indeed, it is not going too far to describe him as a *chef d'école*.

The Cook's Lesson

When the King at last could not manage an erection,
The tables were wiped down and a banquet prepared.
The Cook was a renegade, a master of innuendo,
And was later hanged for some imaginary subversion,
Found laughing in the quarter of the filthy poor.
This, had we known it, was to be his last banquet,
And as such was fittingly dissident and experimental.
Often he had confided to us the tenets of his craft,
How a true artist is obsessed with the nature of his material,
And must make evident the process of creation in preference
To the predictable appearance of the finished product.
The charcoal-burners were lit, the porcelain laid
And the simple broths prepared in which the meal was enacted,
For this was a living meal, a biological history of food.
I cannot remember much. We sweated and fainted and were
    revived
With fragrant towels. We ate furiously and were rewarded
With knowledge of a kind we did not even recognize.
Spawn in the luke gruel divided, gilled and finned,
Swam down flowered channels to the brink of oil

And fell to the plate. Before our eyes
The litter spurted into the fire, picked out by tongs,
Eggs hatched into the soup, embryos bled,
Seeds sprouted in the spoon. As I said, we ate fast,
Far back into life, eating fast into life.
Now I understand that food is never really dead:
Frilled and forked, towered, dusted, sliced,
In mimic aspic or dispersed in sauces,
Food is something that will not willingly lie down.
The bland liquids slid over our tongues as
Heartbeats under crusts, mouthfuls of feathers.

Valentine

The things about you I appreciate
    May seem indelicate:
I'd like to find you in the shower
And chase the soap for half an hour.
I'd like to have you in my power
    And see your eyes dilate.
I'd like to have your back to scour
And other parts to lubricate.
Sometimes I feel it is my fate
To chase you screaming up a tower
    Or make you cower
By asking you to differentiate
    Nietzsche from Schopenhauer.
I'd like successfully to guess your weight
    And win you at a fête.
I'd like to offer you a flower.

I like the hair upon your shoulders,
Falling like water over boulders.
I like the shoulders, too: they are essential.
Your collar-bones have great potential
(I'd like all your particulars in folders
    Marked *Confidential*).

I like your cheeks, I like your nose,
I like the way your lips disclose

The neat arrangement of your teeth
(Half above and half beneath)
    In rows.

I like your eyes, I like their fringes.
The way they focus on me gives me twinges.
Your upper arms drive me berserk.
I like the way your elbows work,
    On hinges.

I like your wrists, I like your glands,
I like the fingers on your hands.
I'd like to teach them how to count,
And certain things we might exchange.
Something familiar for something strange.
I'd like to give you just the right amount
    And get some change.

I like it when you tilt your cheek up.
I like the way you nod and hold a teacup.
I like your legs when you unwind them.
Even in trousers I don't mind them.
I like each softly-moulded kneecap.
I like the little crease behind them.
I'd always know, without a recap,
    Where to find them.

I like the sculpture of your ears.
I like the way your profile disappears
Whenever you decide to turn and face me.
I'd like to cross two hemispheres
    And have you chase me.
I'd like to smuggle you across frontiers
Or sail with you at night into Tangiers.
    I'd like you to embrace me.

I'd like to see you ironing your skirt
    And cancelling other dates.
I'd like to button up your shirt.
I like the way your chest inflates.
I'd like to soothe you when you're hurt
Or frightened senseless by invert-
    ebrates.

I'd like you even if you were malign
And had a yen for sudden homicide.
I'd let you put insecticide
　　　Into my wine.
I'd even like you if you were the Bride
　　　Of Frankenstein
Or something ghoulish out of Mamoulian's
·　*Jekyll and Hyde*.
I'd even like you as my Julian
Of Norwich or Cathleen ni Houlihan.
　　　How melodramatic
If you were something muttering in attics
Like Mrs Rochester or a student of Boolean
　　　Mathematics.

You are the end of self-abuse.
You are the eternal feminine.
I'd like to find a good excuse
To call on you and find you in.
I'd like to put my hand beneath your chin,
　　　And see you grin.
I'd like to taste your Charlotte Russe,
I'd like to feel my lips upon your skin,
I'd like to make you reproduce.

I'd like you in my confidence.
I'd like to be your second look.
I'd like to let you try the French Defence
　　　And mate you with my rook.
I'd like to be your preference
　　　And hence
I'd like to be around when you unhook.
I'd like to be your only audience,
The final name in your appointment book,
　　　Your future tense.

Being

Being not elsewhere now
I wouldn't want to be
    Other than here,
With wine still in the glass,
Watching the year pass.

Being not yet asleep,
The fire glowing steady
    And furred with ash,
I take what was meant,
Receive what was sent.

Being is a wish,
Tilting the final inch
    Against the glow,
That being, once removed,
Need never more be proved.

Being, though, as cold
As it surely will be,
    Proof will be pointless:
Better to treat with caution
The planetary portion.

JAMES FENTON

born 1949

James Fenton has built up a remarkably large reputation on the strength of a very small output. His total output of verse, between 1968 and 1983, amounts to just over 100 pages. Furthermore, some of the poetry is marginal – the cut-up, found materials of the early series of 'Exempla' – or falls into the category of light verse, like the deliciously skilful 'Letter to John Fuller', with its stinging attack on A. Alvarez and the 'Suicide School':

> Should we take hemlock? Too abstruse.
> A punch of deadly nightshade juice?
> A dressing-gown cord for a noose?
>   Strychnine-soaked spats?
> Alas! Warfarin is no more use
>   For poets or rats.

The weightier part of his oeuvre is very various – its central point of reference seems to be the poetry of Auden. Of the poems chosen here 'Dead Soldiers' prompts a reference to Auden's contribution to *Journey to a War*, and 'Nothing' seems to me the equal of Auden's best lyrics.

Dead Soldiers

When His Excellency Prince Norodom Chantaraingsey
Invited me to lunch on the battlefield
I was glad of my white suit for the first time that day.
They lived well, the mad Norodoms, they had style.
The brandy and the soda arrived in crates.
Bricks of ice, tied around with raffia,
Dripped from the orderlies' handlebars.

And I remember the dazzling tablecloth
As the APCs fanned out along the road,
The dishes piled high with frogs' legs,
Pregnant turtles, their eggs boiled in the carapace,
Marsh irises in fish sauce
And inflorescence of a banana salad.

On every bottle, Napoleon Bonaparte
Pleaded for the authenticity of the spirit.
They called the empties Dead Soldiers
And rejoiced to see them pile up at our feet.

Each diner was attended by one of the other ranks
Whirling a table-napkin to keep off the flies.
It was like eating between rows of morris dancers –
Only they didn't kick.

On my left sat the prince;
On my right, his drunken aide.
The frogs' thighs leapt into the sad purple face
Like fish to the sound of a Chinese flute.
I wanted to talk to the prince. I wish now
I had collared his aide, who was Saloth Sar's brother.
We treated him as the club bore. He was always
Boasting of his connections, boasting with a head-shake
Or by pronouncing of some doubtful phrase.
And well might he boast. Saloth Sar, for instance,
Was Pol Pot's real name. The APCs
Fired into the sugar palms but met no resistance.

In a diary, I refer to Pol Pot's brother as the Jockey Cap.
A few weeks later, I find him 'in good form
And very skeptical about Chantaraingsey.'
'But one eats well there,' I remark.
'So one should,' says the Jockey Cap:
'The tiger always eats well,
It eats the raw flesh of the deer,
And Chantaraingsey was born in the year of the tiger.
So, did they show you the things they do
With the young refugee girls?'

And he tells me how he will one day give me the gen.
He will tell me how the prince financed the casino
And how the casino brought Lon Nol to power.
He will tell me this.
He will tell me all these things.
All I must do is drink and listen.

In those days, I thought that when the game was up
The prince would be far, far away –
In a limestone faubourg, on the promenade at Nice,

Reduced in circumstances but well enough provided for.
In Paris, he would hardly require his private army.
The Jockey Cap might suffice for café warfare,
And matchboxes for APCs

But we were always wrong in these predictions.
It was family war. Whatever happened,
The principals were obliged to attend its issue.
A few were cajoled into leaving, a few were expelled,
And there were villains enough, but none of them
Slipped away with the swag.

For the prince was fighting Sihanouk, his nephew,
And the Jockey Cap was ranged against his brother
Of whom I remember nothing more
Than an obscure reputation for virtue.
I have been told that the prince is still fighting
Somewhere in the Cardamoms or the Elephant Mountains.
But I doubt that the Jockey Cap would have survived his good
    connections.
I think the lunches would have done for him –
Either the lunches or the dead soldiers.

Nothing

I take a jewel from a junk-shop tray
And wish I had a love to buy it for.
Nothing I choose will make you turn my way.
Nothing I give will make you love me more.

I know that I've embarrassed you too long
And I'm ashamed to linger at your door.
Whatever I embark on will be wrong.
Nothing I do will make you love me more.

I cannot work. I cannot read or write.
How can I frame a letter to implore.
Eloquence is a lie. The truth is trite.
Nothing I say will make you love me more.

So I replace the jewel in the tray
And laughingly pretend I'm far too poor.
Nothing I give, nothing I do or say,
Nothing I am will make you love me more.

The Killer Snails

The killer snails
Have slung their silver trails
Along the doormat, out across the lawn,
Under the bushes
Where the alarming thrushes
Give night its notice, making way for dawn,
And the obliging lizards drop their tails.

On webs of dew
The spiders stir their pots of glue
And drag their quartered victims to the shade.
Soaked in their rugs
Of grass and moss the slugs
Wind up another night of sluggish trade
And young ingredients get into a stew.

The sorrel bends.
The path fades out but never ends
Where brambles clutch and bracken wipes your feet.
It goes in rings.
Its mind's on other things.
Its way and its intentions never meet.
Meetings of friends?
It gives no undertaking. It depends.

CRAIG RAINE

born 1944

James Fenton's chief rival as the best-known poet of his particular generation, Craig Raine, is also, as Fenton isn't, the leader of a school, the so-called Martians, who take their name from the title poem of his second collection of verse, 'A Martian Sends a Postcard Home'. The poem, which is included here, exemplifies his characteristic poetic method – the use of extravagantly 'conceited' metaphors which make the familiar seem strange and alienated. Perhaps the thing Craig Raine hasn't been given sufficient credit for, even by his admirers, is a plangent sense of melancholy and loss. It appears in another poem chosen here, 'The Onion, Memory'.

A Martian Sends a Postcard Home

Caxtons are mechanical birds with many wings
and some are treasured for their markings –

they cause the eyes to melt
or the body to shriek without pain.

I have never seen one fly, but
sometimes they perch on the hand.

Mist is when the sky is tired of flight
and rests its soft machine on ground:

then the world is dim and bookish
like engravings under tissue paper.

Rain is when the earth is television.
It has the property of making colours darker.

Model T is a room with the lock inside –
a key is turned to free the world

for movement, so quick there is a film
to watch for anything missed.

But time is tied to the wrist
or kept in a box, ticking with impatience.

In homes, a haunted apparatus sleeps,
that snores when you pick it up.

If the ghost cries, they carry it
to their lips and soothe it to sleep

with sounds. And yet, they wake it up
deliberately, by tickling with a finger.

Only the young are allowed to suffer
openly. Adults go to a punishment room

with water but nothing to eat.
They lock the door and suffer the noises

alone. No one is exempt
and everyone's pain has a different smell.

At night, when all the colours die,
they hide in pairs

and read about themselves –
in colour, with their eyelids shut.

Shallots

Seven striped shallots are giving
a silent recital on their sitars

and the magnolia dances motionless,
like a deity with many arms. Bells

bloom on her upturned finger tips.
We inhale the grass

and listen with our eyes
to the long, slow *raga* of summer

bending the air with vibrato . . .
Stoned flowers stare at the sun,

the baby contemplates her navel,
wise beyond words,

the guru of a perfumed garden.
I watch a tabla in your neck

perform its intricate rhythm,
and know that images provide

a kind of sustenance,
alms for every beggared sense –

each an avatar of generosity,
the dustbins bulge like vol-au-vents.

The Onion, Memory

Divorced, but friends again at last,
we walk old ground together
in bright blue uncomplicated weather.
We laugh and pause
to hack to bits these tiny dinosaurs,
prehistoric, crenellated, cast
between the tractor ruts in mud.

On the green, a junior Douglas Fairbanks,
swinging on the chestnut's unlit chandelier,
defies the corporation spears –
a single rank around the bole,
rusty with blood.
Green, tacky phalluses curve up, romance.
A gust – the old flag blazes on its pole.

In the village bakery
the pasty babies pass
from milky slump to crusty cadaver,
from crib to coffin – without palaver.
All's over in a flash,
too silently . . .

Tonight the arum lilies fold
back napkins monogrammed in gold,
crisp and laundered fresh.
Those crustaceous gladioli, on the sly,
reveal the crimson flower-flesh
inside their emerald armour plate.
The uncooked herrings blink a tearful eye.

The candles palpitate.
The Oistrakhs bow and scrape
in evening dress, on Emi-tape.

Outside the trees are bending over backwards
to please the wind: the shining sword
grass flattens on its belly.
The white-thorn's frillies offer no resistance.
In the fridge, a heart-shaped jelly
strives to keep a sense of balance.

I slice up the onions. You sew up a dress.
This is the quiet echo – flesh –
white muscle on white muscle,
intimately folded skin,
finished with a satin rustle.
One button only to undo, sewn up with shabby thread.
It is the onion, memory,
that makes me cry.

Because there's everything and nothing to be said,
the clock with hands held up before its face,
stammers softly on, trying to complete a phrase –
while we, together and apart,
repeat unfinished gestures got by heart.

And afterwards, I blunder with the washing on the line –
headless torsos, faceless lovers, friends of mine.

ANDREW MOTION

born 1952

Very active as an editor – first running *Poetry Review* and then the poetry list at Chatto and Windus – Andrew Motion is an influential figure in British verse. His own poetry shows a fascination with narrative and narrative techniques, and an increasing tendency to use a mask or persona rather than to write in the first person, as he did in the poem 'Leaving Belfast', which makes an interesting comparison with the work of the Irish writers based in that city.

Leaving Belfast
for Craig Raine

Driving at dusk on the steep road
north to the airport, 'Look back,'
you say, 'The finest view of Belfast,'
and point, proud of your choice to stay.

How clear the rows of streetlamps show
which way we came. I trace them slope
by slope through marshlands slipping down
to lanes, and find the roofs again,

their stern geographies of punishment
and love where silence deepens under rain.
Each sudden gust of light explains itself
as flames, but neither they, nor even

bombs redoubled on the hills tonight
can quite include me in their fear.
What does remains invisible, is lost
in curt societies whose deaths become

revenge by morning, and whose homes
are nothing more than all they pity most.
I watch the moon above them, filling rooms
with shadow politics, though whether

voices there pronounce me an intruder,
traitor, or a friend, I leave them now
as much a stranger as I came, and turn
to listen in the twilight for their griefs,

but hear instead the promise of conclusion
fading fast towards me through these miles
of stubborn gorse, until it disappears
at last in darkness, out beyond the coast.

A Dying Race

The less I visit, the more I think
myself back to your elegant house
I grew up in. The drive uncurled
through swaying chestnuts discovers
it standing four square, white-
washed unnaturally clear,
as if it were shown me by lightning.

It's always the place I see,
not you. You're somewhere outside,
waving goodbye where I left you
a decade ago. I've even lost sight
of losing you now; all I can find
are the mossy steps you stood on
– a visible loneliness.

I'm living four counties away, and still
I think of your driving south each night
to the ward where your wife
is living. How long will it last?
You've made the journey six years
already, taking comparative happinesses
like a present, to please her.

I can remember the fields you pass,
the derelict pill-boxes squatting
in shining plough. If I was still there,
watching your hand push back
the hair from her desperate face,

I might have discovered by now the way
love looks, its harrowing clarity.

Writing

After what felt like a lifetime of rent
I bought somewhere my own. But at once,
in less than a week, he was writing:
Dear Madam, I hope you won't mind –

we met when I sold you the house.
It was mine. I gave you the china tea.
I showed you the room where you told me
yes, you could write in that room.

In the home I have now they are cruel.
There are traitors – and spies. I am hoping
my doctor is kind, but what is he doing
to bring me my wife, or give me her news?

Please, if this reaches you, tell her. Say –
if a visit is difficult, letters are fine.
Think of me reading this through at my desk,
throwing it down on my typewriter, frowning,

and wondering was this the room where she died?
Then think of my whisper to answer him:
Dearest heart. Forgive me. I'm ill
and dictating this. But I long for you always,

and when I'm recovered, I'll visit you.
Lazily spinning the phrases out, and finally
writing them, telling myself it was
kindness, and might even turn into love.

Peter Scupham

born 1933

Peter Scupham is considerably older than most of the other writers included in this section, but did not publish his first collection of verse until 1972, which makes him in that sense a member of the younger generation of poets. He is a 'wit' in the sense that he is a learned writer who is also playful. 'I feel with Auden,' he once wrote, 'that poetry is a game of knowledge; and I enjoy the complexity of rules that make the game worth playing.' He also added that 'the game should be played for someone or something else's sake; not for the poet's'. The writers for whom he feels an affinity are James Reeves, Norman Cameron, Louis MacNeice, Richard Wilbur and John Crowe Ransom.

Summer Palaces

How shall we build our summer palaces?
Will the girls bring us sherbet, and our gardens
Brown to the filigree of Chinese lanterns?

The Emperor speaks in a long robe of thunder,
Bruising us cloudily; his combs of rain
Dance out a dance of more than seven veils.

Islands of bird-music; storm-voices dwindle.
Across the blue, cirrus and alto-cirrus
Draw out an awning for our shade pavilion.

Swallows will sew our flying tents together.
We live as nomads, pitching idle camp
Under the white sheets blowing down the line,

Or swing on ropes to somersaults of grass.
The hasps creak upon our airy gallows,
Roofed by light, floored by a crush of earth.

The strong leaves curtain us; we know each scent,
The deep breaths taken behind swaying curtains.
We have become the citizens of green.

Our walls grow firm in fruit and knots of seed.
A dandelion clock rounds out the hour,
Blowing our time away in feathered segments.

The night lies warm upon a wall of shadows.
We lie as naked in our drifting beds
As the close moon, staining us with silver.

Die Ahnherren

Close-lipped, severe, well-fed, Herr Doktor stares
Bleakly across a hundred or so years,
Self-centred in gilt-edged security:
A Lutheran Pastor in his gown and bands,
Partnered by mob-capped wife, pallid and angular.

The Old Ones – two awkward pieces which must fit
A complex tribal jigsaw. Some second cousin
Or genealogic frowst might, perhaps, place them.
We have no skill in family connections.
Disgraced, their custom is to face the wall.

Naming is primal. Features without vocables
Are monstrous as long men without their shadows,
And though names muster to encumber rolls,
Old churchyards, deeds, out-of-date almanacks,
No syllables we try give back identity.

Their loss is irremediable. A teasing flotsam,
Improvidently lacking who, when, where,
Riddles no serious person cares to solve,
They may, with luck, become their time's exemplars:
Minor and tongue-tied ghosts, dwellers in limbo.

To dealers, even such continuance dubious.
Gloomy, unsaleable. By this prognosis
Their stolid self-appraisal stands condemned;
Unlucky ones who chose a black profession,
A dignity which shrouds them to decay.

DAVID SWEETMAN

born 1943

David Sweetman's work recalls that of the poets of the 1930s, but also, with its relish for exoticism, that of the writers who gathered in Cairo and Alexandria during the Second World War. Like David Constantine he exemplifies a new, if subdued, romanticism which has again begun to make itself felt in British verse.

Saidi's Wife

Often Africa seemed quite empty,
the shadows of walls lay on dust roads
sharp and vacant like Nubian pyramids.

Stepping through them, Saidi's wife
would slowly cross our compound
fruit punctuating her scrubbed tray,
adjusting and readjusting the *kanga*
that half-veiled her face, blushing feet
slapping the earth. Then suddenly
a glimpse of nipple,
black as a missionary's biretta.

One day there was gunfire,
no more than the spit and cackle of ice
dashed with strong spirits,
though less than a mile away people died.
As usual Saidi's family worked their fields
so that at any hour the village seemed forgotten,
the thatched huts lying as still as shells
clustered in an abandoned rockpool.

When night came, the palm tree's rotor-blades
whipped up a wind, bamboo telescopes searched
out the stars, and always an electric voice sang
loud but unseen, somewhere in the listening bush.

David Sweetman

Chairpersons

The carnival freaks do it their way:
to the legless man the chairback is a rung
on the ladder he needs to circle the globe,

the Fat Lady covers its insult with a sigh
while for Tom Thumb's Bride it's Carnegie Hall
when, after a deep bow, the Barker steps off.

He alone ignores what they take to be a throne
or a machine, a comment even. Foolishly
he thinks a chair is only a tree sitting down.

DAVID CONSTANTINE

born 1944

The knowledge that David Constantine is a university teacher of
German naturally prompts the reader to look for influences from this
language in his poetry. These exist, but seem to come more from the
literature of the nineteenth century (poets such as Hölderlin) than they
do from anything contemporary. He also seems to take an occasional
glance at Robert Graves. In general, his poetry, like that of David Sweet-
man, hints at a return to romanticism in British verse.

'You are distant, you are already leaving'

You are distant, you are already leaving
You will have seemed here only between trains
And we are met here in the time of waiting
And what you last want is our eyes on you.

We shall have said nothing, we shall have done
Nothing in all that meantime there will
Have been not one gift pleasing us
You will have looked away and only behind
The pane of glass taking your seat with strangers
Being conveyed from here and when there is
No stay of parting you will smile perhaps
And give your face then the small mercy of weeping.

Chronicle

Scabby with salt the shipwreck wondering
Upon what shore, among what manner of savages
He was tossed up, found himself received
With a courtesy near to veneration. Lies
Were ready on his tongue but he found
His rescuers, his hosts, discreet or indifferent

And asking nothing. Only once he was bathed
And dressed in clothes held by for the occasion
There was a pause, a silence, and his fear returned
Imagining sacrifice. Solemnly, deferring,
They led him into the church. The congregation
Was the island's marriageable girls. He must choose,
They said, one for his bride. Any stranger
Showing himself indignant or lascivious
Heard behind him the whetting of knives. The wise man
Walked modestly two or three times
The length of the aisle and among the girls after
The heart's true inclination made his choice.
A priest of the church married them there and then.

Next morning early with a harder courtesy
He was fetched aboard a manned ship and so
Passed back into the sea-lanes. Some thus restored
Put off the escapade, some boasted and some
Wandered thereafter for the one bride. She
According to the custom of the island was courted by the best
And if she were seen to have taken the stranger's seed
Then by the very best, and married in her third month.

The second husbands shone like full moons
In reflected sun, their stepchildren
Were called 'the strangers' and enjoyed
Love and privileges above the rest. The boys
Grew proficient with boats, eyed the horizons
And one morning departed, courting shipwreck. The girls
Excited a restlessness but themselves
Waited, knowing they were most likely to be chosen
When out of the sea one morning a salt man crawled.

'Pity the drunks'

Pity the drunks in this late April snow.
They drank their hats and coats a week ago.
They touched the sun, they tapped the melting ground,
In public parks we saw them sitting round
The merry campfire of a cider jar

Upon a crocus cloth. Alas, some are
Already stiff in mortuaries who were
Seduced by Spring to go from here to there,
Putting their best foot forward on the road
To Walkden, Camberwell or Leeds. It snowed.
It met them waiting at the roundabout.
They had no hats and coats to keep it out.
They did a lap or two, they caught a cough.
They did another lap and shuffled off.

KIT WRIGHT

born 1944

Kit Wright is a rougher, more forthright writer than the other poets with whom I have placed him here. Some of his satires, like the savage poem 'I Found South African Breweries Most Hospitable', suggest a classification with Christopher Logue and Adrian Mitchell among the 'Dissenters'. But his usual tone is more genial. The jolly rhythms and slightly macabre content of some of his most characteristic poems suggest that he is in fact the natural successor to John Betjeman.

The Boys Bump-starting the Hearse

The hearse has stalled in the lane overlooking the river
Where willows are plunging their heads in the bottle-green
   water
      And bills of green baize drakes kazoo.
      The hearse has stalled and what shall we do?

The old don comes on, a string bag his strongbox.
He knows what is known about Horace but carries no tool box.
      Small boys shout in the Cambridge sun.
      The hearse has stalled and what's to be done?

Lime flowers drift in the lane to the baskets of bicycles,
Sticker the wall with yellow and powdery particles.
      Monosyllabic, the driver's curse.
      Everything fires. Except the hearse.

Whose gastric and gastric whinnies shoot neutered tom cats
In through the kitchen flaps of back gardens where tomtits
      Wizen away from the dangling crust.
      Who shall restart the returned-to-dust?

Shrill and sudden as birds the boys have planted
Their excellent little shoulders against the lamented
      Who bumps in second. A fart of exhaust.
      On goes the don and the holocaust.

The Power of Prayer

Very, very little of his garden
  Did God elect to seed.
The rest he leased to utter, outer blankness,
  Invaded by the rankness
    Of not a single weed.

Many, many mansions has his dwelling.
  His own bedsit is small.
A vast and speechless city crumbles round it.
  Never a one has found it
    Anywhere at all.

I Found South African Breweries Most Hospitable

Meat smell of blood in locked rooms I cannot smell it,
Screams of the brave in torture loges I never heard nor heard
  of
Apartheid I wouldn't know how to spell it,
None of these things am I paid to believe a word of
For I am a stranger to cant and contumely.
I am a professional cricketer.
My only consideration is my family.

I get my head down nothing to me or mine
Blood is geysering now from ear, from mouth, from eye,
How they take a fresh guard after breaking the spine,
I must play wherever I like or die
So spare me your news your views spare me your homily.
I am a professional cricketer.
My only consideration is my family.

Electrodes wired to their brains they should have had helmets,
Balls wired up they should have been wearing a box,
The danger was the game would turn into a stalemate,
Skin of their feet burnt off I like thick woollen socks
With buckskin boots that accommodate them roomily
For I am a professional cricketer.
My only consideration is my family.

They keep falling out of the window they must be clumsy
And unprofessional not that anyone told me,
Spare me your wittering spare me your whimsy,
Sixty thousand pounds is what they sold me
And I have no brain. I am an anomaly.
I am a professional cricketer.
My only consideration is my family.

BIBLIOGRAPHY

It is not the intention to list every book and pamphlet published by the poets included in this book, but simply to supply the reader with a list of books which will enable him or her to explore further. Where a good collected edition, or a substantial selected edition exists, this is considered the main source, and only titles covering later work are added. The Scottish poet Ian Hamilton Finlay presents a special problem, since his 'concrete' poems can only be found in innumerable specially designed broadsheets, folders and pamphlets, most of them issued by his own Wild Hawthorn Press. A complete list of these would be almost as long as the whole of the other listings put together, and they are therefore omitted. Two books of 'non-concrete' poetry are included.

A. ALVAREZ: *Autumn to Autumn and Selected Poems 1953–1976*, Macmillan, 1978.

KINGSLEY AMIS: *Collected Poems 1944–1979*, Hutchinson, 1979.

GEORGE BARKER: *The True Confession of George Barker*, Fore Publications, 1950; *Collected Poems, 1930–1955*, Faber & Faber, 1957; *The View from a Blind I*, Faber & Faber, 1962; *Collected Poems, 1930–1965*, October House, New York, 1965; *Dreams of a Summer Night*, Faber & Faber, 1966; *The Golden Chains*, Faber & Faber, 1968; *Poems of Places and People*, Faber & Faber, 1971; *In Memory of David Archer*, Faber & Faber, 1973; *Dialogues etc.*, Faber & Faber, 1976; *Villa Stellar*, Faber & Faber, 1978; *Anno Domini*, Faber & Faber, 1983.

PATRICIA BEER: *The Loss of the Magyar and Other Poems*, Longman, 1959; *The Survivor*, Longman, 1963; *Selected Poems*, Hutchinson, 1979; *The Lie of the Land*, Hutchinson, 1983.

MARTIN BELL: *Collected Poems 1937–1966*, Macmillan, 1967.

FRANCIS BERRY: *Galloping Centaur, Poems 1933–1951*, Methuen, 1952 (second impression, 1970); *Morant Bay*, Routledge, 1961; *Ghosts of Greenland*, Routledge, 1966.

JOHN BETJEMAN: *Collected Poems*, fourth edition, John Murray, 1979; *Uncollected Poems*, John Murray, 1982.

D. M. BLACK: *Rocklestrakes*, Outposts Publications, 1960; *From the Mountains*, Outposts Publications, 1963; *Theory of Diet*, Turret Books, 1966; *With Decorum*, Scorpion Press, 1966; *A Dozen Short Poems*, Turret Books, 1968; *The Educators: Poems*, Barrie & Rockliff, The Cresset Press, 1969; *The Old Hag*, Akros, 1972; *The Happy Crow*, published by *Lines Review*, 1974; *Gravitations*, published by *Lines Review*, 1979.

THOMAS BLACKBURN: *Selected Poems*, Hutchinson, 1975; *Post Mortem*, Rondo Publications, 1977; *Bread for the Winter Birds: the last poems of Thomas Blackburn*, Hutchinson, 1980.

ALAN BOLD: *Society Inebrious*, Mowat Hamilton, 1965; *The Voyage*, M. Macdonald, Edinburgh 1966; *To Find the New*, Chatto & Windus, 1967; *A Perpetual Motion Machine*, Chatto & Windus, 1969; *The State of the Nation*, Chatto & Windus, 1969; *He Will Be Greatly Missed*, Turret Books, 1971; *The Auld Symie*, Akros, 1971; *A Century of People*, Academy Editions, 1971; *A Pint of Bitter*, Chatto & Windus, 1971; *Scotland Yes: World Cup Football Poems*, Paul Harris, 1978; *This Fine Day*, Borderline Press, 1979.

GEORGE MACKAY BROWN: *Selected Poems*, The Hogarth Press, 1977; *Voyages*, Chatto & Windus, 1983.

ALAN BROWNJOHN: *Collected Poems, 1952–1983*, Secker & Warburg, 1983.

BASIL BUNTING: *Collected Poems*, revised edition, Oxford University Press, 1978.

CHARLES CAUSLEY: *Collected Poems, 1951–1975*, Macmillan, 1975.

BARRY COLE: *Blood Ties*, Turret Books, 1967; *Ulysses in the Town of Coloured Glass*, Turret Books, 1968; *Moonsearch*, Methuen, 1968; *The Visitors*, Methuen, 1970; *Vanessa in the City*, Trigram Press, 1971; *Pathetic Fallacies*, Eyre Methuen, 1973; *Dedications*, Byron Press, 1977.

TONY CONNOR: *New and Selected Poems*, Anvil Press, 1982.

DAVID CONSTANTINE: *A Brightness to Cast Shadow*, Bloodaxe Books, 1980; *Watching for Dolphins*, Bloodaxe Books, 1983.

PETER DALE: *The Storms*, Macmillan, 1968; *Mortal Fire*, revised edition, Agenda Editions, 1976; *One Another: A Sonnet Sequence*, Agenda Editions, 1978; *Too Much of Water*, Agenda Editions, 1983.

DONALD DAVIE: *Collected Poems, 1950–1970*, Routledge, 1972; *Collected Poems, 1971–1983*, Carcanet Press, 1983.

DOUGLAS DUNN: *Terry Street*, Faber & Faber, 1969; *The Happier Life*, Faber & Faber, 1972; *Love or Nothing*, Faber & Faber, 1974; *Barbarians*, Faber & Faber, 1979; *St Kilda's Parliament*, Faber & Faber, 1981.

LAWRENCE DURRELL: *Selected Poems*, ed. Alan Ross, Faber & Faber, 1977; *Collected Poems, 1931–1974*, Faber & Faber, 1980.

D. J. ENRIGHT: *Collected Poems*, Oxford University Press, 1981.

JAMES FENTON: *The Memory of War and Children in Exile: Poems 1968–1983*, Penguin, 1983.

IAN HAMILTON FINLAY (non-concrete poems): *The Dancers Inherit the Party*, Migrant Press, 1961; *Glasgow Beasts*, Wild Flounder Press, 1960 (new edition, Fulcrum Press, 1965).

ROY FISHER: *Poems 1955–1980*, Oxford University Press, 1980.

JOHN FULLER: *Fairground Music*, Chatto & Windus, 1961; *The Tree That Walked*, Chatto & Windus, 1967; *The Art of Love*, The Review, 1968; *The Wreck*, Turret Books, 1970; *Cannibals and Missionaries*, Secker & Warburg, 1972; *Epistles to Several Persons*, Secker & Warburg, 1973; *A Bestiary*, Sycamore Press, 1974; *The Mountain in the Sea*, Secker & Warburg, 1975; *Bel and the Dragon*, Sycamore Press, 1977; *Lies and Secrets*, Secker & Warburg, 1979; *The Illusionists*, Secker & Warburg, 1980; *Waiting for the Music*, Salamander Press, 1982; *The Beautiful Inventions*, Secker & Warburg, 1983.

ROY FULLER: *Collected Poems, 1936–1961*, André Deutsch, 1962; *The Individual and His Times: Selected Poems*, ed. V. J. Lee, Athlone Press, 1982.

ROBERT GARIOCH: *Collected Poems*, Carcanet: M. Macdonald, Edinburgh 1977; *Complete Poetical Works*, ed. Robin Fulton, M. Macdonald, 1983.

DAVID GASCOYNE: *Collected Poems*, ed. Robin Skelton, Oxford University Press – Deutsch, 1965; *Collected Verse Translations*, ed. Alan Clodd and Robin Skelton, Oxford University Press, 1970; *Three Poems* privately printed, 1976.

KAREN GERSHON: *Selected Poems*, Gollancz, 1966; *Legacies and Encounters: Poems 1966–1971*, Gollancz, 1972; *My Daughters, My Sisters and Other Poems*, Gollancz, 1975; *Coming Back from Babylon: 24 Poems*, Gollancz, 1979.

HENRY GRAHAM: *Good Luck to You Kafka/ You'll Need It Boss*, Rapp & Whiting, 1969; *Passport to Earth*, Rapp & Whiting, 1971; *Europe After Rain*, Headland Press, 1981.

W. S. GRAHAM: *Collected Poems, 1942–1977*, Faber & Faber, 1979.

ROBERT GRAVES: *Collected Poems, 1975*, Cassell, 1975; *New Collected Poems*, Doubleday, 1977.

HARRY GUEST: *Private View*, Outposts Publications, 1962; *A Different Darkness*, Outposts Publications, 1964; *Arrangements*, Anvil Press Poetry, 1968; *The Cutting Room*, Anvil Press Poetry, 1970; *The Place*, Sceptre Press, 1971; *The Achievements of Memory*, Sceptre Press, 1974; *The Enchanted Acres*, Sceptre Press, 1975; *Mountain Journal*, Rivelin Press, 1975; *A House against the Night*, Anvil Press Poetry, 1976; *English Poems*, Words Press, 1976; *The Hidden Change*, Greylag Press, 1978; *Zeami in Exile*, Sceptre Press, 1978; *Lost and Found*, Anvil Press Poetry, 1983.

THOM GUNN: *Selected Poems, 1950–1975*, Faber & Faber, 1979; *Jack Straw's Castle*, Faber & Faber, 1976; *The Passages of Joy*, Faber & Faber, 1982.

MICHAEL HAMBURGER: *Ownerless Earth: New and Selected Poems*,

Carcanet Press, 1973; *Real Estate*, Carcanet Press, 1977; *Variations*, Carcanet Press, 1981; *Collected Poems 1941–1983*, Carcanet Press, 1984.

TONY HARRISON: *Earthworks*, Northern House, 1964; *The Loiners*, London Magazine Editions, 1970; *From The School of Eloquence and Other Poems*, Rex Collings, 1978; *Continuous*, Rex Collings, 1981; *A Kumquat for John Keats*, Bloodaxe Books, 1981.

LEE HARWOOD: *title illegible*, Writers' Forum, 1965; *The man with blue eyes*, Angel Hair Books, New York, 1966; *The White Room*, Fulcrum Press, 1968; *The Beautiful Atlas*, Kavanagh, 1969; *Landscapes*, Fulcrum Press, 1969; *The Sinking Colony*, Fulcrum Press, 1970; *Captain Harwood's Log of Stern Statements and Stout Sayings*, Writers' Forum, 1973; *Freighters*, Pig Press, 1975; *H.M.S. Little Fox*, Oasis Press, 1976; *Boston–Brighton*, Oasis Press, 1977; *Old Bosham Bird Watch and Other Stories*, Pig Press, 1977 (revised edition, 1978).

SEAMUS HEANEY: *Fieldwork*, Faber & Faber, 1979; *Selected Poems, 1965–1975*, Faber & Faber, 1981; *Station Island*, Faber & Faber, 1984.

JOHN HEATH-STUBBS: *Selected Poems*, Oxford University Press, 1965; *Satires and Epigrams*, Turret Books, 1968; *Artorius, Book I*, Enitharmon Press, 1973; *The Watchman's Flute: New Poems*, Carcanet Press, 1978; *The Mouse, the Bird and the Sausage*, Coelfrith Press, 1978; *Naming the Beasts*, Carcanet Press, 1982.

ADRIAN HENRI: *Autobiography*, Jonathan Cape, 1971; *The Best of Henri: Selected Poems 1960–1970*, Jonathan Cape, 1975; *City Hedges: Poems 1970–1976*, Jonathan Cape, 1977; *From the Loveless Motel: Poems 1976–1979*, Jonathan Cape, 1980; *Penny Arcade*, Jonathan Cape, 1983.

GEOFFREY HILL: *Somewhere is Such a Kingdom: Poems 1952–1971*, Houghton Mifflin, Boston, 1975; *Tenebrae*, André Deutsch, 1978; *The Mystery of the Charity of Charles Péguy*, Agenda Editions, 1983.

PHILIP HOBSBAUM: *The Place's Fault and Other Poems*, Macmillan, 1964; *In Retreat and Other Poems*, Macmillan, 1966; *Coming Out Fighting*, Macmillan, 1969; *Women and Animals*, Macmillan, 1972.

TED HUGHES: *Crow: From the Life and Songs of the Crow*, Faber & Faber, 1970 (revised edition, 1972); *Selected Poems, 1957–1967*, Faber & Faber, 1972; *Gaudete*, Faber & Faber, 1977; *Cave Birds*, Faber & Faber 1978; *Moortown*, Faber & Faber, 1979; *Remains of Elmet*, Faber & Faber, 1979; *River*, Faber & Faber, 1983.

ELIZABETH JENNINGS: *Selected Poems*, Carcanet Press, 1979; *Moments of Grace*, Carcanet Press, 1979; *Celebrations and Elegies*, Carcanet Press, 1982.

BRIAN JONES: *Poems*, Alan Ross, 1966; *A Family Album*, Alan Ross, 1968; *Interior*, Alan Ross, 1969; *The Mantis Hand and Other Poems*, Arc Publications, 1970; *For Mad Mary*, London Magazine Editions, 1974; *The Island Normal*, Carcanet Press, 1980.

DAVID JONES: *In Parenthesis*, Faber & Faber, 1937; *The Anathemata*, Faber

& Faber, 1952; *The Tribune's Visitation*, Fulcrum Press, 1969; *The Sleeping Lord and Other Fragments*, Faber & Faber, 1974; *Introducing David Jones: a Selection of His Writings*, ed. John Matthias, Faber & Faber, 1980.

PHILIP LARKIN: *The North Ship*, Fortune Press, 1945 (revised edition, Faber, 1966); *XX Poems*, privately printed, 1951; *The Less Deceived*, Marvell Press, 1955; *The Whitsun Weddings*, Faber & Faber, 1964; *High Windows*, Faber & Faber, 1974.

PETER LEVI: *Collected Poems 1955–1975*, Anvil Press Poetry, 1976; *Five Ages*, Anvil Press Poetry, 1978; *Private Ground*, Anvil Press Poetry, 1981.

CHRISTOPHER LOGUE: *Ode to the Dodo: Poems 1953–1978*, Jonathan Cape, 1981.

MICHAEL LONGLEY: *No Continuing City*, Macmillan, 1969; *An Exploded View*, Gollancz, 1973; *Man Lying on a Wall*, Gollancz, 1976; *The Echo Gate*, Secker & Warburg, 1979.

EDWARD LUCIE-SMITH: *A Tropical Childhood and Other Poems*, Oxford University Press, 1961; *Confessions and Histories*, Oxford University Press, 1964; *Towards Silence*, Oxford University Press, 1968; *The Well-Wishers*, Oxford University Press, 1974; *Beasts with Bad Morals*, Leinster Fine Books, 1984.

GEORGE MACBETH: *Collected Poems, 1958–70*, Macmillan, 1971; *Shrapnel*, Macmillan, 1973; *A Poet's Year*, Gollancz, 1973; *In the Hours Waiting for the Blood to Come*, Gollancz, 1975; *Buying a Heart*, J–Jay Publications, 1978; *Poems from Oby*, Secker & Warburg, 1982; *The Long Darkness*, Secker & Warburg, 1983.

NORMAN MACCAIG: *Old Maps and New: Selected Poems*, Chatto & Windus, 1978; *A World of Difference*, Chatto & Windus, 1983.

HUGH MACDIARMID: *Complete Poems 1920–1976*, ed. Michael Grieve and W. R. Aitken, Martin Brian & O'Keeffe, 1978.

ROGER MCGOUGH: *Frinck, a Life in the Day of*, (including 'summer with monika'), Michael Joseph, 1967; *Watchwords*, Jonathan Cape, 1969; *After the Merrymaking*, Jonathan Cape, 1971; *Gig*, Jonathan Cape, 1973; *Sporting Relations*, Eyre Methuen, 1974; *In the Glassroom*, Jonathan Cape, 1976; *Holiday on Death Row*, Jonathan Cape, 1979; *Waving at Trains*, Jonathan Cape, 1982.

MEDBH MCGUCKIAN: *Single Ladies: Sixteen Poems*, Interim Press, 1980; *Portrait of Joanna*, Ulsterman Publications, 1980; *The Flower Master*, Oxford University Press, 1982; *Venus and the Rain*, Oxford University Press, 1984.

LOUIS MACNEICE: *Collected Poems*, Faber & Faber, 1966.

DEREK MAHON: *Poems, 1972–1978*, Oxford University Press, 1979; *The Hunt by Night*, Oxford University Press, 1982.

MATTHEW MEAD: *Identities and Other Poems*, Rapp & Whiting, 1967; *The Administration of Things*, Anvil Press Poetry, 1970; *In the Eyes of the People*, Satis, 1973; *Minusland*, Martin Robertson, 1978; *The Midday Muse*, Anvil Press Poetry, 1979.

CHRISTOPHER MIDDLETON: *Poems*, Fortune Press, 1944; *Nocturne in Eden: Poems*, Fortune Press, 1945; *Torse 3: Poems 1949–1961*, Longman, 1962; *Nonsequences: Selfpoems*, Longman, 1965; *Our Flowers and Nice Bones*, Fulcrum Press, 1969; *The Lonely Suppers of W. V. Balloon*, Carcanet Press, 1975; *Pataxanadu: Prose Poems*, Carcanet Press, 1979; *Carminalenia*, Carcanet Press, 1979; *One Hundred and Eleven Poems*, Carcanet Press, 1983.

ADRIAN MITCHELL: *For Beauty Douglas: Adrian Mitchell's Collected Poems 1953–1979*, Allison & Busby, 1982; *On the Beach at Cambridge: New Poems*, Allison & Busby, 1984.

DOM MORAES: *A Beginning*, Parton Press, 1957 (revised edition, 1958); *Poems*, Eyre & Spottiswoode, 1960; *John Nobody*, Eyre & Spottiswoode, 1965; *Poems, 1955–1965*, Macmillan, New York, 1966.

EDWIN MORGAN: *Poems of Thirty Years*, Carcanet Press, 1982; *Grafts/Takes*, Mariscat, 1983.

ANDREW MOTION: *The Pleasure Steamers*, Carcanet Press, 1978; *Independence*, Salamander Press, 1981; *Secret Narratives*, Salamander Press, 1983; *Dangerous Play: Poems 1974–1984*, Chatto & Windus, 1984.

EDWIN MUIR: *Collected Poems*, Faber & Faber, 1960.

PAUL MULDOON: *New Weather*, Faber & Faber, 1973; *Mules*, Faber & Faber, 1977; *Why Brownlee Left*, Faber & Faber, 1980; *Quoof*, Faber & Faber, 1983.

JEFF NUTTALL: *Selected Poems*, Horizon, 1970; *Poems, 1962–1969*, Fulcrum Press, 1970; *Objects*, Trigram Press, 1976; *What Happened to Jackson*, Aloes Books, 1978; *The Patriarchs: An Early Summer Landscape*, Bean and Aloes Arc, 1978; *Grape Notes, Apple Music*, Rivelin Press, 1980.

BRIAN PATTEN: *Little Johnny's Confession*, Allen & Unwin, 1967; *Notes to the Hurrying Man: Poems Winter '66 to Summer '68*, Allen & Unwin, 1969; *Walking Out: The Early Poems of Brian Patten*, Transican Books, 1971; *The Irrelevant Song and Other Poems*, Allen & Unwin, 1971 (revised edition, 1975); *Vanishing Trick*, Allen & Unwin, 1976; *Grave Gossip*, Allen & Unwin, 1979; *Love Poems*, Allen & Unwin, 1981.

TOM PAULIN: *A State of Justice*, Faber & Faber, 1977; *The Strange Museum*, Faber & Faber, 1980; *Liberty Tree*, Faber & Faber, 1983.

SYLVIA PLATH: *The Colossus*, Heinemann, 1960; *Ariel*, Faber & Faber, 1965; *Crossing the Water*, Faber & Faber, 1971; *Winter Trees*, Faber & Faber, 1971; *Collected Poems*, ed. Ted Hughes, Faber & Faber, 1981.

PETER PORTER: *Collected Poems*, Oxford University Press, 1983.

CRAIG RAINE: *The Onion, Memory*, Oxford University Press, 1978; *A Martian Sends a Postcard Home*, Oxford University Press, 1979; *A Free Translation*, Salamander Press, 1981; *Rich*, Faber & Faber, 1984.

TOM RAWORTH: *Weapon Man*, Goliard Press, 1965; *Continuation*, Goliard Press, 1966; *The Relation Ship*, Goliard Press, 1967; *The Big Green Day*, Trigram Press, 1968; *Lion, Lion*, Trigram Press, 1970; *Moving*, Cape Goliard, 1971; *Act*, Trigram Press, 1973; *Ace*, Cape Goliard, 1974; *Heavy Light*, Transgravity Press, 1979.

PETER REDGROVE: *Sons of My Skin: Selected Poems 1954–1974*, ed. Marie Peel, Routledge, 1975; *From Every Chink of the Ark and Other New Poems*, Routledge, 1977; *The Weddings at Nether Powers and Other New Poems*, Routledge, 1979; *The Apple Broadcast and Other New Poems*, Routledge, 1981.

PETER SCUPHAM: *The Snowing Globe*, E. J. Morten, 1972; *Children Dancing*, Sycamore Press, 1972; *Prehistories*, Oxford University Press, 1975; *The Hinterland*, Oxford University Press, 1977; *Summer Palaces*, Oxford University Press, 1980; *Winter Quarters*, Oxford University Press, 1983.

JON SILKIN: *Selected Poems*, Routledge, 1980; *The Psalms with Their Spoils*, Routledge, 1980.

C. H. SISSON: *In the Trojan Ditch: Collected Poems and Selected Translations*, Carcanet Press, 1974; *The Corridor*, Mandeville Press, 1975; *Anchises*, Carcanet Press, 1976; *Exactions*, Carcanet Press, 1980; *Selected Poems*, Carcanet Press, 1981; *Collected Poems*, Carcanet Press, 1984.

IAIN CRICHTON SMITH: *Selected Poems 1955–1980*, Macdonald, 1981; *The Exiles*, Carcanet Press, 1984.

KEN SMITH: *Burned Books*, Bloodaxe Books, 1981; *The Poet Reclining: Selected Poems 1962–80*, Bloodaxe Books, 1982; *Able, Baker, Charlie, Delta – Epic Sonnets*, Bloodaxe Books, 1981.

STEVIE SMITH: *Collected Poems*, Allen Lane, 1975; *Selected Poems*, ed. James MacGibbon, Penguin, 1978; *Me Again: Uncollected Writings*, ed. Jack Barbera and William McBrien, Virago Press, 1981; *A Selection*, ed. Hermione Lee, Faber & Faber, 1983.

BERNARD SPENCER: *Collected Poems*, Alan Ross, 1965; *Collected Poems*, ed. Roger Bowen, Oxford University Press, 1981.

JON STALLWORTHY: *The Apple Barrel: Selected Poems 1956–1973*, Oxford University Press, 1974; *A Familiar Tree*, Chatto & Windus, 1978.

DAVID SWEETMAN: *Looking into the Deep End*, Faber, 1981.

GEORGE SZIRTES: *The Slant Door*, Secker & Warburg, 1979; *November and May*, Secker & Warburg, 1981; *Short Wave*, Secker & Warburg, 1983.

NATHANIEL TARN: *Old Savage/Young City*, Jonathan Cape, 1964; *Where Babylon Ends*, Cape Goliard, 1968; *The Beautiful Contradictions*, Cape

Goliard, 1969; *A Nowhere for Vallejo: Choices, October*, Cape, 1972; *Lyrics for the Bride of God*, Jonathan Cape, 1975; *Alashka/Atitlan: New and Selected Poems*, with Janet Rodney, Brillig Works Press, 1979.

D. M. THOMAS: *Selected Poems*, Secker & Warburg, 1983; *News from the Front*, with Sylvia Kantaris, Arc Publications, 1983.

DYLAN THOMAS: *The Poems*, ed. Daniel Jones, Dent, 1971; *Selected Poems*, ed. Walford Davies, Dent, 1974.

R. S. THOMAS: *Selected Poems, 1946–1968*, Hart-Davis, 1973; *Later Poems, A Selection*, Macmillan, 1983.

ANTHONY THWAITE: *Home Truths*, Marvell Press, 1957; *The Owl in the Tree: Poems*, Oxford University Press, 1963; *The Stones of Emptiness: Poems 1963–1966*, Oxford University Press, 1967; *Inscriptions: Poems 1967–1972*, Oxford University Press, 1973; *New Confessions*, Oxford University Press, 1974; *A Portion for Foxes*, Oxford University Press, 1977; *Victorian Voices*, Oxford University Press, 1980; *Poems 1953–1983*, Secker & Warburg, 1984.

CHARLES TOMLINSON: *Selected Poems 1951–1974*, Oxford University Press, 1978; *The Flood*, Oxford University Press, 1981; *Notes from New York*, Oxford University Press, 1984.

GAEL TURNBULL: *A Trampoline: Poems 1952–1964*, Cape Goliard, 1968; *Scantlings: Poems 1964–1968*, Cape Goliard 1970; *Finger Cymbals*, Satis, 1972; *A Random Sampling*, Pig Press, 1974; *Residues: Down the Sluice of Time*, Grosseteste Press, 1976; *Thronging the Heart*, Aggie Weston's, 1976; *If a Glance Could be Enough*, Satis, 1979; *A Gathering of Poems 1950–1980*, Anvil Press Poetry, 1983

VERNON WATKINS: *Affinities*, Faber & Faber, 1962; *Fidelities*, Faber & Faber, 1968; *Selected Poems 1930–1960*, Faber & Faber, 1967; *Uncollected Poems*, Enitharmon Press, 1969; *I That was Born in Wales*, ed. Gwen Watkins and Ruth Pryor, University of Wales Press, 1976; *Unity of the Stream*, Gomer Press, 1978; *The Ballad of the Outer Dark*, Enitharmon Press, 1979; *The Breaking of the Wave*, Gologonooza Press, 1979.

DAVID WEVILL: *Birth of a Shark*, Macmillan, 1964; *The Christ of the Ice-Floes*, Macmillan, 1966; *Firebreak*, Macmillan, 1971; *Where the Arrow Falls*, Macmillan, 1973.

KIT WRIGHT: *The Bear Looked over the Mountain*, Salamander Imprint, 1977; *Rabbiting On*, Collins, 1978; *Hot Dog*, Kestrel Books, 1981; *Bump-starting the Hearse*, Hutchinson, 1983.

ACKNOWLEDGEMENTS

For permission to reprint the poems in this anthology acknowledgement is made to the following:

For A. ALVAREZ: 'Lost', 'Back' from *Lost*, Turret Books, and 'Mourning and Melancholia', to the author.

For KINGSLEY AMIS: 'The Last War' from *A Case of Samples*, Gollancz, to Curtis Brown Ltd; 'Souvenirs' and 'A Point of Logic' from *A Look Round the Estate*, published in the U.S.A. by Grossman Publishers Inc., copyright © 1967 by Kingsley Amis, to Harcourt, Brace and World Inc. and Jonathan Cape Ltd.

For GEORGE BARKER: 'On a Friend's Escape from Drowning off the Norfolk Coast' from *Collected Poems 1930–1955*, copyright © 1957, 1962 and 1965 by George Granville Barker, to October House Inc. and Faber & Faber Ltd; 'Roman Poem III' from *The View from a Blind I*, to Faber & Faber Ltd.

For PATRICIA BEER: 'Finis' from *The Survivors*, to Longmans Green & Co. Ltd; 'A Dream of Hanging' from *Just Like the Resurrection*, to Macmillan & Co. Ltd and to The Macmillan Company of Canada Ltd.

For MARTIN BELL: 'The Enormous Comics', 'Letter to a Friend' from *Collected Poems*, Macmillan & Co. Ltd, to St Martin's Press Inc., The Macmillan Company of Canada Ltd and Macmillan & Co. Ltd.

For FRANCIS BERRY: 'Hvalsey', 'Vadstena' from *Ghosts of Greenland*, to Routledge & Kegan Paul Ltd.

For JOHN BETJEMAN: 'Indoor Games Near Newbury', 'Devonshire Street W.1', 'N.W.5 & N6' from *Collected Poems*, published in the U.S.A. by Houghton Mifflin Company, to John Murray (Publishers) Ltd.

For D.M. BLACK: 'The Educators', 'Prayer' from *A Dozen Short Poems*, Turret Books, to the author; 'From the Privy Council', from *With Decorum*, to Scorpion Press.

For THOMAS BLACKBURN: 'En Route' from *A Breathing Space*, Putnam & Co. Ltd., to the author.

For ALAN BOLD: 'June 1967 at Buchenwald' from *A Perpetual Motion Machine* to Chatto & Windus Ltd.

For GEORGE MACKAY BROWN: 'Ikey on the people of Helya', 'The Hawk' from *The Year of the Whale*, to Chatto & Windus Ltd.

Acknowledgements

For ALAN BROWNJOHN: 'Office Party', 'The Space' from *The Lions' Mouths*, to Macmillan & Co. Ltd, and 'For a Journey' from *The Railings*, Digby Press, to the author.

For BASIL BUNTING: 'The Spoils' from *Collected Poems*, © 1978 by Basil Bunting, reprinted by permission of Oxford University Press.

For MILES BURROWS: 'minipoet' from *A Vulture's Egg*, to Jonathan Cape Ltd.

For CHARLES CAUSLEY: 'My Friend Maloney' from *Johnny Alleluia*, Rupert Hart-Davis Ltd, to David Higham Associates Ltd.

For BARRY COLE: 'The Domestic World in Winter', 'Reported Missing', to the author.

For TONY CONNOR: 'A Child Half-Asleep', 'From "Twelve Secret Poems": III, VI' from *Kon in Springtime*, to Oxford University Press Ltd.

For DAVID CONSTANTINE: 'Chronicle', 'Pity the Drunks' from *Watching for Dolphins*; 'You are distant, you are already leaving' from *A Brightness to Cast Shadows*, to the author and to Bloodaxe Books Ltd.

For PETER DALE: 'Not Drinking Water', 'Thrush' from *The Storms*, to The Macmillan Company of Canada Ltd and Macmillan & Co. Ltd.

For DONALD DAVIE: 'Housekeeping', 'Green River', 'New York in August', copyright © 1965 by Donald Davie, reprinted from *Events and Wisdoms*, by Donald Davie, to Routledge & Kegan Paul Ltd and Wesleyan University Press, Publishers.

For DOUGLAS DUNN: 'Men of Terry Street', 'A Removal from Terry Street', 'Young Women in Rollers' from *Terry Street*, and 'Witch-girl' from *St Kilda's Parliament*, to Faber & Faber Ltd.

For LAWRENCE DURRELL: 'A Portrait of Theodora', 'Sarajevo', 'Bitter Lemons' from *Collected Poems*, to Faber & Faber Ltd and to E. P. Dutton & Co. Inc.

For D. J. ENRIGHT: 'In Memoriam' from *Addictions*, Chatto & Windus Ltd, to the author, and David Higham Associates Ltd.

For IAN HAMILTON FINLAY: 'Orkney Lyrics', to Fulcrum Press; 'Stones for Gardens', 'Green Waters', to the author.

For ROY FISHER: 'The Hospital in Winter', 'Interior I' from *Collected Poems 1968*, Fulcrum Press, to the author.

For JOHN FULLER: 'The Cook's Lesson' from *The Tree That Walked*, to Chatto & Windus Ltd.; 'Valentine', 'Being' from *Beautiful Inventions* to the author and to Martin Secker & Warburg Ltd.

For ROY FULLER: 'Poem Out of Character', from 'Meredithian Sonnets': II, IX, XIII from *Collected Poems*, to André Deutsch Ltd.

For ROBERT GARIOCH: 'I'm Neutral', 'In Princes Street Gairdens' from *Selected Poems*, to M. Macdonald Printers (Edinburgh) Ltd.

For DAVID GASCOYNE: 'Elegiac Improvisation on the Death of Paul Eluard' from *Collected Poems*, © Oxford University Press 1965, reprinted by permission of Oxford University Press.

For KAREN GERSHON: 'I Was Not There', 'In the Jewish Cemetery' from *Selected Poems*, to Victor Gollancz Ltd.

For HENRY GRAHAM: 'Cat Poem', 'Two Gardens' from *Good Luck Kafka/You'll Need It Boss*, to Rapp & Whiting Ltd.

For W. S. GRAHAM: 'Malcolm Mooney's Land', to the author.

For ROBERT GRAVES: 'Counting the Beats', 'The Straw', 'The Face in the Mirror' from *Collected Poems*, Cassell & Co. Ltd, to A. P. Watt Ltd, and to Collins-Knowlton-Wing Inc.

For HARRY GUEST: 'Two Poems for O-Bon', to Anvil Press Poetry.

For THOM GUNN: 'The Annihilation of Nothing', 'Considering the Snail', 'My Sad Captains' from *My Sad Captains*, and 'Touch' from *Touch*, to Faber & Faber Ltd and to Chicago University Press.

For MICHAEL HAMBURGER: 'Travelling', 'The Jackdaws' from *Feeding the Chickadees*, Turret Books, to the author.

For TONY HARRISON: 'Voortrekker' from *The School of Eloquence* and 'Study', 'Long Distance II', 'Clearing I' from *Continuous*, to the author and to Rex Collings Ltd.

For LEE HARWOOD: 'When the Geography Was Fixed', 'The Final Painting' from *The White Room*, Fulcrum Press, 1968, and *Landscapes*, Fulcrum Press, 1968.

For SEAMUS HEANEY: 'Death of a Naturalist', 'The Barn' from *Death of a Naturalist*, to Oxford University Press and Oxford University Press Inc.; 'Punishment', 'Anahorish', 'The Backward Look' from *Wintering Out* and 'Aisling' from *North*, to Faber & Faber Ltd.

For JOHN HEATH-STUBBS: 'The Last Watch of Empire', 'A Charm Against the Toothache' from *Selected Poems*, to David Higham Associates Ltd.

For ADRIAN HENRI: 'Tonight at Noon' from *Tonight at Noon*, to Rapp & Whiting Ltd and David McKay Co. Inc.; 'The Entry of Christ into Liverpool', to Rapp & Whiting Ltd.

For GEOFFREY HILL: 'In Piam Memoriam', 'To the (Supposed) Patron' from *For the Unfallen*, 'Ovid in the Third Reich' from *King Log*, 'Hymn VI' from *Mercian Hymns*, 'Christmas Trees', 'An Apology for the Revival of Christian Architecture in England' from *Tenebrae*, to the author and to André Deutsch Ltd.

Acknowledgements

For PHILIP HOBSBAUM: 'A Secret Sharer', 'Can I Fly Too?', 'Ocarina', to the author.

For TED HUGHES: 'Wodwo', 'Gog', 'Pibroch', 'Theology' from *Wodwo*, to Faber & Faber Ltd and Harper & Row Publishers Inc.; 'Fifth Bedtime Story', to Miss Olwyn Hughes.

For ELIZABETH JENNINGS: 'Night Garden of the Asylum', 'One Flesh' from *Collected Poems*, to The Macmillan Company of Canada Ltd. and to Macmillan & Co. Ltd.

For BRIAN JONES: 'Husband to Wife: Party-Going', 'Sunday Outing', 'Runner' from *Poems*, to Alan Ross Ltd.

For DAVID JONES: 'A, a, a, Domine Deus', 'The Hunt', to the author.

For PHILIP LARKIN: 'Mr Bleaney', 'The Whitsun Weddings' 'Days', from *The Whitsun Weddings*, to Faber & Faber Ltd; 'Going' from *The Less Deceived*, to Marvell Press.

For PETER LEVI: 'Monologue Spoken by the Pet Canary of Pope Pius XII' from *Fresh Water. Sea Water*, Black Raven Press, and 'To speak about the soul' from *Pancakes for the Queen of Babylon*, Anvil Press, to John Johnson.

For CHRISTOPHER LOGUE: 'From Book XXI of Homer's *Iliad*' from *Songs*, Hutchinson Books Ltd, to the author.

For MICHAEL LONGLEY: 'Ash Keys' from *The Echo Gate*, to the author and to Martin Secker & Warburg Ltd; 'In Memoriam', 'The Third Light' from *Collected Poems*, to The Salamander Press Edinburgh Ltd.

For EDWARD LUCIE-SMITH: 'Looking at a Drawing', 'Silence' from *Towards Silence*, to Oxford University Press; 'The Bruise', 'Night Rain' to the author.

For GEORGE MACBETH: 'Owl' from *A Doomsday Book*, to Scorpion Press; 'The Shell' from *The Colour of Blood*, to The Macmillan Company of Canada Ltd, Macmillan & Co. Ltd and Atheneum Publishers, N.Y.; 'The Bamboo Nightingale', to the author.

For NORMAN MACCAIG: 'Nude in a Fountain' from *A Common Grace*, 'Fetching Cows' from *Measures*, 'Interruption to a Journey' from *Surroundings*, to Chatto & Windus Ltd.

For HUGH MACDIARMID: 'In the Fall', 'Bagpipe Music', 'Glasgow 1960' from *Collected Poems*, to The Macmillan Co., New York.

For ROGER MCGOUCH: 'Let Me Die a Youngman's Death', to Hope Leresche & Steele; Poem 39, from 'summer with monika', from *Frinck*, to Michael Joseph Ltd.

For MEBDH MCGUCKIAN: 'The Aphrodisiac', 'The Sun-Trap', 'Gentians' from *The Flower Master*, to Oxford University Press.

For LOUIS MACNEICE: 'The Wiper', 'The Truisms', 'The Taxis', 'After the Crash', 'The Habits' from *Collected Poems*, to Faber & Faber Ltd and Oxford University Press Inc.

For DEREK MAHON: 'My Wicked Uncle', 'An Unborn Child' from *Night Crossing*; 'Rage for Order' from *Poems* 1962–78; 'In the Aran Islands' from *Lives*; 'Derry Morning', 'The Woods' from *The Hunt By Night*, © Derek Mahon 1982, reprinted by permission of Oxford University Press.

For MATTHEW MEAD: 'Identities II', 'Translator to Translated' from *Identities*, to Rapp & Whiting Ltd.

For CHRISTOPHER MIDDLETON: 'Climbing a Pebble' from *torse 3* and 'Cabal of Cat and Mouse', 'Lenau's Dream' from *nonsequences*, to Longmans Green & Co. Ltd.

For ADRIAN MITCHELL: 'Nostalgia – Now Threepence Off' from *Poems*, to Jonathan Cape Ltd; 'To Whom It may Concern' from *Out Loud*, to Cape Goliard Publishers Ltd. *Out Loud* is distributed in the U.S.A. by Grossman Publishers Inc.

For DOM MORAES: 'Craxton' from *Poems 1955–65*, to The Macmillan Co., New York.

For EDWIN MORGAN: 'From the Domain of Arnheim', 'Opening the Cage', 'Pomander' from *The Second Life*, to Edinburgh University Press.

For ANDREW MOTION: 'Leaving Belfast', 'A Dying Race' from *The Pleasure Steamers*, to the author and to Carcanet Press, Manchester; 'Writing' from *Secret Narratives*, to Salamander Press Edinburgh Ltd.

For EDWIN MUIR: 'The Combat' from *Collected Poems*, to Faber & Faber Ltd and to Oxford University Press Inc.

For PAUL MULDOON: 'Why Brownlee Left', 'Anseo' from *Why Brownlee Left* and 'Glanders', 'The Frog' from *Quoof*, to Faber & Faber Ltd.

For JEFF NUTTALL: 'Insomnia', 'When it had all been told', to the author.

For BRIAN PATTEN: 'Little Johnny's Confession' from *Little Johnny's Confession*, to George Allen & Unwin Ltd; 'Into My Mirror Has Walked', 'It is Always the Same Image' from *Notes to the Hurrying Man*, George Allen & Unwin Ltd, to Miss Olwyn Hughes.

For TOM PAULIN: 'Under Creon', 'To the Linen Hall', from *Liberty Free*, to Faber & Faber Ltd.

For SYLVIA PLATH: 'Blackberrying' from *Uncollected Poems*, Turret Books, to Miss Olwyn Hughes; 'Lady Lazarus', 'Daddy' from *Ariel* to Miss Olwyn Hughes.

For PETER PORTER: 'Death in the Pergola Tea-Rooms' from *Once Bitten, Twice Bitten*, 'Madame de Merteuil on "The Loss of an Eye"', 'The

Great Poet Comes Here in Winter' from *Poems Ancient and Modern*, to Scorpion Press; 'Fossil Gathering', 'An Exequy' from *Collected Poems*, to Oxford University Press.

For CRAIG RAINE: 'A Martian Sends a Postcard Home', 'Shallots' from *A Martian Sends a Postcard Home*, and 'The Onion, Memory' from *The Onion, Memory* to Oxford University Press.

For TOM RAWORTH: 'You Were Wearing Blue', 'I Mean' from *The Relation Ship*, to Cape Goliard Press Ltd; 'Inner Space' from *The Big Green Day*, to Trigram Press Ltd.

For PETER REDGROVE: 'The House in the Acorn' from *The Force*, to Routledge & Kegan Paul Ltd; 'Young Women with the Hair of Witches and No Modesty', 'The Moon Disposes' from *Work in Progress*, 1968, Poet & Printer, 'The Half-Scissors', to the author.

For PETER SCUPHAM: 'Summer Palaces', 'Die Annherren' from *Summer Palaces*, to Oxford University Press.

For JON SILKIN: 'Caring for Animals', 'Dandelion', 'A Bluebell', 'A Daisy', copyright © 1954, 1965 by Jon Silkin. Reprinted from *New and Selected Poems*, by Jon Silkin, by permission of Chatto & Windus Ltd and Wesleyan University Press, Publishers.

For C. H. SISSON: 'Ellick Farm' from *Selected Poems*, 'The Desert', 'A Visitor' from *Exactions*, 'The Consequence' from *Collected Poems* (1984), to the author and to Carcanet Press, Manchester.

For IAIN CRICHTON SMITH: 'Old Woman' from *The Law and the Grace*, to Eyre & Spottiswoode (Publishers) Ltd; 'The Departing Island' and 'Farewell', to the author.

For KEN SMITH: 'Family Group', 'Eli's poem', 'His lament', from *The Poet Reclining: Selected Poems 1962–1980*, to the author and to Bloodaxe Books Ltd.

For STEVIE SMITH: 'Not Waving but Drowning' from *Not Waving but Drowning*, to Longmans Green & Co. Ltd and New Directions Publishing Corporation; 'Tenuous and Precarious', 'Emily Writes Such a Good Letter' from *The Frog Prince*, to Longmans Green & Co. Ltd.

For BERNARD SPENCER: 'Night-time: Starting to Write', 'Properties of Snow' from *Collected Poems* edited by Roger Bowen, © Mrs Anne Humphreys 1981, to Oxford University Press.

For JON STALLWORTHY: 'The Almond Tree' from *Root and Branch*, to Chatto & Windus Ltd and Oxford University Press Inc.

For DAVID SWEETMAN: 'Saidi's Wife', 'Chairpersons' from *Looking Into the Deep End*, to Faber & Faber Ltd.

For GEORGE SZIRTES: 'North Wembley', 'The Girls', from *November and May* to the author and to Martin Secker & Warburg Limited.

For NATHANIEL TARN: 'Last of the Chiefs' from *Old Savage/Young City*, by Nathaniel Tarn, copyright © 1964 by Nathaniel Tarn. Reprinted by permission of Random House Inc., and Jonathan Cape Ltd; 'Markings' from *Where Babylon Ends*, to Cape Goliard Press Ltd.

For DYLAN THOMA: 'Over Sir John's Hill' from *Collected Poems*, copyright © 1952 by Dylan Thomas. Reprinted by permission of New Directions Publishing Corporation, New York, and of J. M. Dent & Sons Ltd.

For D. M. THOMAS: 'Missionary', to the author.

For R. S. THOMAS: 'The Welsh Hill Country', 'The Mixen' from *Song at the Year's Turning* and 'The Country Clergy', 'Evans' from *Poetry for Supper*, to Rupert Hart-Davis.

For ANTHONY THWAITE: 'Mr Cooper', from *The Owl in the Tree*; 'Butterflies in the Desert', 'Letters of Synesius: VI' from *The Stones of Emptiness*, to Oxford University Press.

For CHARLES TOMLINSON: 'The Snow Fences', 'The Fox', 'A Given Grace' from *American Scenes*, to Oxford University Press; 'Tramontana at Lerici' from *Seeing is Believing*, copyright © 1958 by Charles Tomlinson, reprinted by permission of Astor-Honor Inc., New York, and Oxford University Press.

For GAEL TURNBULL: 'Homage to Jean Follain', 'George Fox, From His Journals' from *A Trampoline*, published in the U.S.A. by Grossman Publishers Inc., to Jonathan Cape Ltd.

For VERNON WATKINS: 'A Man With a Field', 'Great Nights Returning' from *Cypress and Acacia*, copyright © 1959 by Vernon Watkins, reprinted by permission of New Directions Publishing Corporation, and of Faber & Faber Ltd; 'The Razor Shell' from *Fidelities*, to Faber & Faber Ltd.

For DAVID WEVILL: 'My Father Sleeps', 'Groundhog' from *Birth of a Shark*, 'Winter Homecoming' from *A Christ of the Ice-Floes*, to St Martin's Press Inc., The Macmillan Company of Canada Ltd, and Macmillan & Co. Ltd.

For KIT WRIGHT: 'The Boys Bump-starting the Hearse', 'The Power of Prayer', 'I Found South African Breweries Most Hospitable', from *Bump-starting the Hearse*, to the author and to Hutchinson Publishing Group Limited.

INDEX OF POETS

INDEX OF POEM TITLES

INDEX OF FIRST LINES

MORE ABOUT PENGUINS, PELICANS AND PUFFINS

For further information about books available from Penguins please write to Dept EP, Penguin Books Ltd, Harmondsworth, Middlesex UB7 ODA.

In the U.S.A.: For a complete list of books available from Penguins in the United States write to Dept DG, Penguin Books, 299 Murray Hill Parkway, East Rutherford, New Jersey 07073.

In Canada: For a complete list of books available from Penguins in Canada write to Penguin Books Canada Ltd, 2801 John Street, Markham, Ontario L3R 1B4.

In Australia: For a complete list of books available from Penguins in Australia write to the Marketing Department, Penguin Books Australia Ltd, P.O. Box 257, Ringwood, Victoria 3134.

In New Zealand: For a complete list of books available from Penguins in New Zealand write to the Marketing Department, Penguin Books (N.Z.) Ltd, Private Bag, Takapuna, Auckland 9.

In India: For a complete list of books available from Penguins in India write to Penguin Overseas Ltd, 706 Eros Apartments, 56 Nehru Place, New Delhi 110019.

Poetry in King Penguin

THE MEMORY OF WAR
AND CHILDREN IN EXILE

Poems 1968–83

James Fenton

'Fenton is 33, Rochester's age at death, so it is not too soon to hail his achievement and celebrate his voice ... a magician-materialist ... his assemblages bring with them tragedy, comedy, love of the world's variety, and the sadness of its moral blight' – Peter Porter in the *Observer*

'He is alone among his contemporaries in having a great deal to write *about* ... a vision of recent history, and his own personal place in it ... a view of life that is stylish, wary, provisional, always intelligent, never breast-beating' – Jonathan Raban in the *Sunday Times*

'Utterly arresting, alive from first to last with inventive wit' – John Lucas in the *New Statesman*

'James Fenton is a poet I find myself again and again wanting to praise ... light and skilful, assured in his forms and also compassionate and grave' – Geoffrey Grigson in the *Listener*

WAR MUSIC

An Account of Books 16 to 19 of Homer's *Iliad*

Christopher Logue

'A work of great virtuosity ... the perfect introduction to Homer ...

'Faithful in tone and spirit to the essential Greekness of the old poem. More than this, the characters who figure are drawn with economy and clarity – they spring off the page ... a small triumph of skill and beauty' – Lawrence Durrell in the *London Magazine*

'Pent-up violence, and the strange delicacy which accompanies it, find their expression at last in the extraordinary *War Music* sequence ... Less a translation than an adaptation. Less an adaptation, in fact, than an original poem of considerable power' – Derek Mahon in the *Observer*

A Choice of Poetry in Penguins

CORNWALL IN VERSE

Edited with an introduction by Peter Redgrove

Everyone who is visiting, living in or remembering Cornwall will find something to enjoy in this anthology of verse, chosen and introduced by Peter Redgrove. In Thomas Hardy's Lyonesse and John Betjeman's Trebetherick; with verses by Charles Causley, Geoffrey Grigson and D. M. Thomas, this delightful book gives you a map of the landscapes and draws out their flavours in poetry that, like Cornwall itself, is full of the rhythms of the sea.

OXFORD AND OXFORDSHIRE IN VERSE

Edited with an introduction by Antonia Fraser

'And that sweet city with her dreaming spires, She needs not June for beauty's heightening.' So wrote Matthew Arnold and, as this anthology richly demonstrates, the meadows, bells and quadrangles of Oxford have been an inspiration to all our poets in all centuries and seasons.

Compiled by Antonia Fraser, who spent her youth there, this book forms a fascinating guide to the city and its lovely countryside. Here is the Oxford of W. H. Auden and Graham Green, Hopkins, Belloc and William Morris, in a poetic A–Z that will be a pleasure to every visitor and connoisseur, student and lover.

PENGUIN POETRY

☐ *The Penguin Book of American Verse*
  Ed. Geoffrey Moore   £5.95

'A representative anthology which will give pleasure to the general
reader and at the same time presents a full range of American poetry
of all periods' – *The Times Literary Supplement*

☐ *Selected Poems* **Pasternak**   £2.50

Translated from the Russian by Jon Stallworthy and Peter France.
'These translations from *My Sister Life* and the other famous collec-
tions are the best we have, faithful to the originals, and true poems in
their own right' – *The Times*

☐ *The Penguin Book of Bird Poetry*
  Ed. Peggy Munsterberg   £3.95

'Beautifully produced and intelligently compiled. Peggy Munster-
berg has done a fine job. Her anthology will please lovers of birds
and of poetry alike' – *The Times Literary Supplement*

☐ *The Complete Poems* **Jonathan Swift**   £10.95

A new, authoritative edition of the poems of this great satirist,
pamphleteer and author of *Gulliver's Travels*. With an introduction,
notes and a biographical dictionary of Swift's contemporaries by the
editor, Pat Smith.

☐ *London in Verse* **Ed. Christopher Logue**   £2.95

Nursery-rhymes, street cries, Shakespeare and Spike Milligan trace
a route through the streets, sights and characters of London in this
lively anthology, which has a linking commentary and illustrations
chosen by Christopher Logue. 'A rare and delightful book' – *Country
Life*

☐ *The Penguin Book of Spanish Civil War Verse*
  Ed. Valentine Cunningham   £4.50

Poetry and prose making up 'an outstanding piece of historical
reconstruction . . . a human document of absorbing interest' – *The
Times Literary Supplement*

PENGUIN POETRY

☐ *The Penguin Book of Women Poets*
Ed. Cosman, Keefe and Weaver   £3.95

From Sappho and Li Ching-chao to Emily Dickinson and Anna
Akhmatova, this acclaimed anthology spans 3,500 years and forty
literary traditions; it also includes a biographical/textual note on
each poet.

☐ *Selected Poems* **William Carlos Williams**   £2.95

Poems extracted by Williams from small-town American life, 'as a
physician works upon a patient, upon the thing before him, in the
particular to discover the universal'. Edited and introduced by
Charles Tomlinson.

☐ *The Memory of War* and *Children in Exile*
James Fenton   £2.25

Including 'A German Requiem' and several pieces on the Vietnam
War, this collection of Fenton's poems 1968–83 is a major literary
event. 'He is a magician-materialist . . . the most talented poet of his
generation' – Peter Porter in the *Observer*

☐ *Poems of Science*
Ed. John Heath-Stubbs and Phillips Salman   £4.95

This unusual anthology traces our changing perceptions of the
universe through the eyes of the poets, from Spenser and
Shakespeare to Dannie Abse and John Updike.

☐ *East Anglia in Verse* **Ed. Angus Wilson**   £2.95

The sea, flat wheat fields and remote villages of East Anglia have
inspired poets as diverse as John Betjeman, Thomas Hood, Edward
Lear and Horace Walpole. Containing theirs and many other poems,
this is a collection 'full of small marvels' – *Guardian*

☐ *Selected Poems* **Lorca**   £2.50

With music, drama, the gypsy mythology, and the Andalusian folk-
songs of his childhood, Lorca rediscovered and infused new life into
the Spanish poetic traditions. This volume contains poems, plus
excerpts from his plays, chosen and translated by J. L. Gili.

PENGUIN POETRY